URBAN LIFE AND URBAN LANDSCAPE SERIES

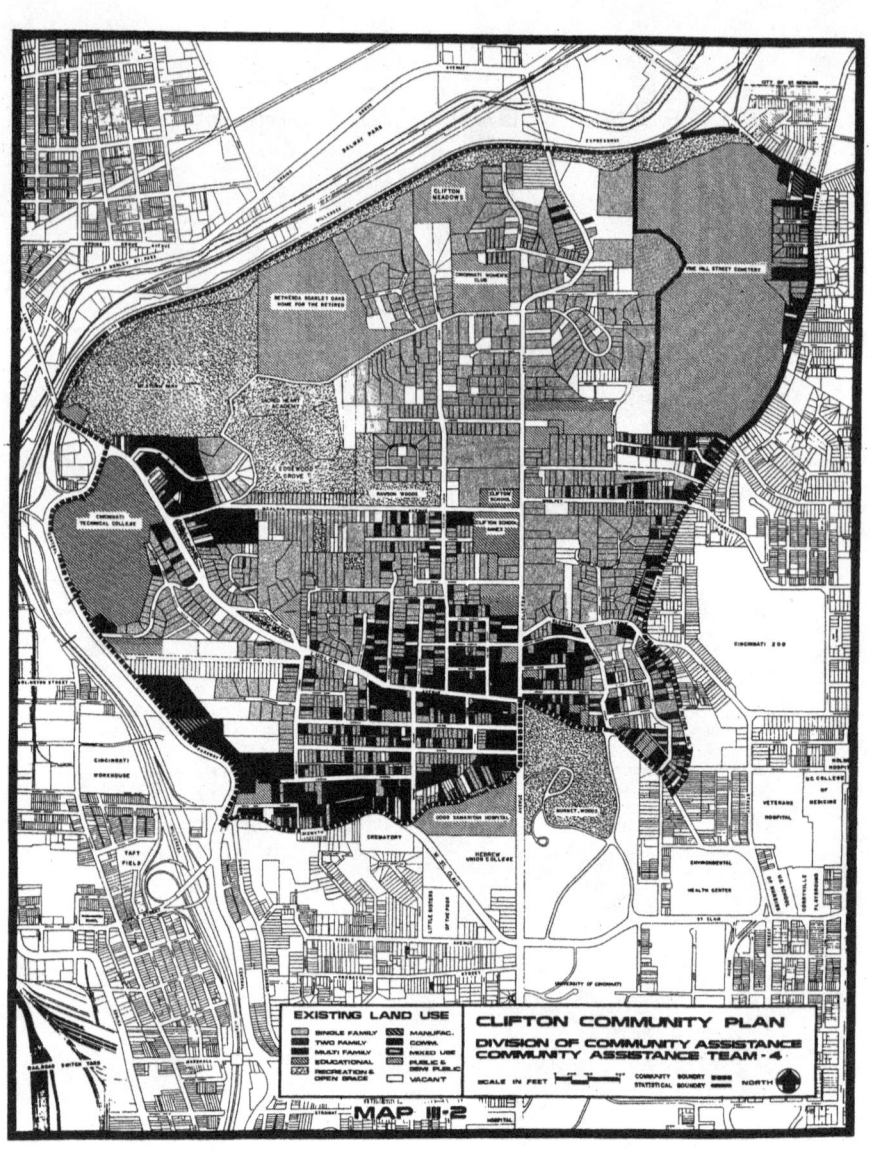

VISIONS OF PLACE

The City, Neighborhoods, Suburbs,
and Cincinnati's Clifton, 1850–2000

Zane L. Miller

OHIO STATE UNIVERSITY PRESS
COLUMBUS

Frontispiece: Clifton Land Use Map, 1981.

Copyright © 2001 by The Ohio State University.
All rights reserved.

Library of Congress Cataloging-in-Publication Data

Miller, Zane L.
   Visions of place : the city, neighborhoods, suburbs, and Cincinnati's Clifton, 1850–2000 / Zane L. Miller.
      p. cm. — (Urban life and urban landscape series)
Includes bibliographical references and index.
    ISBN 0-8142-0859-2 (alk. paper)
   1. Neighborhood—Ohio—Clifton (Cincinnati)—History. 2. Cities and towns—Ohio—Clifton (Cincinnati)—Growth. 3. City planning—Ohio—Clifton (Cincinnati)—History. 4. Clifton (Cincinnati, Ohio)—History. 5. Clifton (Cincinnati, Ohio)—Social conditions.   I. Title. II. Series.
   HT168.C52 M55   2001
   307.3'362'0977178—dc21

00-012825

Paper (ISBN: 978-0-8142-5740-1)

Text and jacket design by Paula Newcomb
Type set in Adobe Minion by G&S Typesetters, Inc.

To Nancy K. Shapiro, 1939–1985 (in memoriam),
and her CTM friends

Contents

Preface
ix

Introduction
1

1 Transforming Clifton: The New Suburban and Neighborhood Idea, 1870s–1910s
7

2 Preparing for the Worst: Comprehensive Planning for the End of Clifton, 1910s–1950s
37

3 Establishing Clifton as an "In-town Suburb," 1955–1964
68

4 Toward Community Control, 1964–1974
93

5 Making a Comprehensive Neighborhood Plan, 1974–1982
113

6 Implementing the Plan: The Politics of Neighborhood Autonomy
132

Epilogue: Race and the Future
161

Appendix: Methodological Note on "Liberation" History
167

Notes
169

Bibliography
201

Index
209

Preface

This book on Cincinnati's Clifton (first a suburb and then a neighborhood of the Queen City), like many research projects, started by accident, took a long time to produce, and appears in a form not originally envisioned. In 1975, someone in the Clifton Town Meeting (CTM), Clifton's community council, proposed the publication of a short history of Clifton as a brochure for distribution during the 1976 version of the annual house tour sponsored by CTM as a fund-raising venture. Since 1976 also marked the bicentennial of the American Revolution, the idea of doing something not only historical but also more durable than a tour caught on among other members of the organization. But "normal" Cliftonites found the doing of such a history a daunting prospect. So several of them asked me as a resident of Clifton and as a professional historian who specialized in American urban history with special reference to Cincinnati to take on the assignment pro bono. This struck me as an appropriate undertaking, for it would help fulfill both my civic obligation as a resident of Clifton and my community service obligation to the University of Cincinnati, where I taught history in the McMicken College of Arts and Sciences.

This task seemed also an easy one because of the availability of some helpers. Henry D. Shapiro, also a Clifton resident and a historian, and I had started an undergraduate research seminar in 1973 called the Laboratory in American Civilization,[1] in which we tried to teach our students how to do history rather than merely lead them in reading and discussing other people's studies of the past, and to do it by using Cincinnati as a convenient test case. So we signed on to produce with the aid of our students a little history of Clifton for CTM, a project that yielded in the spring of 1976 a forty-four-page illustrated booklet.

This item sold very well, as did its reprint edition (1981), and we decided to expand it into a book, aimed at professional historians as well as general readers, especially Cliftonites, but also for other Americans, most of whom live or have lived in a suburb or neighborhood and who might as a consequence view such a book as a matter of personal concern. By 1998 we had a robust manuscript containing five chapters by Shapiro on Clifton in the nineteenth century and seven chapters and an epilogue I had completed concerning Clifton since the mid-nineteenth century. In a process too long and tedious for the purpose of this preface, our critics who read this manuscript (one of whom called it "half-baked") for two university presses persuaded us that we had written two books, or parts of two books, and Shapiro persuaded me that I should take the next step, the writing of one book, while he figured out what to do with his part of the manuscript. I agreed, and decided to do so by deleting rather than reworking Shapiro's five chapters, by significantly revising the first three of my seven chapters, and by writing an introduction to the final product.

So here it is, at last, the outcome of an effort that may be said to have begun in the mid-1970s, and for the completion of which I've drawn on the assistance of a large number of people. The first of these, of course, is Shapiro himself, with whom, as he once put it, I've engaged since 1967 in a more or less continuous discussion of how to do history, and with whom on occasion I've combined to do some of it together. As a consequence I think of Shapiro as mentor as well as friend, a person from whom I've learned more than he thinks and from whom I've borrowed ideas and, as he sometimes complains, distorted them, even though I failed in the application of those ideas to notice the distorting.

I wish also to acknowledge my debt to our students in the Laboratory in American Civilization, who asked provocative questions and whose naivete forced me and Shapiro to clarify our notions, especially conceptual and process notions, about the American past in general and Cincinnati's past in particular. The students of the mid-1970s also did much of the preliminary research that informs this study: Christopher Noell, Tracy Thomas, Patricia Tighe, Mark Winfield, Carl Grunenger, Gail Jordan, Michael Nauer, Missi Meyer, Amy Peters, Susan Stein, Gayle M. Hansen, Tom Kordish, Paul Davis, Andy Marko, Lloyd Terrell, and especially Martha Reynolds and Betsy Schwartz.

We also worked closely with members of the Clifton Town Meeting in preparing the 1976 and 1981 booklets and with others who helped us by virtue of their jobs, but way beyond the call of duty. Special accolades go to Shirley Richfield, Harriet Van Ginkel, Jean Shelblessy, and Daniel J. Ransohoff, Clifton civic volunteers extraordinaire, and to Sidney Weil, who helped me unravel the legal niceties of a complicated zoning and planning dispute. Webster Posey, longtime and now retired clerk of the Cincinnati City Council, made available invaluable governmental documents, not only council records but also the minutes of Clifton Village from its incorporation in 1850 until its annexation by the City of Cincinnati in 1896. Staff members at the Cincinnati Historical

Society, especially Laura Chace, Dottie Lewis, Frances Forman, and Steven Wright, dug out photos and led our students and us through the Society's vast collections of printed and archival materials. The staff of the Department of Archives and Rare Books, University of Cincinnati Libraries, during the mid-1970s, most notably Helen Slotkin and Alice Cornell, and in the 1980s and 1990s, Cornell and Kevin Grace, proved indispensable, not only in helping find collections and items within collections but also in acquiring or assisting in the acquisition of collections particularly useful for this project, especially the records of the Clifton Town Meeting. I called, too, on Karen Kottsy and Sally Moffitt, government documents librarian and history bibliographer, respectively, in the Langsam Library, University of Cincinnati Libraries, on an anonymous (to me) staff member at our incredibly well-funded and first-rate Public Library of Cincinnati and Hamilton County, and on Fred Krome, assistant to Dr. Gary Zola, the head of the American Jewish Archives on the Cincinnati campus of the Hebrew Union College.

I'm also indebted to the folks at Ohio State University Press for their patience and assistance. The process of preparing the manuscript for publication began in one regime, Barbara Hanrahan's, and concluded in another under the supervision of acquisitions editor Darrin Pratt, who handled the task serenely and effectively. Freelance copy editor Elaine Otto turned in a first-class job. I quibbled with a few of her suggestions and blanched when she spotted examples of what she called "jargon." But she seemed mostly on the mark in her efforts to make the prose more readable and to shorten the length of the story, in part (and impressively) by reducing significantly the space consumed by endnotes, tedious but invaluable work. She also for the convenience of readers compiled a bibliography.

A few others deserve special accolades. Evelyn Schott, my faithful typist over the years, patiently transformed the sloppily composed versions of this story, including the longish but futile "half-baked" one, and skillfully juggled errant footnotes as I added and deleted materials for reasons that sometimes must have seemed whimsical to her. Janet A. Miller not only put up with me but also listened and talked back in intellectually constructive ways as I worked my way through the fun and frustration of research, writing, and living in the interstices of these and other professional activities. Two cats, M.K. (now deceased) and A.K., made life more amusing than otherwise would have been the case, and also listened, but without talking back, at least not in a language I could fathom.

I thank all of these helpers and apologize to those I've overlooked. And I absolve them in addition of any responsibility for errors of fact, infelicities of expression, shortcomings of judgment, and interpretive extravagances. I tried hard to eliminate these, but long experience with press and journal reviewers persuades me that I've slipped here and there, and maybe egregiously in the view of some critics. So it goes, as Kurt Vonnegut Jr. taught us to say (albeit about more serious matters).

Introduction

THE United States experienced in the mid-nineteenth century a boom in the proliferation and growth of suburbs, some occupied mostly by people who worked in the city, some mostly by people who both lived and worked in the suburb but traded or spent leisure time in the city, and some by a more or less even mixture of commuters and noncommuters. For the first time, however, respectable people from various classes moved into these suburbs, which contemporaries defined as suitable localities for those who wanted to participate in the economic, social, and cultural life of cities but who sought to avoid their higher susceptibility to taxes and/or epidemic diseases.[1] And while these suburbs differed in their demographic structures and land use patterns, contemporary discussion of human behavior discounted the significance of the internal social and physical environments of cities and suburbs in molding the behavior (or misbehavior) of their residents. Instead, that discussion centered on the civilizability of city dwellers and suburbanites, who seemed equal, or potentially so, in their capacity for building a strong character and acquiring and maintaining habits appropriate for successful participation in various aspects of American civilization, regardless of the social and physical environments of their neighborhoods, whether in a suburb or a city.[2]

Clifton, which lay three miles from Cincinnati's northern municipal boundary on the northwestern section of a large hilly ridge surrounded by valleys, ranked at midcentury as one of the Queen City's commuter suburbs. Its development began in the mid-1840s, when some wealthy Cincinnati civic leaders built or redesigned country estates in the northern part of Clifton for full-time use rather than as summer residences. But they intended also to promote Clifton as a year-round home for other prosperous and respectable commuters who wanted to be of but not in the city.[3] As part of this scheme, Clifton's founders subdivided some vacant land into lots as small as one acre but reserved space for baronial homes in the northern part of Clifton on plots of fifteen acres and more. And in 1850, as the population grew, Clifton's promoters incorporated the locality as a village capable of providing modest but important services, including street construction and improvement, sewers, law enforcement, fire protection, land use regulations banning saloons and factories, and a public school called the Resor Academy, named after the man who gave money to offset the cost of putting up the building.

By some accounts, all of Clifton ranked in the last three decades of the nineteenth century as a purely residential and parklike suburb for exceptionally wealthy "American stock" people, despite the presence since the 1850s of large numbers of first- and second-generation immigrants (see table 1) and despite the appearance after 1860 of large numbers of small detached houses and apartments.

These contradictions present a problem, though not an inexplicable one. The elegant northern portion of Clifton of the nineteenth century attracted visitors. But accounts of parklike Clifton as the whole of Clifton necessarily overlooked south Clifton, which contained very little open space. This oversight

Table 1
Clifton Population According to Federal and Village Records, 1850–1880

| | Youth 5–21 | | Adults | | | | | Parents | |
| | | | | | | | Native | Foreign | Foreign |
	M	F	M	F	Total	Voters	Born	Born	Born
1850		135							
1851	125								
1852	54	90	126	114	384	56			
1853	52	114	144	115	425	60	250		175
1854	64	89	166	151	470	85	253		217
1855	82	95	341		518	89			
1856	82	99	404		585	86	314		271
1857		182							
1858	83	93							
1859	92	108							
1860	89	116							
1870	248	235	308	313	1104	291	485	235	384
1880	200	235	235	332	1002		390	318	276

Source: Henry D. Shapiro and Zane L. Miller, *Clifton: Neighborhood and Community in an Urban Setting. A Brief History* (Cincinnati: Laboratory in American Civilization, Department of History, McMicken College of Arts and Sciences, University of Cincinnati, 1976), 12.

suggests the power of the new metropolitan vision of the city as a system of functionally and structurally differentiated groups and parts, a vision so powerful that it led even close and honest observers to concoct concepts of reality compatible with the "need" to assign special roles to each of the parts of the city and to ignore contradictory evidence or to gloss over perceptions dissonant with those concepts.

Village government served Clifton well for the rest of the nineteenth century, even as development accelerated and Clifton took directions unanticipated when it incorporated as a village in 1850. Within thirty years, Clifton became what we now think of as a quintessential city neighborhood with lots much smaller than an acre dominating the southern half of the suburb and a shopping strip for village residents on Ludlow Avenue, the southern boundary of the municipality. Landlords and building owners along the strip rented two to four floors of flats above the street-level stores, and real estate operators constructed apartment buildings of four to six floors, some compact and some in sprawling edifices, among the modest single-family homes and duplexes set close to the street and close to one another in the few blocks next to and north of the little shopping district.

Clifton's political status also changed in the late nineteenth century, for in 1896 the city of Cincinnati annexed the village and several other suburbs, and Clifton, like the others, lost its political independence. The Queen City had tried earlier to annex Clifton. The first attempt, which targeted an even larger swath of suburban territory, failed in 1870. Yet that effort deserves our special notice. It provided one of the first manifestations of a new way of thinking about cities and suburbs that yielded profound consequences, not only for the metropolis as a whole, including the new view of all suburbs as properly a part of the city of Cincinnati, but also for Clifton, including its eventual annexation and the differing patterns of development in its northern and southern portions during the late nineteenth century.

The new mode of thought about cities abandoned the mid-nineteenth-century habit of downplaying the taxonomic importance of the interior social and physical environments of particular neighborhoods and suburbs. Instead, it stressed the utility of closely assessing the social and physical character of suburbs and neighborhoods to establish their identities for policy makers and to establish for purposes of comparison their relationship to other such places and to the city as a whole. For these reasons, proponents of the new mode of thought sought to separate urban activities according to broad categories of endeavor and to separate groups of people according to their diverse levels of prosperity and the cultural baggage they carried with them. It also sought to place each urban activity and each group of people in an appropriate and distinctive social and physical environment.

In more particular terms, the new mode of thought defined cities as metropolitan social and physical systems composed of differentiated and interdependent social and physical environments. Each city had a particular mission and a land use pattern compatible with that mission, including, for example, some districts for commercial purposes, some for industry, some for vice, and some for civic uses. Residentially, this systematizing urge assigned some neighborhoods to poor people, immigrants, and white migrants from rural America, some neighborhoods to African Americans regardless of their incomes or other diverging traits, some to other persons of color, some to whites with just enough resources to move out of the poor, immigrant, and white rural migrant districts, some to middle- and upper-income whites living in single-family detached homes, and some to very wealthy "American stock" persons living on large estates in parklike settings that would serve in fact as parks for residents of and visitors to the city (hence the ubiquity of the word *park* in the names of American suburbs).[4]

The metropolitan residential taxonomy also drew an invidious distinction between suburban and "old" city neighborhoods that depicted suburban ones as superior places in which to live. It represented suburban neighborhoods as harbors from the turbulence of the "old" city, the city of intensely mixed land uses and peoples crammed into unsightly areas unsegregated by income, race, or ethnicity. By contrast, suburban neighborhoods looked greener, cleaner, calmer, tidier, and more spacious in their spatial segregation of manufacturing activities (for suburbs that contained factories) and in their residential segregation of various classes of inhabitants (within suburban places that accommodated various groups of people).[5]

Our story starts in the late nineteenth century, when the new way of thinking about cities sparked efforts to create new city and suburban neighborhoods that contrasted with residential living quarters in the "old" city. The story focuses first on the definition of Cincinnati as a metropolitan social system and on Clifton as one element in the metropolitan system of differentiated neighborhoods, and concentrates thereafter on changes in those definitions and how they affected the relationship between Clifton and Cincinnati. On that score, our most important actors believed that the distinct interests of the districts and neighborhoods of the city should be subordinated to the welfare of the whole, a vision that took one form from the 1870s into the 1910s (chapter 1) and another from the 1910s into the 1950s (chapter 2).[6]

But the apotheosis of the welfare of the whole lost out after 1950 to a view of the city as a congeries of different sections with interests superior to any sense of the whole. That concept formed the central assumption behind the neighborhood revolution of our times (since 1950), an upheaval that pitted big city and suburban neighborhoods against each other and the core cities of metropolitan areas against both unincorporated and incorporated suburban places in fights for economic and human resources. Protagonists in these contests virtually ignore the idea of the welfare of the whole, despite abundant recent talk about the virtues of "regionalism," a term which stresses the need for voluntary cooperation among submetropolitan governments and neighborhoods, not the need for political consolidation or federation or for a diminution of drives for neighborhood autonomy and suburban independence. And even the voluntary cooperation talk stops precipitously when someone raises the delicate question of race,[7] a major issue in the Clifton story after 1950.

This book also seeks to present a useful history of Clifton as an outer-city neighborhood, a residential category virtually ignored by the many historians now working the urban and suburban scene. We know a great deal about inner-city and suburban neighborhoods and how they became what they are. But we know precious little about the thousands of outer-city neighborhoods that sit between the oldest districts at the center and the newer ones on the peripheries of American metropolitan areas. We know that such outer-city neighborhoods vary in design and in population composition, and that city officials regard them as valuable economic, social, and civic resources because of the high income and educational levels of most of their residents. We also know that many outer-city neighborhoods, like Clifton, took shape in the early nineteenth century as unincorporated affluent suburbs, acquired village governments, and then gained a more dependent status as urban neighborhoods because of their annexation by big city municipalities.

Yet we know little about the social, economic, civic, and land use experience of outer-city neighborhoods in the same period. Worse still, we know even less about the more recent past of outer-city neighborhoods, about how they fared, for example, during the suburban boom of the 1920s, the stagnation of urban growth and the municipal fiscal pinch of the 1930s, and the enormous population shifts of World War II and afterward, especially the expansion of African American inner-city neighborhoods toward the edge of the city that engulfed some outer-city neighborhoods and threatened to engulf others. Did outer-cities in these contexts benefit or suffer from the invention between the 1910s and 1950s of comprehensive planning and zoning, slum clearance and redevelopment, and neighborhood conservation and rehabilitation? How did they cope with the suburban boom of the 1950s, the long hot summers of racial violence in the 1960s, and "stagflation" in the 1970s? Did they embrace or eschew new urban policies and programs, including the war on poverty, model cities schemes, environmental conservation and historic preservation districting, housing rehabilitation, neighborhood empowerment, and other responses to aspects of the "urban crisis" of our times, especially the continuing flight of large numbers of outer-city residents to ever more distant suburbs? And how stands Clifton today, and what might its civic leaders take as its most serious problem?

This study offers answers to these questions. But it also situates the analysis in the context of changing ideas about the role of place in social theory and practice and seeks to present a history of such a neighborhood as a place itself, rather than as a story or a series of chapters about how transcendent national events, such as the Civil War, the Gilded Age, the Progressive Era, social and geographic mobility, racism, sexism, or anti-Semitism, played themselves out in a particular locale presented as a setting rather than as an object of action and/or an actor in the drama. As a consequence, this book explores various meanings of neighborhood and community and their relationship to shifting definitions of the city in the United States from the 1870s through the 1990s, an approach that marks it as a characteristic product of the "Cincinnati school" of urban history, which centers on the role of taxonomies of social reality in shaping the processes by which people define and solve problems.[8]

The body of this book contains also an epilogue consisting of comments and suggestions by me as citizen/historian on race relations since the mid-twentieth century (preachy, one reviewer called this section of the study, perhaps because it cites the Golden Rule). The epilogue contends that black-white relations are our country's central public policy problem because we have failed to make more room for stable, racially integrated neighborhoods. Our metropolitan pattern of virtual residential apartheid not only separates and estranges blacks and whites but also keeps alive a civil rights crossfire of accusation and counteraccusation that distracts attention from and deters action on a broad range of domestic issues and undermines our credibility in dealing with ethnic territorial conflicts overseas.

I have concluded with a methodological note that lays out the principal theoretical ideas on which the book rests. These ideas define what I call "liberation" history, a way of approaching the past to make it speak meaningfully to the present and future without projecting into the past our present assumptions about the way the world works or ought to work. This methodological note may be of most interest to academics, but I like to think of it as useful to anyone who wants to "do" history in one form or another or to handle more critically the histories done by others.

1

Transforming Clifton: The New Suburban and Neighborhood Idea, 1870s–1910s

OBSERVERS of the rapid growth of Cincinnati in the mid-nineteenth century noted the appearance of suburbs. The best remembered were Clifton, Avondale, Mount Auburn, and Walnut Hills, hilltop settlements one to three miles from the city, and Glendale and Wyoming, fifteen miles from the city along the Cincinnati, Hamilton, and Dayton Railroad tracks in the Mill Creek Valley.[1] But Cincinnati's mid-nineteenth-century building boom did not immediately produce a separate literature on the phenomenon or attempts to distinguish suburbs from each other or from city neighborhoods. Guidebooks did not tout suburbs as "sights" that visitors should not miss. They did not draw invidious distinctions between city and suburban living, except to note that some suburbs enjoyed cleaner air and water. These midcentury guidebooks also did not report on the ethnic, religious, or economic class composition of the populations of particular suburbs, or on the fraternal organizations or types of manufacturing carried on in some of them, or on the "taste" of their residents, the design of buildings, the work of landscape architects, or specific improvements, such as horticultural gardens or the kinds of churches or schools (except for colleges). Nor did mid-nineteenth-century guidebooks treat suburbs as entities interdependent with the city. They saw suburbs as detached from Cincinnati, as settlements suitable for self-government by individuals who worked or traded more or less regularly in the city.[2]

Similarly, Clifton's founders in the 1840s did not articulate a particular vision of what Clifton as a suburb might be, might become, or ought to become. This absence of a fixed image of Clifton or of suburban ideals generally fostered an aimless developmental drift in the 1850s and 1860s that permitted real

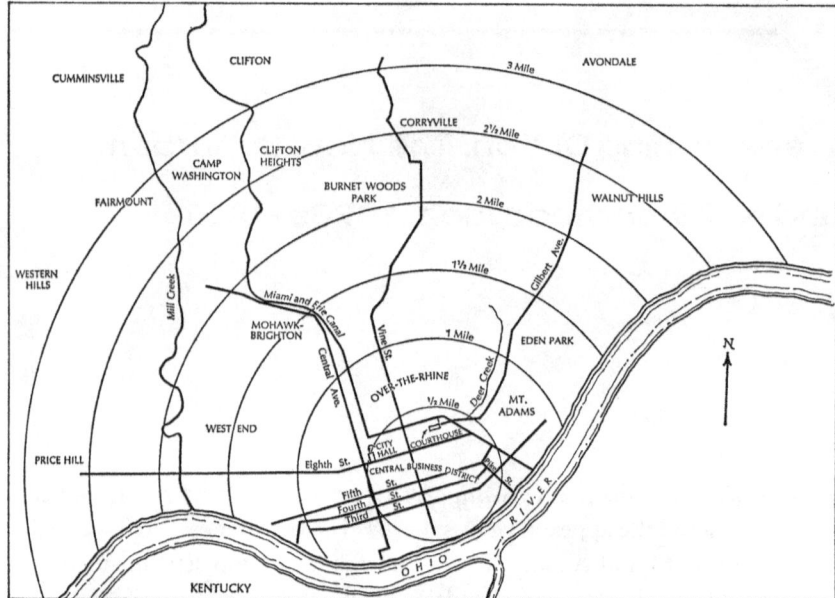

Map 1. Cincinnati in 1875.

estate investors to pursue policies that supported not only the construction of more big homes on big estates but also the subdivision of lots into parcels of one acre and smaller. This made Clifton accessible to persons much less wealthy than the barons who occupied the "castles" along Lafayette Avenue on the northern edge of Clifton and the grand homes on upper Clifton Avenue.[3] Village authorities also adopted policies that encouraged the growth and diversification of the population. As a consequence, when the number of residents in Clifton rose from 700 in 1860 to 1,100 in 1870, village officials expressed concern for Clifton's reputation and identity as they sought to combat new kinds of misbehavior, such as vandalism, vagrancy, burglary, and the miscellaneous unsavory acts of lewd and disorderly persons, worries that, unlike the stray animals and unruly schoolboys who earlier aroused their ire, provoked a sense of beleaguerment.[4]

In this perplexing context of directionlessness and concerns for internal disarray, some Clifton residents sought to develop a sense of the village as a special kind of suburban place for the civic inspiration of its residents and as a way of providing a service to other inhabitants of the metropolis by promoting the development of a particular social and physical environment which they could visit for their edification. One of the first expressions of this new imagery came in 1869 in the midst of another worrisome situation, Cincinnati's first effort to annex Clifton (a campaign which netted for the Queen City four suburbs, but not Clifton). The new vision of the potential nature and role of Clifton came from Flamen Ball as he retired from the village mayor's office after almost twenty years. Ball noted that Clifton comprised 1,200 acres "adorned . . . with rare and beautiful trees and shrubbery, and with costly and elegant buildings." Such a site, Ball argued, if suitably improved with pedestrian walkways and additional plantings in public places, could become "the largest and most beautiful park in the United States, if not in the world," a place of repose, aesthetic inspiration, and recreation for its residents and for those of Cincinnati, who could enjoy it without paying additional taxes for construction of parks then proposed or under construction on the Queen City's hilltop territory.[5]

At the same time publisher George E. Stevens, one of Cincinnati's premier boosters, set down descriptions of the appropriate social and physical characteristics of suburbs close to Cincinnati and treated Clifton, despite its varied landscapes, as a prime example of a suburban type by applying to it Ball's park imagery, a misleading picture of Clifton that persisted for thirty years in guidebooks about Cincinnati and its various suburbs. Stevens's 1869 guidebook stands also as the first work to manifest the new vision of the city as a metropolitan system of differentiated social and physical environments. Although subtitled in the traditional guidebook way as a compilation of "Cincinnati's attractions, advantages, institutions and internal improvements," Stevens's book divided the city into socially and physically unique "quarters" and stressed the interiors and visibly distinctive features, sometimes activities, sometimes buildings, sometimes people, that gave each part a particular character and role. These places consisted of Third Street, the location of "most of the banks, insurance offices, agencies, lawyers' offices, etc.," Fourth Street, Cincinnati's "fashionable promenade" and site of "magnificent retail establishments," the West End, which "includes the larger number of handsome and comfortable dwellings," and Over-the-Rhine, a district north of the Miami and Erie Canal so called because it contained "a population of almost entirely German descent or birth."[6]

In the same way, Stevens called Clifton, Mount Auburn, and Walnut Hills "unequalled in beauty by those [suburbs] of any city of the world" and announced proudly that the Prince of Wales had called these suburbs "the finest he had ever seen." Among the three he ranked Clifton as tops, "the pride of Cincinnati. Its parklike grounds, its beautiful drives, its magnificent prospects [views], its splendid residences, make it a chief point of interest among tourists," and its "charming reticence," unlike other kinds of suburbs, "has been invaded by nothing in the shape of shop or store." Instead, it featured residences of "palatial elegance and size, and surroundings which present every thing beautiful which taste and wealth can furnish."[7]

Sidney Maxwell, an officer of the Cincinnati Chamber of Commerce, took further the process of sorting out the city and its various suburbs by treating both parklike and suburbs of all sorts as better residential places than city neighborhoods. His book appeared in 1870 near the climax of Cincinnati's effort to annex twenty-seven miles of outlying territory, including Clifton, an addition that would expand the city's ambit to forty-five square miles. Maxwell thought it desirable to preserve the history of these suburbs, "famous now, but soon to be merged into the common history of a great city."[8]

Yet Maxwell's work reached much further than this. It ranks as the first extended treatment (186 pages) of Cincinnati's suburbs as a separate and single object of study, notable for emphasis on their variety and for its handling of them, like Stevens, as de facto city neighborhoods of a new kind, residential areas identifiable by their internal social and physical characteristics housing a distinctive element or a particular mix of the population elements of the metropolis. Maxwell covered eleven of the incorporated villages targeted for annexation as well as "suburban places" thirty or forty miles from Cincinnati. Some of these seemed likely subjects of annexation proceedings, and some of them, particularly the several Kentucky localities across the Ohio River from Cincinnati, seemed unsuitable for annexation because they fell under the jurisdiction of another state. Maxwell also included as suburbs some places long since annexed, as if to bolster his contention that after annexation suburbs remained—whether industrial or more purely residential—greener, more spacious, and healthier than city neighborhoods. In the city proper, he contended, even the large houses of the wealthy sat on small lots so close to the street and to each other that they provided little if any room for lawns, shrubs, or trees, and they stewed in an atmosphere he described as polluted by "the maelstrom of business . . . and the dust and smoke and heat inseparable from a great city."[9]

In all this, Maxwell reveled in the variety of suburbs and in their internal diversity. He pointed out valley and hilltop places, turnpike and railroad suburbs, suburbs in which omnibuses (horse-drawn passenger coaches) took commuters to their trains, horsecar suburbs (horse-drawn coaches on street rails), bridge and ferry suburbs, suburbs with and without Protestant churches, suburbs with and without Catholic churches, suburbs with both Protestant and Catholic churches, old suburbs and new suburbs, suburbs with and without a large contingent of Germans, suburbs (such as Cumminsville) recovering from their tarnished reputations for vice and crime and from their association with noxious industries (some people, he wrote, still called Cumminsville Tanyard because of its long-standing tannery), suburbs occupied by rich people, and suburbs occupied by working-class people (and some occupied by both). He especially gauged the level of "improvements" in various suburbs, which meant churches, schools, well-kept homes and grounds around the buildings, and the dominance of law-abiding residents and solid citizens pushing for additional improvements.[10]

Maxwell made no attempt to taxonomize the suburbs, but proceeded anecdotally while insisting that all of them contained large numbers of people who worked in Cincinnati or who went there on business. Indeed, the number and variety of suburbs he described defy classification, but they included Covington, Kentucky, on the south bank of the Ohio River, with a population of 30,000 people who supported fourteen Protestant congregations, including a Welsh and a German one, three Catholic churches, five lodges of the Independent Order of Odd Fellows, eight Masonic bodies, two iron rolling mills, a large glass factory, "and other manufactures." Maxwell expected that silk-stocking Mount Auburn on Clifton's southeast flank would soon "teem with a population that will demand a [real] park," and described Corryville, southeast of Clifton, as a suburb "generally settled by persons of moderate means, who purchased small lots and erected such dwellings as their ability would allow." Here "the German element" ran "very strong," as it did in part of Woodburn, to the east of Clifton, where German Catholics "had built a settlement about the church [St. Francis] of neat houses and pleasant surroundings."[11]

In this labyrinth of a book, Maxwell did not lay down a particular suburban ideal. He helped establish a way of thinking that legitimized a focus on the internal and changing social and physical characteristics of particular suburbs and of the city they surrounded, that encouraged law-abiding people and solid citizens pushing for local improvements, regardless of their other traits, to seek out affordable suburban domiciles, and that urged established suburbanites to accept newcomers as the good neighbors they intended to be. "In all directions," he concluded, "the city is moving on to conquer, the flower of her

12 • Chapter One

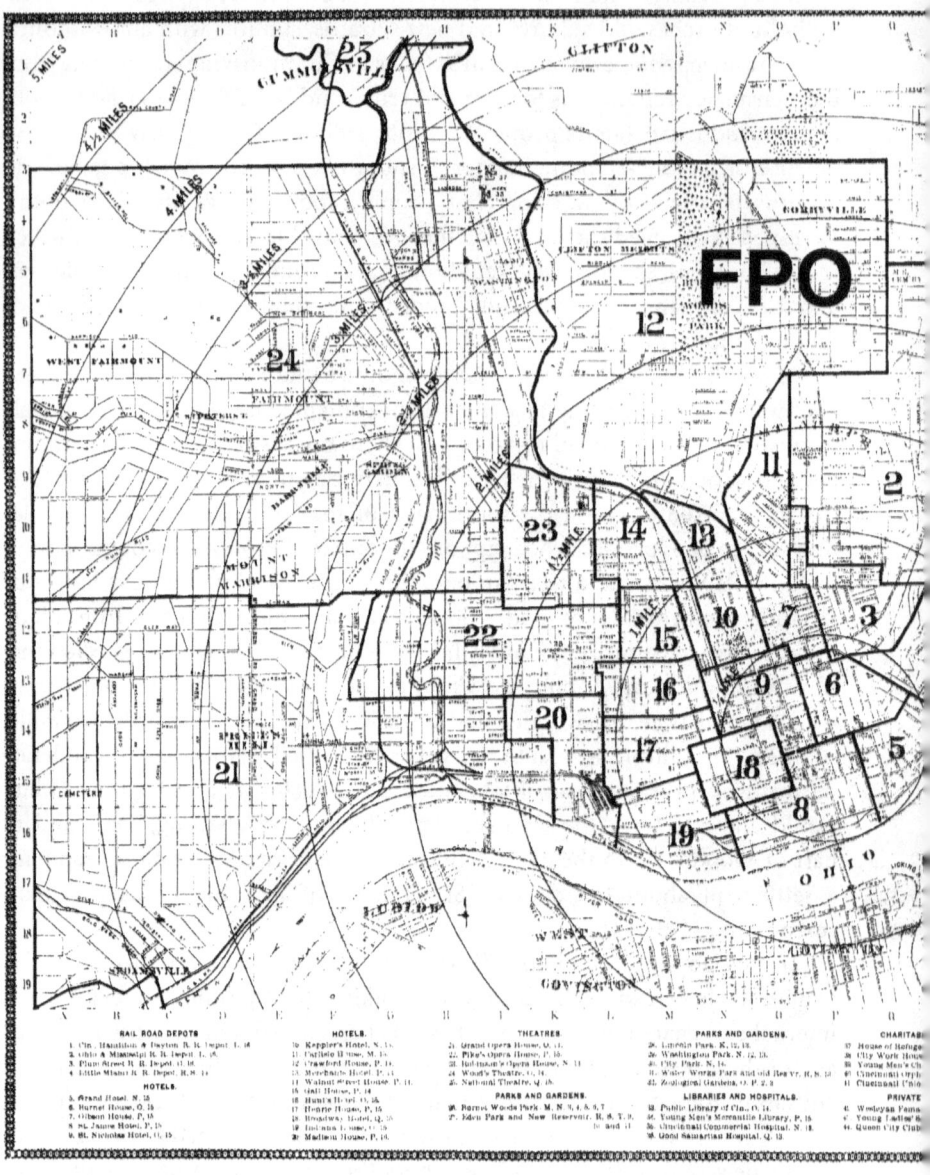

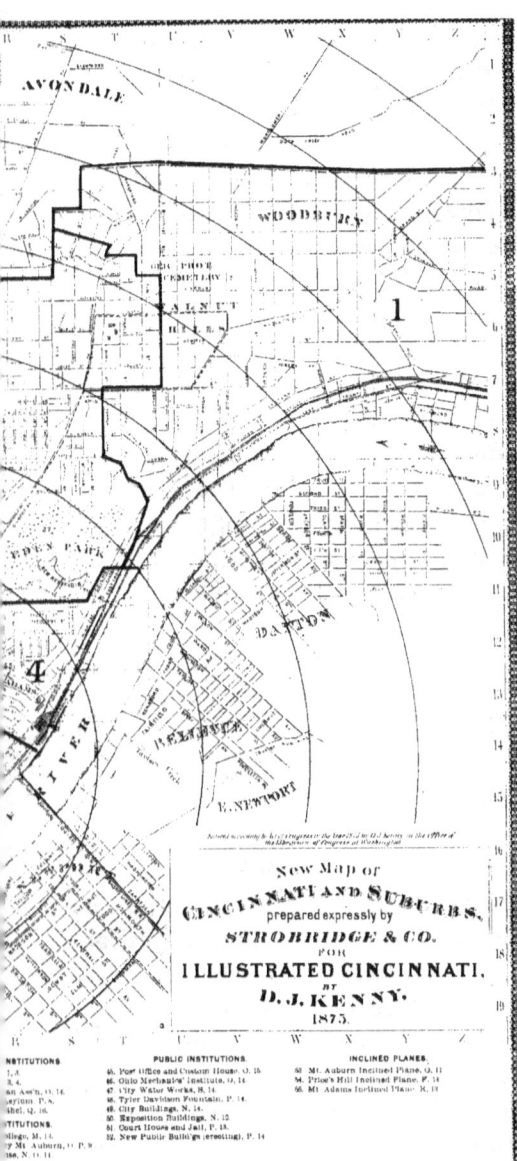

Map 2. Cincinnati and Its Suburbs (including those in Kentucky), 1875. This map looked excessively busy even before its reduction from its original size of 13¾ by 11 inches. But writers of late nineteenth-century guidebooks liked to include very detailed maps to assist travelers, businessmen, entertainers, conventioneers, and local residents themselves in finding their way around the rapidly expanding metropolis and its "sights" and utilitarian buildings, even at the expense of excluding more remote but noteworthy locales, such as the outer suburbs of Glendale and Wyoming. The large numbers on the map identify wards, the biggest of which comprise recently annexed peripheral territory of the city, a pattern that gave the new periphery of the city fewer representatives on the city council than the smaller and more numerous "old" city representative districts. *Source:* Daniel J. Kenny, *Illustrated Cincinnati* (Cincinnati: Robert Clarke, 1875).

population deployed as skirmishers, who steadily advance upon a country that little thinks or knows what powers of expansion and absorption belong to the cities." But suburbanites should not fear annexation, because his survey indicated that even as the residents of annexed suburbs grew and diversified, those places remained healthier, more comfortable, and less congested places of residence than those available in the city. Maxwell offered special solace to Cliftonites, whose suburb he depicted as different from most others described in his book. Clifton, he contended, remained "a purely residential place" with "nothing of the town about it, . . . neither store, grocery, mechanic's shop nor saloon." And in Clifton's case, he predicted soothingly, it would be "many years" before "the general character of the place" would change.[12]

Maxwell erred on that score, for Clifton changed rapidly after 1870 because public officials and suburban real estate developers took steps that made it a split-level neighborhood, the rich for the most part above McAlpin Avenue in spacious "north" Clifton, and the not-so-rich below McAlpin in less spacious and increasingly crowded "south" Clifton. Indeed, after 1870 Clifton not only became a split-level neighborhood but also took its place in a new urban setting, a shift encouraged by the spreading out and sorting out of the compact and intense mixture of peoples and land uses characteristic of the "old city." This spreading and sorting deposited an industrial corridor and a string of neighborhoods and suburbs for workers below the hill along Clifton's western and northern flanks, a large concentration of African Americans in the lower West End, a colony of recently arrived immigrants farther north in the same section of the city, and a growing enclave of Jews in Avondale to the east and north of Clifton.

But the spreading and sorting also introduced a distinction in residential land use patterns within Clifton that symbolized the class differentials between the inhabitants north of McAlpin Avenue and those south of McAlpin. In addition, the spreading and sorting established a broader pattern of land use in which detached single-family houses set back from the street on residential lots accumulated in the center of Clifton and commercial establishments on its periphery, especially along Ludlow Avenue where a little business strip took shape that catered particularly to neighborhood residents. And for three or four blocks north of that strip, developers created a more tightly packed array of residential structures, including duplexes, many apartment buildings, some of them massive, and small virtually yardless houses set very close to the street and very close to one another in an array looser than but reminiscent of "old city" neighborhoods.

The spreading and sorting out of the metropolis stemmed from the new way of thinking about cities as social systems of differentiated groups and parts, and from the accompanying urge, seldom wholly satisfied, to create a more uniformly decongested metropolis and a large variety of distinctive physical and social environments. But the incompletely realized spreading and sorting also yielded inescapably visible and worrisome daily reminders of the diversity within Clifton and the city, a diversity that seemed more intractable than ever before and more nettlesome because it clashed with the overriding assumption in the late nineteenth and early twentieth centuries that residents of Clifton and Cincinnati ought to share with other Americans a common culture, a total way of life. The accomplishment of this vision of homogeneity, given the apparent reality, intensity, and irrepressibility of the cultural differences that divided the city into mutually suspicious groups, seemed unlikely in the foreseeable future. Community leaders in Clifton and Cincinnati, as a consequence, sought to create mechanisms that would imbue the diverse residents of the city in their diverse physical and social environments with a shared sense of civic identity and loyalty that would transcend their enduring differences along class, ethnic, racial, religious, and residential lines. From this effort to use civic identity and loyalty for the promotion of social coherence and tranquillity emerged two new and related phenomena: the city's first territorial-based civic organization movement, and attempts to develop new municipal programs and citywide plans to provide Cliftonites and other residents with an abundance of shared civic experience and education in the form of public services and monumental public works projects, including a system of parks and parkways and a proposed complex of public buildings on the northern edge of Cincinnati's central business district.

But the spreading and sorting came first in a process abetted by the village of Clifton and the city of Cincinnati, both of which granted franchises for the use of public rights of way to rapid transit entrepreneurs seeking alternatives to horse-drawn streetcars, a technology introduced during the 1850s. Two decades later, the horsecars seemed too slow to people accustomed to steam railroads and inadequate for climbing the steep hills surrounding the "old city." In addition, the horses required feeding and stabling, fell ill and sometimes died in harness, occasionally stepped on, trampled, or kicked people, and polluted the streets and atmosphere with tons of urine and manure each year.[13]

Rapid transit entrepreneurs overcame the shortcomings of the horsecars by developing and installing three new modes of public transportation. In the 1870s and 1880s, they promoted the "inclined plane" (a trestle and track on the

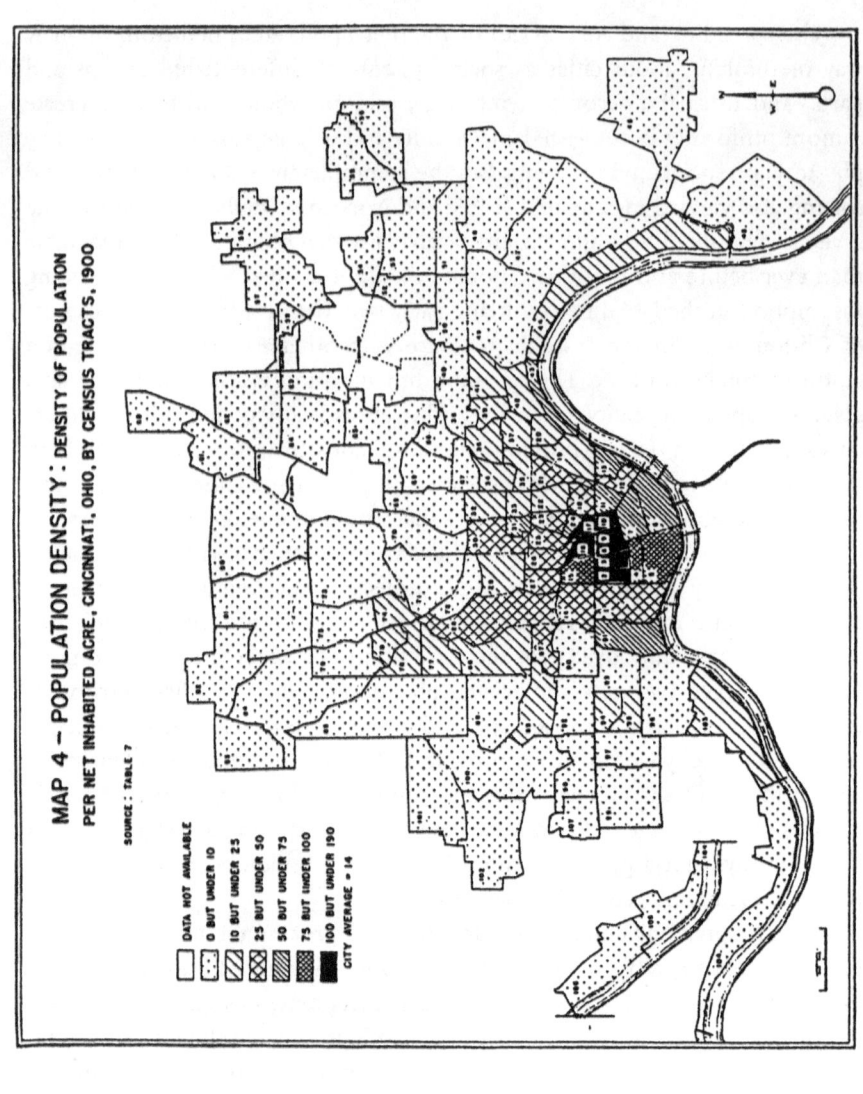

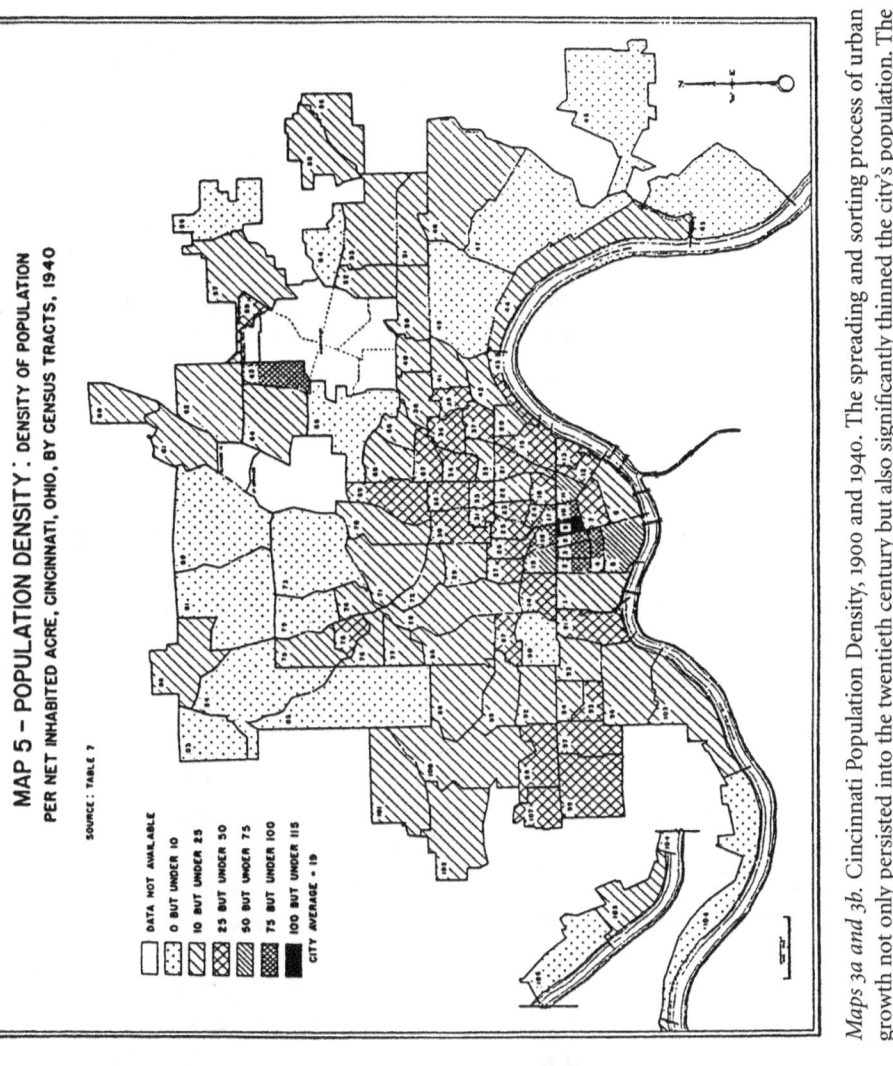

Maps 3a and 3b. Cincinnati Population Density, 1900 and 1940. The spreading and sorting process of urban growth not only persisted into the twentieth century but also significantly thinned the city's population. The density of Clifton's (census tracts 70, 71, and 72) population, however, increased, although it remained in 1940 among the most thinly settled set of neighborhoods in the Queen City. *Source:* James A. Quinn, Earle Eubank, and Lois E. Elliot, *Population Changes: Cincinnati, Ohio, and Adjacent Areas, 1900–1940* (Columbus: Bureau of Business Research, Ohio State University, 1947), between pp. 26 and 27.

side of a hill, up and down which a stationary steam engine and cable pulled a platform for carrying street railway cars, pedestrians, and freight) and the cable car (a horseless streetcar pulled by a steam-driven underground cable over level terrain and modest hillside grades). In the 1880s and 1890s, they equipped streetcars with trolleys that transferred electricity from an overhead wire to motors under the car.

The urban transportation revolution came to Clifton in the 1870s. Two inclined planes opened shop in Cincinnati: the Main Street or Mount Auburn line and the Bellevue or Clifton line. By 1880, horsecar lines running from the top of these inclines linked the once remote hilltop suburbs of Mount Auburn and Clifton directly with the street railway system serving the commercial, industrial, and residential complex in the "basin" below the hilltops (the "old city"). One line started at the Mount Auburn incline terminal and proceeded by way of Auburn Avenue to Vine and Jefferson as far as Brookline on the eastern edge of Clifton. The other started at the Clifton incline and ran up Ohio and Calhoun to Vine, thence to Jefferson where it dead-ended at Brookline on the southern edge of Clifton. Those transit improvements sparked the rapid settlement of Clifton Heights and Corryville to the south of Clifton, but Clifton proper still stood just beyond the street railway system.

What remained of Clifton's isolation, however, ended in 1888. In that year the Cincinnati Street Railway Company, after receiving authorization from Clifton Village authorities, tied into the hilltop connections by running a cable line from Vine to Jefferson to Ludlow and formed a loop in "south" Clifton by cutting north on Middleton to Bryant, east from Bryant to Telford, south on Telford to Ludlow, and back via Jefferson to Vine. The cable line then followed Vine down the hill into the central business district where it terminated at Fifth Street. In 1890, it took riders twenty-five minutes, including a transfer at the Jefferson-Vine powerhouse, to make the trip from Clifton to Fountain Square in the very heart of the city.[14]

The advent of streetcars combined with the village council's ambitious "good roads" campaign of avenue, gutter, curb, sewer, and sidewalk improvements sparked a subdivision development boom, mostly in south Clifton, during the 1880s and early 1890s. A Cincinnati newspaper story in 1891 described a twelve-acre subdivision on Cook (now Telford), Thrall, Middleton, and Bryant Avenues, a second of nine acres on Ludlow and Linden (now Whitfield), a third of fifty acres on Linden, a fourth of fourteen acres on Prospect (now Hosea) and Brookline, a fifth of ten acres on Brookline, and a sixth of ten acres on Resor. The same article noted the first subdivision action north of and

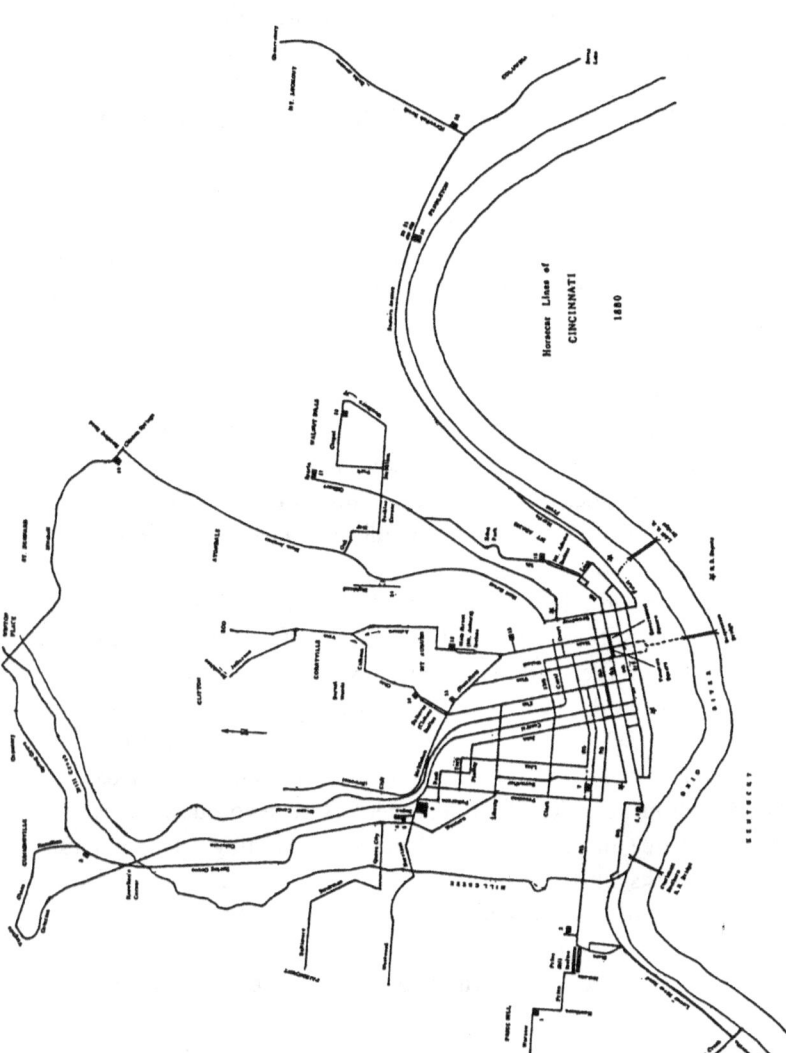

Map 4. Streetcar Lines and Incline Planes Serving the City and Its Suburbs, 1880. The dark boxes identify the locations of horsecar barns. The streetcar system included a circumferential route that skirted Clifton and Avondale by going out the Mill Creek Valley, cutting east to the corner of Reading Road and Clinton Springs, and then dropping down southwesterly to Broadway. Source: Richard M. Wagner and Roy J. Wright, Cincinnati Streetcars, No. 1. Horsecars and Steam Dummies, 2d ed. (Cincinnati: Wagner Car Company, 1972), 17.

downhill from the baronial estates on Lafayette Avenue: the creation of an "Amazon Park" subdivision of small lots along a single street halfway down the hillside.[15]

By the 1890s, then, both Clifton's twentieth-century transportation network and the familiar lines of its present-day land use pattern had taken shape. One streetcar line stretched along Ludlow Avenue, the southern boundary of Clifton, down to the Miami and Erie Canal on the village's western edge, and another ran along Vine Street, the eastern boundary of the village, as far out as Mitchell, where it intersected with a line that came down the hill from Avondale along Mitchell Avenue. Only one branch of the transit system's network cut through Clifton (as in 1888), and it ran up Middleton to McAlpin and over to a dead-end on Clifton Avenue,[16] a route that provided service accessible by foot to both north and south Clifton. All the nonresidential addresses in Clifton, except for Adrian's florist shop on McAlpin, lay close to the streetcar lines clustered in the southern edge of the neighborhood. At the bottom of the Ludlow Avenue hill sat a boat building establishment, a combination saloon and grocery, and a florist. Farther east on Ludlow, beyond McAlpin, came the Jewish cemetery. From there nothing broke the residential continuity until one reached the corner of Ludlow and Clifton. There a saloon stood on the south side of Ludlow half a block west of Clifton, and across the street stood a confectioner and two groceries. A drug store on the northeast corner of Clifton and Ludlow and a candy manufacturer on the south side of Ludlow closer to Clifton Avenue than Brookline completed the neighborhood shopping district. The only other businesses occupied sites well removed from this area on the east side of Vine Street, starting with two florist shops, a marble works, and a saloon concentrated, and perhaps not fortuitously, in the vicinity of the German Evangelical Protestant cemetery. Farther north, on Mitchell near the canal, stood a brick manufacturer and another saloon, and on Harriet (later called Wuest) between Kessler and Vine, a shoemaker's shop.[17]

By the 1890s, Clifton had become a new kind of place. It sported a new land use pattern, and its residents pursued a more diverse range of occupations: fewer bankers and merchants, more people engaged in manufacturing, salaried white-collar posts, and small businesses, but also gardeners, domestic servants, and handymen for the grand homes on Lafayette and upper Clifton Avenue. It was also transformed politically into a dependency of the city of Cincinnati, then and for a decade to come under the control of the legendary George B. Cox, the "boss" of the Republican Party, the dominant factor in

Cincinnati politics from the 1880s into the 1920s, and himself a Clifton resident for almost two decades.

The élimination of Clifton Village occurred because the state legislature enacted in 1893 the so-called Lillard Law, which changed the rules of the annexation game. Before this, suburban villages could not be annexed unless their citizens voted in favor of it. The new rules counted the suburban and city vote together, and Clifton, which voted no, became part of the city of Cincinnati, as did four other villages, including Avondale, by a total vote of 49,467 to 4,467 (two of the annexees, however, voted yes).

Clifton now became a ward, the unit of political representation on Cincinnati's city council, and its representatives tried to look out for its interests during city hall battles in which Cox and his allies sought to balance the interest of the city's many wards in ways that both protected them and subordinated them to the welfare of the whole. A boss, Cox once said, was "not necessarily a public enemy,"[18] and Clifton, as it turned out, fared reasonably well in the give and take of welfare-of-the-whole politics. By 1910, when the population had edged up from 3,555 in 1895 to 4,375, the incidence of nonresidential land uses had become more frequent, but the city government did nothing to change the general pattern. Six businesses gathered below the intersection of McAlpin and Ludlow near the canal, and only the Jewish cemetery, a business at Lyleburn, and a professional office on Whitfield near Ludlow Avenue interrupted the residential character of the street between McAlpin and Middleton. By this time, however, the business-commercial strip from Middleton to Brookline had filled out considerably. That strand accommodated nineteen businesses on both sides of the street, and five apartment buildings stood along the Ludlow commercial strip. Five others were also located in north Clifton: three on Middleton (one at the corner of Shiloh, another at Bryant, and the third at Resor), the fourth on Hosea at Clifton Avenue, and the fifth on the south side of Hosea one-third of the way to Brookline. The streetcar routes followed the same paths as in 1896, all the commercial places and apartments on or near the strip huddled close to the mass rapid transit facilities, and the entire core of the community remained devoted to residences, churches, and schools.[19]

The residential core of detached houses also displayed a differentiated land use pattern as a consequence of developments in the late nineteenth and early twentieth centuries. Churches hugged Clifton Avenue, which also formed a corridor that proved attractive to the founders of private schools. The first of these, the Bartholomew-Clifton School for girls and women, opened on Evanswood in 1900, and Helen Gibbons Lotspeich established the Clifton Open Air

Fig. 1. The Roanoke apartment building is one of several constructed in the late 1800s and early 1900s. Another large one, also brick but of a different design, stands on the south end of Middleton Avenue. Photo (1998) courtesy of Jon Hughes.

School on Resor in 1916. The sites of both institutions lay within walking distance of Clifton Avenue and not far from the Clifton School on the corner of McAlpin and Clifton Avenue.[20]

A third school, this one on Clifton Avenue, grew out of the establishment of a Catholic parish for Clifton. Before then, six parishes, at least three of which served predominantly poor congregations, cared for various parts of Clifton. But the Roman Catholic Archdiocese in 1910 laid down boundary lines for a new parish (Annunciation) that coincided roughly with the old Clifton Village boundaries, except that they extended south of Ludlow Avenue to Dixmyth. Father James Kelly and twenty-five to thirty Catholic residents of Clifton proper, including cigar manufacturer Michael Ibold, Dr. William Wenning, millionairess Louisa Hanks, and advertising agent J. C. Kelley, took charge of organizing the parish. The priest first held services in a rented storeroom on Ludlow Avenue across from the fire station, but the congregation soon purchased from the Sisters of Charity part of a piece of property on Clifton and Resor (375 feet on Clifton and 470 feet on Resor) on which the order had opened in 1903 a temporary annex of the Good Samaritan Hospital, which stood at Sixth and Locke Streets in the more crowded part of the city below the hilltop suburbs. The frame church opened in 1910, and four years later the parish purchased the remainder of the hospital property and refitted the hospital building for a priest's residence and school. The congregation did not grow rapidly, however, because of "the high price of property in the locality," according to Father Kelly. By 1919 the school had 115 students enrolled in nine grades,[21] but it took the congregation until 1931 to raise sufficient funds for the construction and dedication of an imposing stone building. It was a "beautiful edifice," according to the *Cincinnati Catholic-Telegraph,* the archdiocesan newspaper, "a modern conception of early Christian architecture" that "brings full realization of the dreams of the pastor, Rev. James M. Kelly."[22]

The development of improvements in Clifton after annexation, however, derived not only from nongovernmental initiatives but also from actions of Cincinnati's city government as part of its effort to enhance living standards and bolster civic loyalty and social coherence both within neighborhoods and on a citywide basis. The fire department, for example, constructed a new station at Clifton's edge, on the southwest corner of Clifton and Ludlow. (Before annexation, the village's fire equipment had been kept in the center of the residential area, at Clifton and McAlpin.)[23] Equally important, action by the city helped establish a sharp boundary for the community on the west side and at the same time prevented intensive development of that section. That end of Clifton still contained "The Windings," occupied since 1876 by the Sacred Heart Academy for girls, and the home of Mr. and Mrs. Max Fleischmann, a wedding gift presented to them by another of the "barons" of Lafayette Avenue, George K. Schoenberger. Next to the Fleischmann house, at the turn of the century, loomed Mount Storm, a great white marble Italian villa built in the mid-1860s by Robert Bonner Bowler, an attorney, former mayor of Clifton, Democratic candidate for the first congressional district seat, and assistant treasury secretary under President Grover Cleveland. Bowler delighted in entertaining heads of state, especially royalty. His gardener, Adolph Strauch, who designed the replica of Venus's Temple of Love that stands as the last vestige of the estate, started his career as a protégé of Prince Herman von Pückler-Muskau of Silesia. After Bowler's unfortunate death in a runaway carriage accident on Sycamore Street, the city of Cincinnati purchased 66.74 acres of land in 1911 from a Bowler heir for $115,270, a step which preserved the site from commercial or residential development and provided the west end of Clifton with a park.[24]

Mount Storm Park did for Clifton's northwest side what Burnet Woods Park did for its southern boundary east of Clifton Avenue. Burnet Woods Park began to take shape in 1872, when Robert Burnet and his sister's husband,

William S. Groesbeck, leased their heavily wooded 165-acre tract of hilly land to the Cincinnati Board of Park Commissioners. Adolph Strauch, who now served as superintendent of both Spring Grove Cemetery and the city's parks, oversaw the installation of roadways and a lake, and the new park opened to the public in 1874. The city purchased the grounds in 1881 and, eight years later, set aside forty-three acres at the southeastern corner of the park, well removed from Clifton, as a site for the municipally supported University of Cincinnati, which moved from its old quarters on the Clifton Avenue hillside near Vine Street into several architecturally imposing buildings constructed on the Burnet Woods campus in the late 1890s and early 1900s.[25]

The city also improved the Clifton School after the turn of the century. Merger with the city meant that taxes for school purposes increased in Clifton from 3 mills to 4.1 mills. (In other annexed suburbs, school taxes declined from higher rates—5 mills in Avondale, 8 mills in Westwood, 9 mills in Linwood, and 11 mills in Riverside—to the new rate of 4.1 mills.)[26] It also meant greater educational opportunities for the children of the village, since the Cincinnati Board of Education was obligated to supplement the existing district and intermediate schools by allowing Clifton youngsters to enroll in the city's comprehensive public high schools, one of which, Hughes High School, moved from the west end to a site across Clifton Avenue from the University of Cincinnati in 1911.[27] In addition, the board agreed to maintain Clifton as a separate elementary school district and to rent the now useless Clifton Village council chamber in the Resor Academy facility for school purposes.[28]

With the rapid growth in Clifton's population, however, the Resor Academy building soon became inadequate. At first the board erected temporary buildings to house an overflowing school population, which grew from 251 pupils in 1896 to 350 in 1901.[29] But these soon proved "so frail that they were a menace to the health of the children," especially in wet weather. "The roofs were put on so that the water would not run off properly," parents complained, and when "the tar paper roofing rotted, . . . the children were either forced to sit in the rain or use umbrellas." Luckily for Cliftonites, between 1903 and 1905 the Cincinnati Board of Education launched a major building program to provide new facilities and to modernize older buildings, thereby completing a program of school development which it hoped would—and in fact did—make the Cincinnati system one of the most up-to-date and best equipped in the nation.[30]

The board decided to build a Clifton school on the site of the Resor Academy. When finished in 1907, the new edifice, an architecturally imposing civic monument called the Clifton School, cost in excess of $143,500 and featured not only an elegantly embellished exterior but also spacious corridors, a basement with playrooms and lavatories, fourteen classrooms, an auditorium, a gymnasium, and a library. The board of education spent $3,692 on new equipment to furnish the school and announced with civic pride that "the citizens of Clifton have raised a fund amounting to $3,000 for interior decoration [which] has been used to purchase statuary and pictures. . . . This building has been pronounced by educators from other cities . . . the most beautiful in structure and equipment that they have seen."[31]

Clearly, then, Clifton garnered a variety of civic movements but experienced few essential changes in the fifteen years following annexation. Since the 1870s it had become much more a part of the city than before, and the idea of it as a parklike suburb faded in the 1890s. Mass rapid transit provided close connections between it and the heart of the city. Now it drew directly on the municipal corporation for parks, education, and fire and police protection, and it contributed taxes to the municipality in return for these and other services. In a fashion more direct and unmistakable than in the past, the fate of the city and the former suburb of Clifton seemed inextricably intertwined. Cliftonites, like others from similar neighborhoods, responded by seeking to control the fate of the city of which they were now irrevocably a part and with which their own future seemed so intimately connected. Urban politics now became a compelling interest of Clifton's civic-minded citizens.

Cliftonites registered their views in city politics during the first quarter of the twentieth century in two ways. One was through participation in citywide elections. In a manner characteristic of political tendencies in Cincinnati and other cities during these decades, Cliftonites joined in periodic efforts to purge the city of boss rule. In every reform effort between 1897 and the adoption of the city-manager system of government in the mid-1920s, those who led the charge against control of the city and its schools by the dominant Republican machine found their staunchest supporters in neighborhoods like Clifton, Mount Auburn, Avondale, Hyde Park, and Walnut Hills.[32]

Residents of these and similar localities in other cities also angled for political influence through local improvement associations. These tended to support political candidates, regardless of their party affiliation, who advocated a generous array of public improvements while haranguing citizens and property owners about the virtues of undertaking private improvements in the physical and social environment. The associations concentrated on local development in part from their conviction that "improvements" (a term defined loosely to cover everything from alley design and cleaning to smoke abatement) steadied and enhanced property values. But they also advocated the carrying out of improvements throughout the city and the development of a general sense of civic loyalty and vision, ideals they disseminated across the United States through the National League of Improvement Associations (1900), which changed its name in 1902 to the American League for Civic Improvement and then, after merging in 1904 with the American Park and Outdoor Association, to the American Civic Association.[33]

The neighborhood improvement association movement in Cincinnati began in the late nineteenth century as a drive for influence by recently annexed outlying districts that felt underrepresented in a city council dominated by politicians from the smaller and more numerous wards of the "old city." Clifton joined the cause in 1896, the year of its annexation, with the establishment of the Clifton and Burnet Woods Improvement Association. Its constitution, like those of similar organizations, identified its concerns in broad terms as "the advance of all modern improvements" and especially the "opening of streets, extending rapid transit, beautifying, sprinkling, and lighting of parks and avenues, improving walks, schools, etc."[34] It also carved out a generous territory for itself by claiming to work for the benefit of citizens not only of Clifton but also of Mount Auburn and Corryville, a territory contiguous with the boundaries of the Twenty-eighth and Thirty-first Wards, and touted the assets of its "sphere" by listing on the first page of its magazine the University of Cincinnati, Burnet Woods, "beautiful" Clifton Avenue, the Cincinnati Zoological Gardens (established by a corporation and opened in 1875 on a site east of Clifton between McAlpin and Ludlow and designed by the ubiquitous Adolph Strauch), the German Protestant Orphan Asylum, the German Home for the Elderly, the Jewish Home and Hospital, the Cincinnati Crematory, and the North Cincinnati Turner Hall, none of which, except for the "beautiful" northern segment of Clifton Avenue, lay within the boundaries of the former village of Clifton.[35]

The association's journal, the *North Cincinnati and Clifton Advocate*, edited by a "press committee" of six members, all of whom lived within the boundaries of the former village of Clifton, supported improvements throughout the journal's "sphere." In its fourth issue, for instance, it condemned the delay in the construction of Middleton Avenue (which forced some people to trespass on private property to reach streetcar stops), criticized two property owners for not repairing their sidewalks, and called for the extension of Rochelle Avenue and Charleton Street through a ravine in Corryville to shorten the time for firefighters to get to burning buildings on the other side of the gulch. The same issue announced that the Clifton and Burnet Woods Improvement Association, the Cincinnati Turner Society, and several singing societies hoped to build a Saengerfest Hall on "our hill," a "suburb" that offered a variety of advantages, including suitable grounds near the zoo, "plenty large enough for all purposes, level, beautifully located, and convenient to street cars," and a site the several groups had also "proposed to the G.A.R. people for camping . . . next year." [36]

This journal sought to prompt civic pride in Cincinnati and support for its improvement, often by comparing its progress to that of other cities. "Chicago's greatness has come," asserted one column, "because it makes miles of improvements while we make inches." Or, as another writer put it, "we have not made near enough improvements" and "are far behind any large or even smaller city, as anybody who has ever traveled beyond the confines of Cincinnati is painfully aware." To drive home the point, the author contended that an "improving city is invariably a growing and prosperous city; witness Washington, Detroit, Buffalo, Cleveland, Indianapolis, Dayton, etc., all of which cities have spent thousands to our hundreds." Indeed, this writer came down for "modern improvements of all kinds" and chided those who opposed municipal expenditures as reactionary "reformers" who "prefer to live like their grandfathers before them on mud streets, visit each other with lanterns, fetch the water in buckets from the river, go to bed by candlelight, go to town in omnibuses, be without sewers." Such people "should move to some backwoods settlement, the farther back the better. As for us, we want some of the good things of modern civilization in our lifetime while we can enjoy them." [37]

This same spirit of civic boosterism pervaded the journal's approach to political issues it deemed worthy of support by "Improvers." In one issue, for example, it urged the construction of school playgrounds and the municipal ownership of transportation and lighting facilities, the expansion from $1,000 to $25,000 of the city's "condemnation fund" for the acquisition of private property for public purposes, and the lowering of assessments on property owners for street and alley improvement, in part by changing the law requiring approval of such improvements by the owner or owners of three-fourths of the square footage affected (rather than by three-fourths of the property owners). The journal also called for a constitutional amendment, if necessary, for the institution of a flat tax on land, developed or not, and for the abolition of taxes on improvements made upon the land, such as the construction or expansion of a building. In urging support for this cause it urged officeholders to help the journal "and with it the city at large, in its onward march for public and private improvements, seeking the welfare of our neighbors, our people, our children, our children's children, and let us place your name on the scroll of honor, that your own posterity may be proud of you, instead of being pointed out as public enemies."[38]

As it turned out, the Clifton and Burnet Woods Improvement Association did not last long. Yet the rage for "improvements" it embodied persisted into the twentieth century, modified by efforts to discipline the chaos of neighborhood competition at city hall for the delivery of improvements to particular localities. This drive took place in the context of the tendency to think of the city in functional terms as a collection of interrelated parts that formed systems and produced a tendency to plan for the future development of particular systems rather than particular localities. This kind of planning defined the systems of the city as mechanically interdependent so that a defective system could be isolated and treated separately. Sewer, transit, and park systems ranked as favorite targets of this kind of planning, characteristically performed by an out-of-town expert consultant whose out-of-town-ness might help shield the expert from local pressures within the city and from partisan political pressure.

This kind of planning caught on in Cincinnati during the early twentieth century and yielded a plan for a park system that seemed likely to improve and beautify Clifton along lines proposed by the park board in the 1890s and in ways satisfactory to the leaders of the now defunct Clifton and Burnet Woods Improvement Association. The board assigned to its proposed system of various *kinds* of parks the tasks of beautifying the city, promoting good citizenship, and improving the health and morals of park users. The board said a proper park system should consist of several elements, each with a special mission: small parks, squares, or playgrounds for relieving the congestion of the "old city," larger parks to help attract people to the new style urban neighborhoods, such as Clifton, and connecting drives or parkways for linking the parks. The board, however, did not treat all these elements in the system as equal. It assigned top priority to the smaller parks for the "old city" because they provided "the greatest good for the greatest number" and because of their strong potential for promoting social and civic stability. People playing in crowded city streets, noted the superintendent of parks in 1897, led invariably to "an interference on the part of the police, which in time engenders a feeling of hostility between children and the guardians of public order, and the growth of the criminal class, causing misery, poverty, and danger to society."[39]

The park commissioners made some headway in realizing this vision of a park system, especially after 1903, when city council authorized the expenditure of $500,000 for park improvements and for the acquisition of additional parks. But civic leaders from Clifton and other neighborhoods also put together an organization called the Greater Park League to lobby for the establishment of a plan to guide the commission's work. Council approved this in 1906, and commissioners promptly hired George E. Kessler, a landscape architect from Kansas City with expertise in urban park system planning, to prepare a plan for Cincinnati, a document he released in 1907.[40]

Kessler came up with a proposal for a park system almost identical to one suggested by the park commission in the 1890s. Kessler's plan called for small parks with playgrounds for organized and supervised play activities in the neighborhoods of the "old city," larger parks in the new style urban neighborhoods, such as Clifton, even larger parks farther out for use by all the residents of the metropolis, and a system of parkways linking all parts of the system and thereby linking all the neighborhoods of the city to one another and to the central business district. That last function seemed especially important because Kessler proposed to add on the northern edge of downtown another kind of "park" for everybody's use and edification, a pedestrian mall flanked by public and semipublic buildings, including the courthouse on one end and city hall on the other in a "group plan" intended to impress tourists and inspire a sense of civic pride and loyalty among the diverse groups, classes, and neighborhoods that formed the heterogeneous population and social geography of the metropolis.[41]

Kessler intended this downtown feature of the plan, as well as its metropolitan parks, to serve Clifton as well as other neighborhoods. But several other proposals in the plan concerned Clifton and Cliftonites more directly. Kessler wanted to move the Miami and Erie Canal into the Mill Creek Valley and replace it with "a main, central artery from the heart of the business portion of the city, connecting it with every residence district," an artery that would be the city's "most important parkway." Kessler called this artery Central Parkway and proposed a broad path for it running all the way from downtown along the western edge of Clifton, a route that separated Clifton from Mill Creek and its industrial corridor but also connected Clifton to locations north and south of it. Kessler also proposed a new park in the northwest corner of Clifton called Clifton–Lafayette View Park (established by the city in 1911 as Mount Storm Park) and two additional parkways significant for Clifton. One would run from the western hills across a viaduct over Mill Creek Valley to Burnet Woods by way of Dixmyth Avenue and open up not only Burnet Woods but also Clifton Avenue and Ludlow Avenue to traffic from the west side of town. In addition,

Kessler proposed the construction of "a central east and west parkway" from Central Parkway to McAlpin and along it through Clifton onto Forest Avenue to the eastern side of the city, a thoroughfare that would have divided more sharply "north" Clifton from "south."[42]

The park board approved of Kessler's proposal, but city council gave it a cool reception, especially the proposals for a civic center and for parks and parkways for new style city neighborhoods, including Clifton. Council accepted Kessler's plan but said that it rather than the park commissioners would "select parcels of ground which may be designated for park purposes, especially in the districts that are thickly congested with the population of a large number of tenement houses." Council also resolved that it would "endeavor at the proper time to give the citizens of Cincinnati any assistance they might desire relative to the carrying out of the proposed park scheme."[43]

By the time of the release of the Kessler plan (1907), the local improvement enthusiasm, which provided much of the impetus for developing the plan, had reached its second stage. In the late nineteenth century, that enthusiasm yielded the organization of associations that covered rather broad territories, like the Clifton and Burnet Woods Improvement Association, which claimed "north Cincinnati" for its special sphere even as it encouraged improvements throughout the city. In the early twentieth century, however, such organizations usually carved out narrower territories, a process that yielded a proliferation of associations that might properly be called neighborhood institutions because of their more restricted turfs. The Clifton Improvement and Welfare Association, for example, kept watch in the 1900s and 1910s over an area bounded by the corporate lines of the former village of Clifton plus Clifton Avenue south of Ludlow to McMillan Street. But this association, like its more ambitious predecessor, pushed for a variety of improvement projects, including the organization of a clean-up and paint-up campaign, the rebuilding of Clifton Avenue from Ludlow northward, and the lighting of both sides of Clifton Avenue from Ludlow to McMillan with boulevard lights, not only to illuminate the street but also to remove the wooden poles on which hung the older style arc lights. The association also wanted to reduce to two gentle curves the twenty "bad ones" on Ludlow Avenue between Cornell Place and the canal, in part to make streetcar travel more comfortable and to allow the introduction of double tracks, and in part to fill in a ravine to open for building purposes the property south of the avenue in its curvy stretch. The city government implemented these Ludlow Avenue improvements between 1912 and 1914. It also built a Ludlow Avenue viaduct for trolleys, autos, and pedestrians that

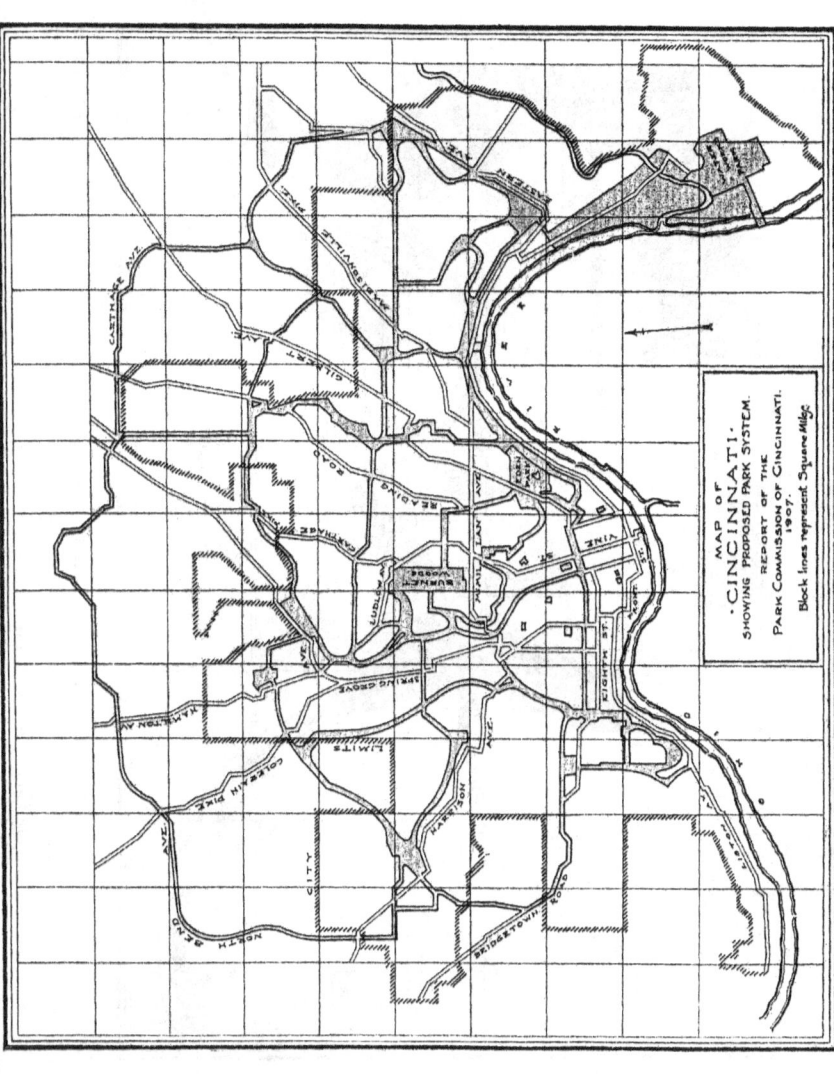

Map 5. Kessler's elaborate park and transportation plan sought to make the city more beautiful and efficient and also to kindle and sustain both neighborhood and citywide civic pride in the Queen City's diverse population. He aimed in addition to make the plan itself an object of civic inspiration for its elegance and its colorful appearance, the recurring motif of which consisted of green and grey illustrations. *Source:* Cincinnati Park Commission, *A Park System for the City of Cincinnati* (Cincinnati: 1907).

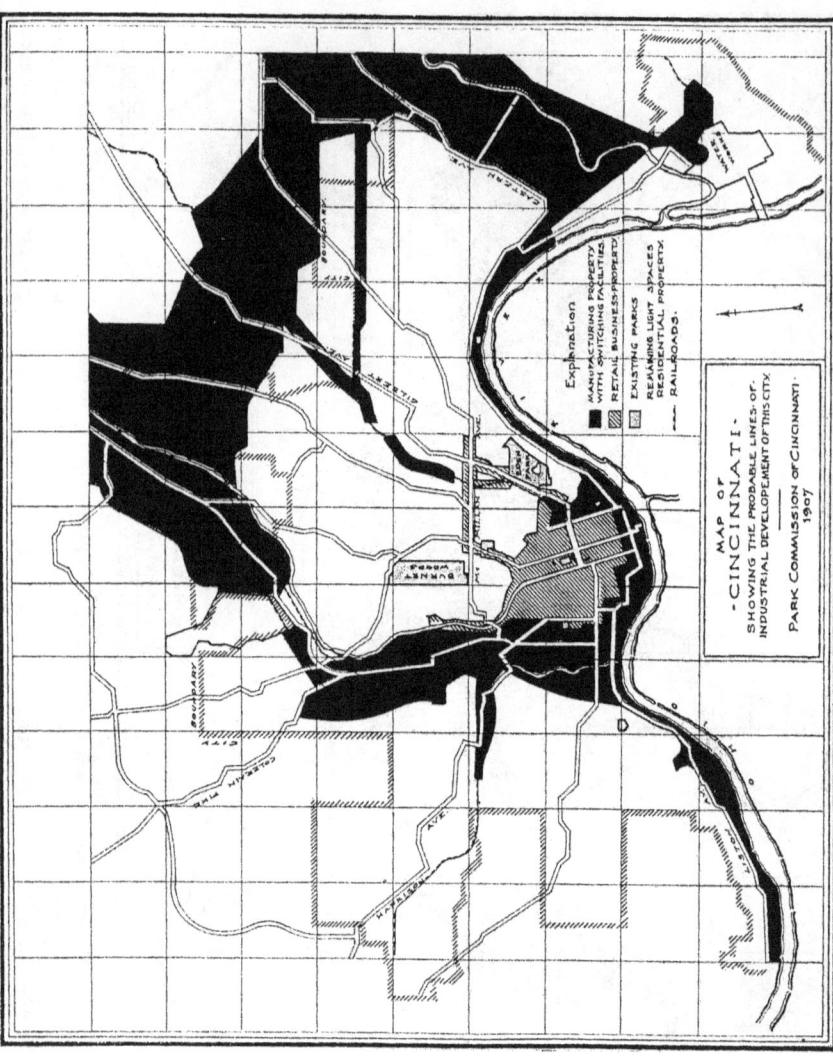

Map 6. In this map Kessler projected the growth of industry and the central business district, neither of which in his view threatened Clifton's future as a residential neighborhood. *Source:* Cincinnati Park Commission, *A Park System for the City of Cincinnati* (Cincinnati: 1907).

crossed the Cincinnati, Hamilton and Dayton Railroad railway tracks and Mill Creek at the bottom of the street. These public works projects created additional lots for residential construction on both sides of Ludlow in Clifton, below Cornell Place, and established a thoroughfare connecting outer and suburban neighborhoods to the northwest and north both to Clifton and to Cincinnati's central business district via Clifton Avenue or Jefferson Avenue and Vine Street.[44]

The failure of city council to embrace the Kessler plan also did not dim the push by Clifton civic leaders and others for a more systematic and citywide approach to handling park system and other improvements and beautification projects. Representatives of the Clifton Improvement and Welfare Association met on May 9, 1907, to consider the formation of a federation of such organizations, a meeting which selected W. G. Franz of the Clifton association as secretary and which designated J. D. Frey of Clifton as a member of the committee to draft a constitution and bylaws for the federation.[45] The conferees hoped that a federation would make the associations more effective than under the old arrangement when each section of the city looked out "for its own pet projects." The constitution followed that line by committing the federation to the promotion of "the general welfare of Cincinnati and particularly of the... residence districts by giving special attention to municipal improvement and all that relates to the beautification of those sections and convenience and comfort of the inhabitants." It opened membership to organizations outside of Cincinnati within Hamilton County and established committees on law and legislation, streets and sidewalks, parks and forestry, beautification, schools and public buildings, steam and electric railways, lighting, publicity, smoke, and "other nuisance abatement."[46]

The constitution dubbed the new organization the Federated Improvement Associations of Hamilton County, which caught on at once and flourished. Founded by just seven neighborhood improvement associations, it claimed by 1913 thirty-six constituent societies representing eight thousand members. Its rapid growth made a deep impression on the Rev. Charles Frederick Goss, the author of a two-volume history of Cincinnati and a promoter of "philopolism," the spirit of city love represented and sparked, he thought, by the federation. "To attend a meeting of these delegates from associations representing every suburb and natural division of the city," he wrote in 1912, "is to be made profoundly certain that a civic consciousness of some kind is actually being born; that the soul of the city is awakening to new and nobler life.... Today that comprehension is penetrating the minds of men, women, children, and institutions in an amazing manner."[47]

The federation undertook a variety of projects, including the protection of the public welfare, by prioritizing the demands of its constituent societies for improvements within their neighborhoods. In one such case, the federation's streets and viaducts committee refused to approve and support the Clifton association's request for the construction of a viaduct over a steep declivity between Jefferson Avenue and Vine Street. The committee described this improvement as too expensive, especially because the proposed viaduct was merely a measure of convenience to reach a location accessible by other routes, which meant it could not be justified as a way to save lives in case of fires or other emergencies.[48]

But the federation committee also wanted to make city government more effective at picking and choosing rationally among neighborhood improvement projects. It thought this possible, as one federationist put it, because city dwellers held "many interests in common, such as the use of streets, police, fire, and health protection." As a consequence, they "learn best how to work together, learn the great truth that each must give up something for the good of all." But that could not happen, this federationist argued, unless the state legislature gave up its control of city charter making and turned over to citizens "home rule" authority to write charters for their cities.

That opportunity materialized in 1911, when Ohio voters approved a "home rule" constitutional amendment, after which the federation joined other reformers in a two-year drive to create a home rule charter. The alliance favored a variety of then fashionable reforms in city government, including a strong mayor, a small council elected at large, the nonpartisan nomination and election of all municipal officers, a short ballot, a civil service system, and, as a federationist put it, "other such simplifications of the machinery of government as will tend to make it more efficient and responsive to the city's needs," including that "powerful trinity of democracy," the initiative, referendum, and recall, measures to enable voters to legislate and to remove from office unpopular elected representatives.[49]

The home rule alliance also proposed to rationalize the selection of public works projects in ways protective of the public welfare by developing a single city plan that would weed out proposals for making public improvements in the various city systems and that would by the elegance and beauty of its vision promote civic pride and loyalty among the various groups, classes, and neighborhoods of the city. Sometimes private associations paid for the drawing up of a single city plan of improvements and then tried to sell their implementation to the voters and the municipal government, as in the famous Burnham Plan for Chicago.[50]

But after 1910, planning advocates more often tried to secure for municipalities the authority to develop as well as to carry out a single plan for all improvements. The first attempt in Cincinnati to protect and promote the public welfare by shifting the coordination of improvement proposals from the private to the public sector came through a campaign in 1914 to secure voter approval for a new charter for the city that established a strong mayor elected by the voters. The proposed charter gave the mayor authority to appoint all department heads (except public finance) and board and commission members, but required the selection of individuals with demonstrated expertise in their fields of responsibility. The charter also required the mayor each year to draw up and submit to city council both an operating and a public improvements budget. The charter gave the mayor assistance in compiling public improvements budgets by giving the mayor a nonvoting seat on the planning commission (the first proposed in the history of the city), which would oversee the preparation of a long-term plan for public improvements (including their design) and regulate subdivision platting both within the city and in unincorporated areas contiguous to the city for an area three miles from the city's corporate boundaries. The charter in addition gave the mayor a nonvoting seat on city council, not merely as an observer but explicitly as a site from which to participate in discussions, make recommendations, and introduce and veto ordinances (council members could override mayoral vetoes and planning commission recommendations by a two-thirds majority).[51]

The adoption of such a scheme of city government would not have removed neighborhood improvement associations from the process of making improvements, for they could lobby the planning commission, mayor, and city council just as they had in the past lobbied department heads, boards and commissions, mayors, and city council members. But this kind of coordination would have reduced the number of prime players and streamlined the process. Most important, it gave the mayor the dominant voice in determining which and what kind of public improvements best served the public welfare, not only because of the charter's administrative provisions but also because it reduced significantly the role of political parties in electoral matters and provided for a relatively small (fifteen-member) city council elected at large rather than by wards.

The voters, however, rejected this strong mayor charter and put off until the 1920s the idea of revising city government and giving it the authority to develop a single plan for public works projects in Clifton and other neighborhoods. By that time a new vision of the city had spawned new notions about city government and planning, and by that time, too, changes in and uses along

Clifton Avenue south of Ludlow created ambiguity about Clifton's boundaries and led some to identify Clifton as the special home of professors and physicians and as an urban neighborhood responsible for providing higher educational and medical services to the entire metropolis.[52] The move in the 1890s of the University of Cincinnati into the south end of Burnet Woods Park constituted one such change of land use, as did the construction after 1900 of additional buildings on the Burnet Woods campus and the erection in the 1910s of a new city hospital a few blocks east of the university as a teaching facility for the university's college of medicine. New educational and medical institutions began to appear on the west side of Clifton Avenue across from the university and the park. The new Hughes High School building (1910) was placed next to Deaconess Hospital (1903); the Reform Jewish community started the Hebrew Union College (1913) near the north end of Burnet Woods on what had been the site of the Clifton Golf Club (nine holes); and Roman Catholics built Good Samaritan Hospital (1915) just north of Hebrew Union College.[53]

These new higher educational and medical facilities attracted new kinds of residents to both south and north Clifton, a development that diminished without eliminating the class distance between them and gave a cosmopolitan reputation to the area as a symbol of Cincinnati's alleged character in the 1920s, 1930s, and 1940s as a serene city of intergroup understanding and tolerance.[54] They also reinforced Clifton's status as a place both of and in Cincinnati with a future bound up with the future of the city and came to be seen as anchors of Clifton and bulwarks against the "blighting" conditions that created slums, conditions that metropolitan planners sought to eradicate in the second quarter of the twentieth century by razing and redeveloping such neighborhoods.

2

Preparing for the Worst: Comprehensive Planning for the End of Clifton, 1910s–1950s

THE defeat of the home rule charter of 1914 did not demoralize advocates of establishing a single government planning agency to coordinate the development and implementation of public works projects for the city's neighborhoods. Instead, they launched another and eventually successful effort, but one that rested on a new idea of the city and the processes and patterns of city growth. And the new understanding of the city suggested that all the city's existing neighborhoods, including Clifton, would eventually decay socially and physically to the point that they would have to be razed and rebuilt on "modern" and pluralistic principles of community building in the name of protecting the welfare of the whole metropolis.

The creation of institutions and programs compatible with the new understanding of the city took time, but not much. Advocates of the new view helped create in 1918 a slightly revised city charter that established a planning commission, but one lacking the resources for the hiring of experts to take on the major task of drawing up a plan for the future of the entire city. Planning advocates led by Alfred Bettman, a supporter of the failed home rule charter of 1914, and an emerging national and international authority on planning and zoning, organized as a consequence the United City Planning Committee (UCPC) to conduct a campaign for the financing and writing of such a plan for the future of the city. As a part of this effort, the UCPC brought to Cincinnati in 1920 the annual meeting of the national Conference on City Planning, for which event the Municipal Art Society of Cincinnati prepared and presented a city plan for Cincinnati. Although called a city plan, it differed little from the Kessler park plan, and it explicitly endorsed some of the elements of that document, including the Central Parkway with a civic mall, the parkway from Burnet Woods and Clifton Avenue across Mill Creek Valley into the western hills, the park at the west end of Lafayette Avenue, and the parkway through Clifton on the McAlpin and Forest Avenue route. To these proposals the Municipal Art Society plan added a thoroughfare running from the northwest corner of Burnet Woods down the hill on a southwest angle to Central Parkway.[1]

Yet the Municipal Art Society de-emphasized the importance of its city plan by calling it "a contribution toward working out a real plan for Cincinnati," one both "reasonable and logical" and one "indicating the steps by which gradually we may make improvements from year to year." And the Society stressed that this kind of planning, unlike its own, and other plans done in the past, should start from a "searching analysis" into the local topography, the history of the city "and its tendencies of growth, the industrial possibilities of the region, the character of its population, its interest in culture, education and the arts, its conservative pursuit of ideals of home and business life."[2]

With these scientific sounding words about the possibility of cultural engineering through city planning, the Municipal Art Society acknowledged both the shortcomings of its own plan and the emergence by 1920 of a new concept of city planning. The new breed planners disdained both the idea of diversity as a regrettable condition requiring a transcendental general sense of civic pride as the basis for social and political coherence and the idea of municipal planning for particular systems, such as streets, rapid transit, schools, public health clinics, sewers, parks and parkways, recreation facilities, and neighborhoods. The new breed planners touted comprehensive "master" planning, treated group, class, and neighborhood diversity as normal and permanent, and placed local pride on an equal plane with metropolitan pride as the best means of protecting and promoting the public welfare. In doing so they focused on metropolitan regions rather than municipalities and defined the metropolis not as a collection of systems with mechanically interrelated parts but as an ecologically interdependent system of systems in which a defective part not only disrupted the functioning of its system but threatened the vitality of all the other systems, including the system of neighborhoods composed of specialized residential components.

The advent of comprehensive metropolitan master planning also brought with it fundamental changes in the structure and direction of local government and a new neighborhood policy with profound implications for the future of Clifton.[3] In the late 1910s, Cincinnati's city government consisted of a directly elected mayor and large city council elected by districts in winner-take-all partisan contests, an arrangement jettisoned in the fall of 1924 by the Queen City's self-styled reformers, whose support, as in the past, ran strongest in peripheral neighborhoods such as Clifton. But both the charter committee, which engineered the charter reforms of 1924 and then won a council majority in the fall of 1925, and its adversaries now displayed a keen interest in a larger unit, the metropolis. Good government advocates, for example, sought both to annex suburban territory and to reform county government by running candidates for county office who advocated the strengthening and "rationalizing" of the structure and functions of county government.[4] Meanwhile, the as yet unreformed Cincinnati City Council adopted in 1925 a comprehensive plan suggesting the wisdom of regional planning "in the interest of the proper development of the metropolitan area of Cincinnati and communities adjacent to it," a proposal picked up by planning advocates who persuaded eleven units of local government in Hamilton County to set up a planning commission in 1929.[5] In the same period, moreover, politicians, planners, and government administrators touted a metropolitan strategy of razing slum neighborhoods and of promoting inner-city and suburban public housing and the development of suburban new towns, such as Mariemont and Greenhills, as invaluable supplements to big city tenement and housing regulations.[6]

All these efforts, though metropolitan in scope, rested on an intense concern with neighborhoods, but with neighborhoods conceived in a new way. By 1920, neighborhoods no longer seemed merely residential locations requiring "traditional" services, "improvements," and protection from crime, vice, and disease by the elimination or control, for example, of saloons and tenements, or by the education of backward people in civics and hygiene.[7] Now people tended to think about and act on neighborhoods as if they were functional "community" units and to concentrate on their internal socio-civic fabric and esprit while continuing to worry about their relationship to other residential neighborhood communities and to other functionally differentiated systems and units of the metropolis, such as factory and warehouse districts, transportation corridors for the movement of people conceived in functional terms ("labor," "consumers," or "white-collar workers"), and the central business district, the functionally and symbolically central and dominant unit of the larger metropolitan community. But these various units now seemed related in an ecologically interdependent way in which a defect in one impaired not only it but also *each* of the other units. In this context of multilateral and multivariate community interdependence, then, neighborhoods could not fend for themselves, and the city could not safely attack its problems, such as sewage systems, or transit, or parks, or tenements, or housing, as discrete problems responsive to particular and essentially separate and cumulative reforms. Only a simultaneous and pluralistic effort to secure the social and civic coherence of each of the subcommunities of the metropolis and of the metropolitan community itself seemed sufficient and efficient.

Planning advocates and their allies not only brought to their cause this new vision of the city. They also secured the adoption of a new city charter in 1926 that recognized the normality of class, ethnic, and residential diversity and defined the role of the planning commission as the guardian of the master plan and the welfare of the whole. The new charter diffused the power of the mayor as proposed in the aborted charter of 1914 by giving most of the administrative/executive functions of that office to an unelected official, a city manager appointed by city council. This left the city with a "weak" mayor and a chief executive officer (the city manager) lacking the clout of a direct mandate from the voters. The mayor, to be sure, could appoint members of most boards and commissions (including the "citizen" members of the planning commission), but the mayor as a creature of fellow council members rather than "the people" lacked the influence to exercise a significant degree of control over mayoral appointees, a factor which contributed to the practice of referring to the planning commission as "independent." The new charter also gave a seat on the planning commission to the city manager, but the manager brought to that seat no electoral mandate from "the people" and lacked therefore the political authority to do more than try and reason with commission members about the wisdom of this or that measure. In short, the new charter leveled the playing field in planning matters by inhibiting the development of a single position in city government with the ability to define the public welfare by exercising a significant influence in planning decisions.[8]

The "independence" of the planning commission from political influence, of course, also reduced the influence on it of aggrieved social and civic minority groups. But the final say in planning matters (as in others) rested with city council, a position designed to deflect to city council the maximum of "heat." The new charter made council a small one (nine members) elected at large on a nonpartisan basis, another attempt to reduce the role of political parties in policy making. But the charter also established a system of proportional representation voting that ensured a seat on council for any candidate securing one-ninth plus one of the total votes cast, a system designed to ensure a strong role in policy making for social or civic minorities possessing a sufficient sense of both self-consciousness and grievance to express politically their hopes and fears.

The Cincinnati metropolitan master plan of 1925, however, provided the first effort to make an attack on the problems of the city as defined by the new conception of the metropolis and its parts and groups. The plan intended to produce a coherent metropolitan community by ensuring the integrity of the functional units that formed the various metropolitan systems and by connecting the systems into a functionally efficient system of systems. This was the first comprehensive plan adopted by a city the size of the Queen City or larger, and although it contained no chapters on neighborhoods or metropolitan communities as such, an implicit concern for these entities permeated the document and manifested the dominant concerns of those who formulated municipal policy and the master plan.

That policy and plan was metropolitan in spirit if not consistently in substance. The master plan of 1925, for example, contained estimates of population growth for Cincinnati, Hamilton County, adjacent Kentucky counties, and for an area included within a fifty-mile radius of Cincinnati.[9] And while the plan held legal force only for Cincinnati and for the regulation of subdivision plats both within the city and in unincorporated areas within a three-mile radius of it in Ohio, the plan's authors contended that "the Comprehensive Plan cannot be cut off sharply at the purely arbitrary political boundaries of the city," for the "physical, the economic and the social problems of Cincinnati extend beyond these imaginary lines, just as though they did not exist."[10]

Although concerned with the metropolis and its region, the plan's chief explicit preoccupation lay with the functionally differentiated units of the metropolis and with both separating and connecting them. A principal instrument for attaining that goal was zoning, a new legal mechanism designed to secure the integrity of neighborhoods and districts by defining them functionally and prescribing land use patterns for each. A section entitled "The Need for Zoning" noted that "hundreds of stores, public garages and even industrial plants had invaded home neighborhoods. Each case was tending to lower neighboring real estate values, with a corresponding loss to the city in ratables [taxes, and therefore services]." Elsewhere, a "number of apartment houses were invading open detached home districts, hundreds of buildings were found to blanket their neighbors by projecting well in front of them," and "garages and billboards were located anywhere, regardless of their effect on neighboring property."

The plan also noted that the courts insisted on the reasonableness of zoning, which meant that the zoning ordinance should be "based on a thorough knowledge of the facts as they affect every property in the city," and that "the proper growth of industry, business, and multiple dwellings must not be stifled just because there happens to be a popular prejudice against them." And the planners asserted that zoning gave "every citizen" the kind of protection available to "the wealthy man," who "could buy up surrounding property to protect" his residence or "pay a fancy price for a plot in a highly restricted private development."[11]

In this view the absence of zoning threatened even the most affluent sections in a city made up of neighborhoods which, like north and south Clifton, might possess a purely residential core—or nearly so—but found within that core a variety of *residential* land uses and around the core a periphery of mixed land uses, especially commercial ones encroaching on residential ones. The problem was how to assert control by the city so it could "determine in black and white ... just what could and could not be done on every lot in the whole 72 square miles of the city." The answer seemed to be zoning carried out

> as an integral part of the rest of the City Plan, for all the parts of the plan are inter-related. Thoroughfares determine the location of future business, industrial and apartment house districts. They control the bus lines, present and proposed, and fix the location of business and apartment houses. The type of subdivision layout controls the type of residences. Parkways attract apartment houses, especially near the center of the city. Schools and playgrounds should be surrounded by residence districts, as should also parks and play fields. In general, it was found that unless the zoning plan is studied jointly with the rest of the City Plan, it would be likely to be just a good guess and continuance of existing conditions, rather than a creative force for the logical and orderly development of the growing city.[12]

According to the plan of 1925, judicious zoning would help protect Clifton at least until midcentury as a desirable community, for it already possessed other attributes deemed appropriate by the planners for a "home" neighborhood. Mount Storm Park, Burnet Woods Park, and the Clifton School, scheduled by the plan for enlargement by the addition of 640 seats and three acres of play space by 1950, provided Clifton with adequate neighborhood parks, playfields, and educational facilities, although the plan recommended the erection by 1950 of a park on the Clifton hillside facing Mill Creek, the construction of a South Clifton grammar school on Lowell, and the establishment of a West Clifton high school in Mill Creek Valley by 1970. The planners viewed these additions as part of the school system's new commitment to the idea of most modern educators "that physical and social conditions in the city call for the geographical distribution of high schools" rather than for their segregation by types of curricula such as classical, liberal arts, or vocational studies. The plan of 1925 also proposed for Clifton and other neighborhoods a local traffic system of "home streets" connected to but not penetrated by either the

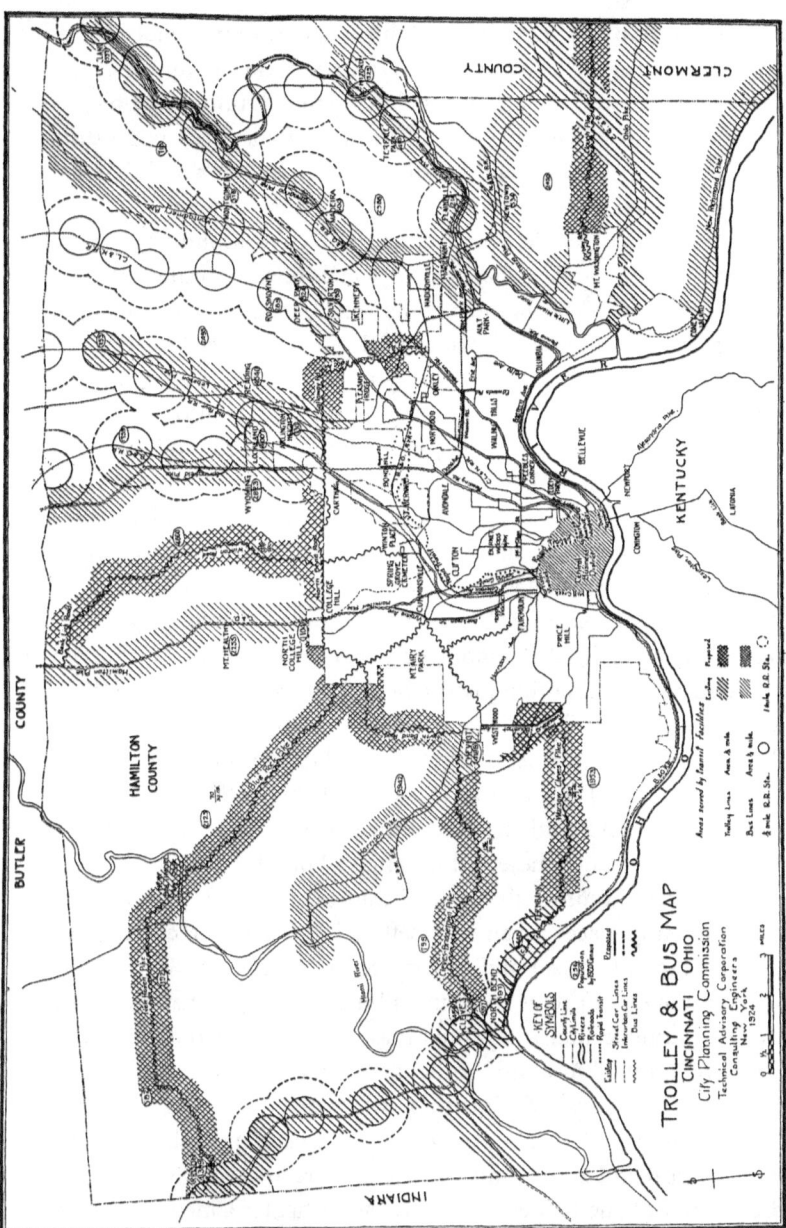

Map 7. This 1924 trolley and bus map dramatizes Clifton's remoteness from the spreading neighborhoods/suburbs farther out and its proximity to the expanding central business district and inner-city slums, as if to document the plan's claim about the prospects for demographic changes in Clifton in the indeterminate future. Source: *Official Plan of the City of Cincinnati* (Cincinnati: City Planning Commission, 1925), 112.

surrounding "spiderweb" of metropolitan thoroughfares for trolleys, buses, and trucks or by the projected surrounding system of parkways for cars.[13]

Other alterations in outlying neighborhoods stemmed from the plan's projection of a continuous albeit slow rate of growth of the city's population, which to the planners meant inevitable change in the population and character of metropolitan neighborhoods. In some cases these changes would be fundamental, as for the 120,000 people who lived in the "basin" around the central business district, the "natural" expansion of which blighted inner-city residential neighborhoods and which, the plan reckoned, required the reservation through zoning of the entire basin for industrial and commercial uses.[14]

But growth also provided an opportunity for perfecting other residential neighborhoods by the remodeling of outlying business strips into community centers, an issue treated in the plan's chapter on public and semipublic buildings and tracts. One portion of that chapter pointed out "several scores of local business centers outside of the 'Basin.'" Each "tends to become a local community center for the surrounding tributary residence districts" and a "focal point to which everyone gravitates who lives within easy walking distance of it." Here "local buildings," such as "branch libraries, public baths, public comfort stations, fire stations, local telephone exchanges, police stations, churches and clubs, as well as stores, motion picture houses, bowling alleys and billiard parlors" will "tend to locate."[15]

The planners approved this tendency for neighborhoods to become communities with central points for face-to-face contact among those living in the locale. But the plan also noted that, "except for stores, garages, filling stations and commercial amusements, these various kinds of buildings should, in their own interest, be located outside the actual business center, for they demand quiet, adequate parking space and an open setting." So the plan recommended that "in locating each of these buildings as needed, special consideration be given to . . . grouping them so as to secure all the advantages that may come from a local community center where buildings, related in function, may form part of a common group." As a model, the plan pointed to the suburban new town of Mariemont, just east of Cincinnati, where the "grouping of various public and semi-public buildings . . . offers a striking example of how this can be done in a practical and at the same time, in a more artistic way." The plan then cited examples of the tendency in thirteen particular Cincinnati neighborhoods, and urged improvement associations in these places "and in any others that have a real homogeneity" to pursue the goal of creating functionally grouped community centers as places of local identity and social and civic intersection.[16]

The plan did not list Clifton as one of the places showing a tendency to develop a community center, but that did not mean that the planners perceived Clifton or similar places as *immediately* endangered by the process of city growth and neighborhood change. Almost nonchalantly the plan predicted that the "highest cost and most open type of housing, such as found today in the Grandin Road district [in Walnut Hills], and in Clifton, will always be limited in quantity and in a sense, can look out for itself." In fact, the document found "considerable room for expansion of the same type in Clifton and to a lesser extent, in Avondale." For the immediate future, this segment of the plan concluded, "all this should be encouraged," but added casually, almost as an afterthought, that "it is obvious from the history of other cities that the older developments [such as Clifton] will gradually give place to more intensive development and the best type of housing will move farther out." Peering into that future, the planners proposed to encourage the location of "the best type of housing" outside of Cincinnati in Indian Hill, in "sparsely settled areas north and west of Wyoming, north and west of Mt. Airy Forest, and along the heights back from the river in Delhi, southwest of Price Hill."[17]

The prospect of having to move to these places must have seemed remote to Cliftonites in the 1920s. Had they not, through their enlightened participation in municipal and metropolitan politics and the unselfish activities of their neighborhood improvement association, helped endow the city with the most efficient, businesslike municipal government yet devised in America and with one of the nation's first comprehensive plans for metropolitan growth? Had they not, during the preparation of the zoning section of that plan, persuaded city council to change the proposed designation of Clifton Avenue from Lafayette to Glenmary from a two-family to an exclusively single-family home district?[18] And could they not, through such political influence, both defend Clifton's interests and assist in the noble task of guiding public policy along a path that coordinated and controlled neighborhood growth to foster the balanced and healthy growth and cohesion of the metropolis, that larger organic community of which Clifton itself formed such an important part? To those in the 1920s who rode along the broad, cool expanse of Clifton Avenue, strolled or skated in Burnet Woods at the edge of the neighborhood, sipped soda in the Busy Bee delicatessen, or shopped for hardware in the Ludlow Avenue business strip, Clifton must have seemed, as the plan of 1925 suggested, quite able to care for itself.

So it must have seemed also to those who in the 1920s let the Clifton Improvement Association drop out of the Federated civic association and disappear.[19] And so it seemed seven years after the promulgation of the plan of

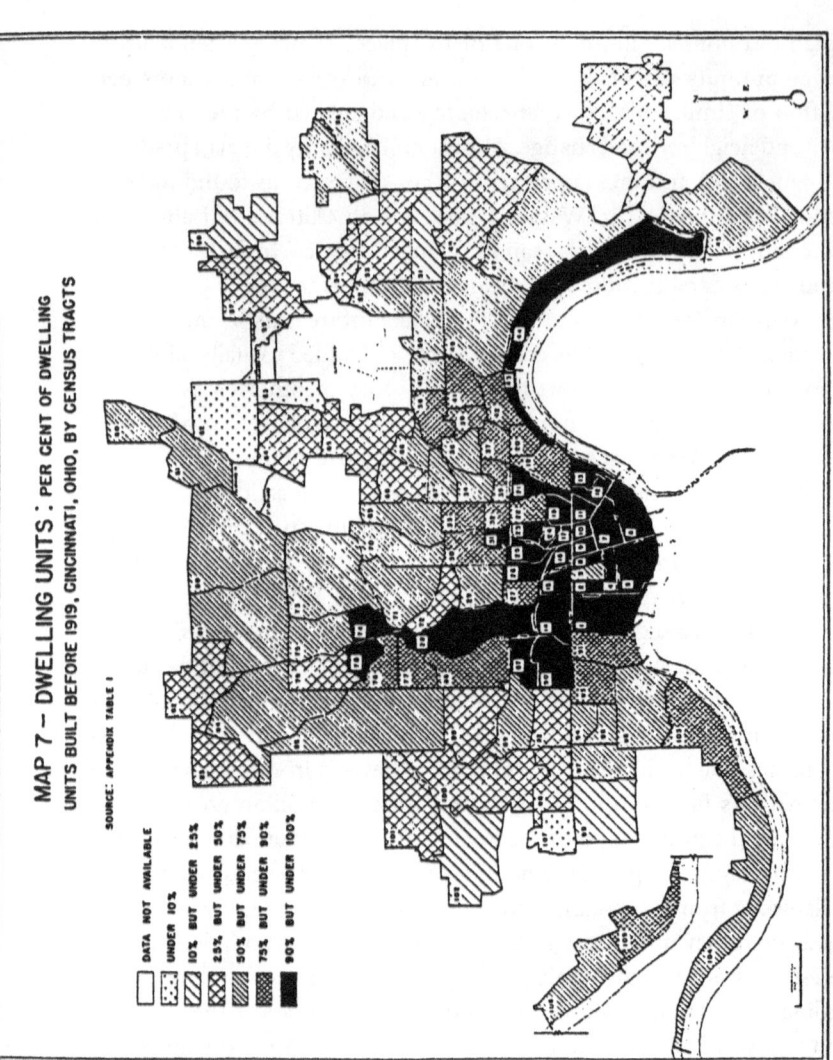

Map 8. By 1920, the housing stock in what had been the village of Clifton (census tracts 70 and 71) ranked it among the third oldest set of neighborhoods in Cincinnati. The area south of Ludlow Avenue (tract 72) that came to be seen as part of the Clifton neighborhood had a lower score. *Source:* James A. Quinn, Earle Eubank, and Lois E. Elliot, *Population Changes: Cincinnati, Ohio, and Adjacent Areas, 1900–1940* (Columbus: Bureau of Business Research, Ohio State University, 1947), facing p. 33.

1925, despite the great economic slump that followed the stock market crash of 1929. A survey in 1932 of Cincinnati's neighborhood business districts ranked Clifton, with Hyde Park and Avondale, as one of the city's "very best residential districts," and assigned it a population of 6,150, much smaller than that of either Avondale (22,900) or Hyde Park (17,350). The survey also noted that such top-notch residential districts contained business districts that occupied less space in proportion to the population they served than those in such "inferior" neighborhoods as Cumminsville, Fairmount, Corryville, Carthage, or Elmwood Place, which in the mind of the surveyor lacked the ideal balance between residential population and business frontage, a "fact" which projected such "inferior" places as objects of remediation.[20] But the survey concentrated on neighborhood business districts rather than entire neighborhoods, and contended that every "large city has its downtown, or central business district," and "a number of neighborhood business districts . . . serving the more common and immediate needs of the neighborhoods."[21] The survey identified all secondary commercial centers by street intersections (Clifton and Ludlow in Clifton's case), and classified the business districts according to the number and types of businesses within them. It defined a "major" center as one containing at least eighty-five establishments and thirty-five types of businesses, and a "minor" center as one with less than thirty establishments and thirty types of businesses. Clifton's neighborhood business district fell in the "intermediate" category, one with thirty or more establishments representing at least twenty types of businesses. Specifically, the survey counted in the Clifton commercial center fifty-nine establishments falling into twenty-nine types of businesses (66 percent retail and 34 percent services), an assemblage that occupied a business frontage of 1,586 feet (see table 2).[22]

This secondary commercial survey, with its distinctions between the central and secondary business districts and between neighborhood business and residential districts, resembled the plan of 1925 conceptually. Both defined the metropolis as an entity composed functionally of differentiated parts, one of them residential, and treated them as equal or potentially equal according to some "scientific" ideal about the composition of the parts and their relationships to other parts. Both regarded the residential units as communities, each of which possessed or should possess a civic "center" and commercial district appropriate to the population of the residential area, and each of which could be categorized on a scale ranging from older to newer and inferior to superior, standards by which to assess each community for its distance from the ideal. And both documents not only gave Clifton high marks as a community

Table 2
Businesses Represented and Not Represented in Clifton's Secondary Commercial Center, 1932

Represented	Not Represented
groceries	meat-fish-poultry
gas stations	auto sales
barber shops	shoe store
1 confectionery	electric-radio
restaurants	billiards
dry cleaners	bank
drug stores	tire and battery
shoe repair	ice
garages	undertaker
delicatessen	jewelry store
bakeries	upholsterer
1 dry goods	women's shop
1 building and loan	paint store
beauty shops	men's shop
hardware	millinery
1 fruit and vegetable	ten cent store
1 plumber	furniture
1 tailor	auto supply
1 roofer-tinner	wall paper
1 cigar store	printer
1 florist	bowling alley
1 laundry	department store
1 theater	

Source: William Applebaum, *The Secondary Commercial Centers of Cincinnati* (Cincinnati: Institute for Industrial Research, for the Commercial Club of Cincinnati, June 10, 1932), 109.

approaching equality with the ideal but also laid out in public a conception of Clifton as a community of diverse but segregated land uses.

But this conception also shifted Clifton's "center" from the mid-nineteenth-century locus at Clifton and McAlpin, the site of Clifton School, to the business strip along Ludlow Avenue where it intersected with Clifton Avenue. This conception of the neighborhood business district as the "center" of Clifton suggested without saying so that Clifton's boundaries properly included territory south of Ludlow Avenue, and pointed to an identification—or a potential identification—of Clifton with the University of Cincinnati's Burnet Woods campus. And this connection of Clifton with the university became explicit and a matter of public record in 1943 with the publication in the American Guide Series, sponsored by the Work Projects Administration, of a guide to metropolitan Cincinnati.[23]

The guide sought to introduce residents and tourists to Cincinnati conceived as a metropolis which, like other metropolises, displayed a particular personality. The book opened with a "Cincinnati Profile" that sought to single out the city's distinctive traits. This section, written by Harry Graff, a Cincinnatian and the state supervisor of the Ohio Writers' Program, asserted that Cincinnati differed from "such typical midwestern places as Cleveland, Columbus, Detroit, Indianapolis, and Chicago" and resembled Pittsburgh and St. Louis only in "physical layout." Graff acknowledged frequent comments by visitors indicating that Cincinnati's "appearance and the habits of its people are reminiscent of New York, Boston, New Orleans, and San Francisco." But the imperfection of these analogies seemed obvious to Graff and, in the way he dismissed them, should have been evident to others. "The truth is, of course, that the city has its own very distinctive character, formed by a definite set of influences." [24]

Graff stressed four factors as decisive influences in the formation of Cincinnati's character, two of which he associated with the Ohio River. First, the river made Cincinnati a boomtown during the mid-nineteenth century, giving the city a "lustiness which still lingers." Second, the river provided the economic base for the great fortunes which in the late nineteenth century established philanthropies and the city's varied art and music institutions.[25] Third, German and Irish immigrants brought a "fresh, liberal point of view that tempered the Presbyterian stringency on the one hand and the boomtown irregularity on the other." These immigrants also established "strong religious institutions and endowed them with a tolerance . . . distinctly noticeable in Cincinnati today," contributed to the "blossoming of the arts," and through their interest in physical well-being "provided the broad base for the city's famed recreation and park program." [26]

But the most influential factor, claimed Graff, had been the city's hilly topography, because of which "Cincinnati is largely composed of scores of suburbs, each . . . once a separate community isolated from its neighbors by steep hillsides, deep valleys, and thick ravines." Annexation brought many of these into the city itself, he observed, and transportation lines drew them together "but failed to erase their insularity. Even today each suburb is different from its neighbors in its architecture and the economic and social levels of its people." And this "tendency toward decentralization has created a certain cosmopolitan flavor, noted particularly in the Basin, where all these people from distinctive suburbs among the hills every day brush shoulders in work and fellowship." Indeed, asserted Graff, the hills of Cincinnati "shut off" the city from the rest of Ohio, rendering state news and politics irrelevant to

Cincinnatians, and discouraged intersuburban socializing, "except on Sundays, when . . . families visit one another or go for long drives, streetcar rides, or walks along the broad hilltop boulevards or in the famous parks that ripple over the edges of practically every suburb, often on the riverside."[27]

For Graff, then, Cincinnati formed a region unto itself, one of the nation's great metropolises, pluralistic and tolerant, but with a well-integrated personality of its own. Within that region flourished subregions, and the Cincinnati guide, after a section on the history of the region devoted largely to explicating the influence of the wealthy and immigrants in the development of the city, presented a series of tours of the subregions that consumed four-fifths of the text. These consisted of nine basin tours, twenty-five city suburban tours, three Hamilton County tours, and two Kentucky tours (one of Covington and its neighbors and one of Newport and its neighbors). With each tour Graff sought to present, through text and illustrations, the personality of the subarea derived from an analysis of its architectural, institutional, and economic and social history.

The WPA guide's tour of Clifton, though written after the Great Depression and during World War II, took a sanguine view of Clifton's status and future prospects and offered an expanded set of boundaries and an identity for the place that linked it to the University of Cincinnati and made it a neighborhood with a special character. Instead of using Ludlow Avenue as Clifton's southern boundary, the tour selected West McMillan Street, a commercial artery one block south of the southern edge of the university, and included as part of Clifton a broad swath of land between Jefferson Avenue on the east and Central Parkway on the west, strokes that stretched the territory of Clifton well beyond the village boundaries of the mid-nineteenth century. And instead of lumping Clifton with other old yet "superior" residential districts, such as Avondale or Hyde Park, the tour called Clifton "a distinctive suburb greatly influenced by the University of Cincinnati." Indeed, Graff noted in the first paragraph that the shops along McMillan and in the Ludlow neighborhood business district catered to college students and that many Clifton residents boarded college students in their homes. As for the streets turning off Clifton Avenue below Ludlow, they possessed "the traditional quiet associated with study."[28]

The introduction to the Clifton tour further defined it as a suburban neighborhood within the city, once "an exclusive residential section, a suburb of mansions and huge estates," but now a place fundamentally altered "by the expansion of the city and the macadam pavements, the trolley cars and the bus lines, that now make it easily accessible to the rest of the city." With these transportation innovations came other changes to Clifton. "Many of the groves

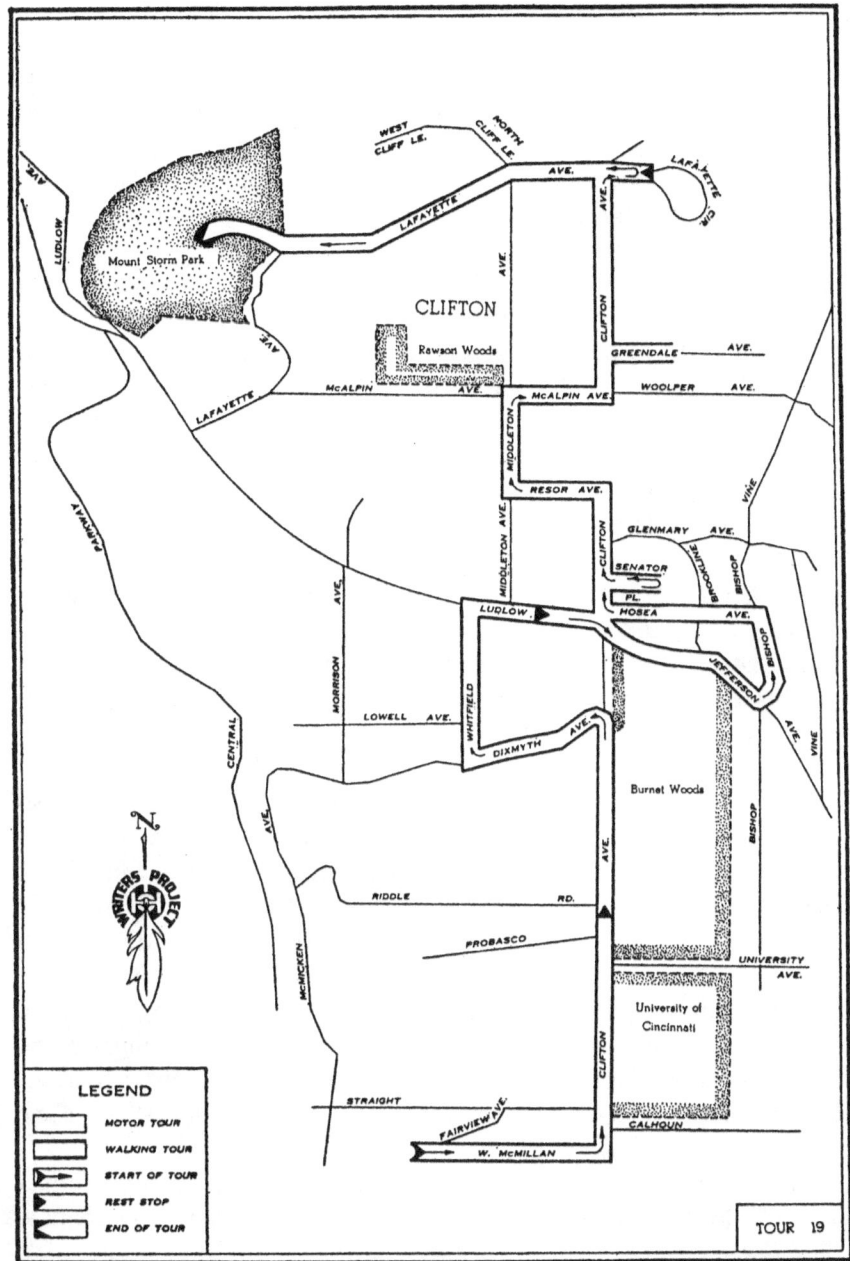

Map 9. WPA Guide's Tour of Clifton, 1943. During the second quarter of the twentieth century, many people defined Clifton as occupying a space that stretched south from Lafayette Avenue to McMillan and as a place identified with the University of Cincinnati, a view acknowledged in the WPA's tour of the neighborhood. *Source:* Ohio Writers' Project of the Work Projects Administration in the State of Ohio, *Cincinnati: A Guide to the Queen City and Its Neighbors* (Cincinnati: Wiesen-Hart Press, 1943).

that shaded vast lawns and drives have been cut down and the ornate homes removed to make room for smaller and more modern residences. Some of the old homes remain, however, and add to the dignity of the suburb," a dignity enhanced by the academic as well as the architectural ambiance of the place.[29]

In keeping with this approach, the tour started with an institutional bias, emphasizing the University of Cincinnati. The tour began at the corner of Fairview Avenue and West McMillan (in what is now known as the University Heights/Fairview neighborhood, or neighborhoods, depending on your source) at the site of St. Monica's Cathedral (which served briefly in 1938 as the seat of the Roman Catholic Archdiocese of Cincinnati), and marched down the west side of Clifton Avenue past Hughes High School and Deaconess Hospital. The guide then turned across the street and offered a history and tour of the university's campus that consumed more than one-third of the Clifton entry (twenty pages). The text stressed not only the university's grand buildings but also its size (ten colleges, 11,500 students, and six hundred faculty) and its "special features," such as its cooperative program of work and study, its status as a privately endowed and municipally supported institution, and its research and graduate programs in pediatrics, pathology, applied physiology, leather and lithographic research, and its recent archaeological expeditions to the site of ancient Troy, which had "recovered many artifacts of the pre-Christian era."[30]

After leaving the university grounds, the guide did not stick to purely residential sections but mixed them with institutions, as if to emphasize the diversity of Clifton and its combination of residential charm with educational, scientific, medical, and social welfare institutions. The tour moved from the university back to Clifton Avenue's west side and proceeded northward past the Hebrew Union College, the Good Samaritan Hospital, and the Cincinnati Crematory on Dixmyth and Clifton Avenue. The route then went to Whitfield and north to Ludlow, then back east on Ludlow along "the shopping and amusement district for upper Clifton," where "students . . . , university faculty members and their wives, and long-time residents mingle in neat shops and on the busy pavements."[31]

From there, the guide led sightseers up Jefferson Avenue past the former home of "Boss" George B. Cox, then down Bishop and around Hosea back to Clifton Avenue, where the tour took them north along this "purely residential" street, one "absolutely quiet" because of the absence of streetcars. This section of the guide carried entries for five mansions on Clifton Avenue, as well as commentaries on the Church of the Annunciation, Clifton Public School, Calvary Episcopal Church, and Rawson Woods, a bird preserve maintained by the city after 1923. Next came a brief side trip on Greendale for views of and remarks about the Resor home and the former residence of Francis Pedretti, an Italian immigrant who came to Cincinnati in 1854 and earned a comfortable living painting frescoes in public buildings and in the homes of wealthy merchants. Then the tour moved down Clifton for two turns around Lafayette Avenue, the conclusion of the event. Here the tour proceeded from grand mansion to grand mansion, as the guide offered commentary on the transformation of some of the buildings to institutional uses, such as the Bethesda Home for the Aged, the Convent of the Sacred Heart, and the Abbe Meteorological Observatory, a scientific facility for the study of the weather named after Cleveland Abbe, a Cincinnatian, the founder of the first regional weather service in the United States and the country's first "weather chief," the head of the U.S. Weather Bureau (1870). The tour terminated in Mount Storm Park, where Robert B. Bowler once lived and entertained such visitors as Dom Pedro, emperor of Brazil, and the Prince of Wales, later King Edward VII of England.[32]

The WPA guide presented a view of Clifton very different from that in the late nineteenth-century guidebooks, a portrait of a cosmopolitan urban and urbane neighborhood, bustling in parts but leisurely and quiet in others, and deeply influenced by its connections with the University of Cincinnati and other institutions along Clifton Avenue and elsewhere, a sketch drawn in terms that might have been applied to Cambridge, Massachusetts, in the same period. This Clifton seemed above all stable, and that sense of security persisted even after the appearance in the 1940s of some of the sorts of changes which frightened and inspired the Clifton anti-annexationists in the 1890s, and after the adoption by the Cincinnati City Council of the metropolitan master plan of 1948, which proposed to merge Clifton into the projected new "community" of Clifton Hills, an entity composed of several very different neighborhoods.

Clifton's population reached 9,800 in 1940 and rose sharply over the next five years, largely as a consequence of increased apartment construction on its southern edge near and along Ludlow Avenue. Between 1940 and 1945, a total of 220 dwelling units were built in Clifton, but only 60 were single-family houses. Of the rest, 24 housed two to three families, 88 accommodated four families, and 48 contained five to nine families.[33] Yet Clifton's situation seemed far from critical, even for the experts who prepared the metropolitan master plan of 1948, which anticipated that Clifton, like all neighborhoods of the metropolis, would eventually deteriorate to a point requiring its razing and "redevelopment" in the interest of the welfare of its inhabitants and the metropolis. But looking only as far ahead as 1970, the experts scheduled Clifton for "protection" rather than "redevelopment," or "conservation" (a treatment for deteriorating areas designed to retard "blight" and forestall "redevelopment" for up to twenty years), or "preparation for growth."[34]

These schemes for the treatment of neighborhoods rested on a domino theory about the natural life cycle of neighborhoods similar to but more elaborate than that suggested in the plan of 1925. The planners of 1948 pictured the metropolis as constructed of concentric circles of older and newer neighborhoods, with the older neighborhoods at the core, the middle-aged in the next ring, and the new ones on the periphery. The theory regarded the old neighborhoods of the core as nearing the end of their life cycles, and hence depicted a declining core, with its poor white and black residents gradually leaving the oldest residential neighborhoods as they fell to nonresidential uses and moving into declining residential neighborhoods nearby. Each neighborhood, said the plan, had a distinct life cycle, and the urban area consisted of "a vast patchwork of neighborhoods which had their origins at different points in time." Each experienced a period of growth, shortly after the initial subdivision, then a period of stability "during which the neighborhood tends to retain its original character." Then came "decline" as "the sale of homes rises again, with changes in the type of population coming into the neighborhood" and "a shift from owner to tenant occupancy, accelerated perhaps by the conversion into smaller apartments of larger homes," changing land use patterns, heavier traffic, more institutions, and the incursion of industry or commercial facilities.[35]

By these standards Clifton seemed middle-aged rather than old, and the master plan of 1948 suggested only minor modifications in and immediately around it, most of them related to traffic control and education. The plan described Clifton as an area with "many single-family high-cost residences and fine old mansions," added that "some of the original estate tracts have been sub-divided and expensive new residences erected," and noted without comment the cluster of "large apartments" near the business center at Ludlow and Clifton Avenues.[36] Even Cliftonites themselves seemed unconcerned about the neighborhood's future, for at this date Clifton had no civic organization, and no one in 1948 thought it appropriate to organize one to protest or praise the provisions of the plan.

Cliftonites, then, apparently shared the view of the planners of 1948 both about the metropolis and about the role of Clifton in that larger entity, a view based on assumptions quite compatible with those implicit or enunciated less systematically in the plan of 1925. Both documents, that is, took the metropolis as the basic unit of concern and the problem of maintaining the cohesiveness of that "natural" entity as the principal problem. Both, moreover, saw the

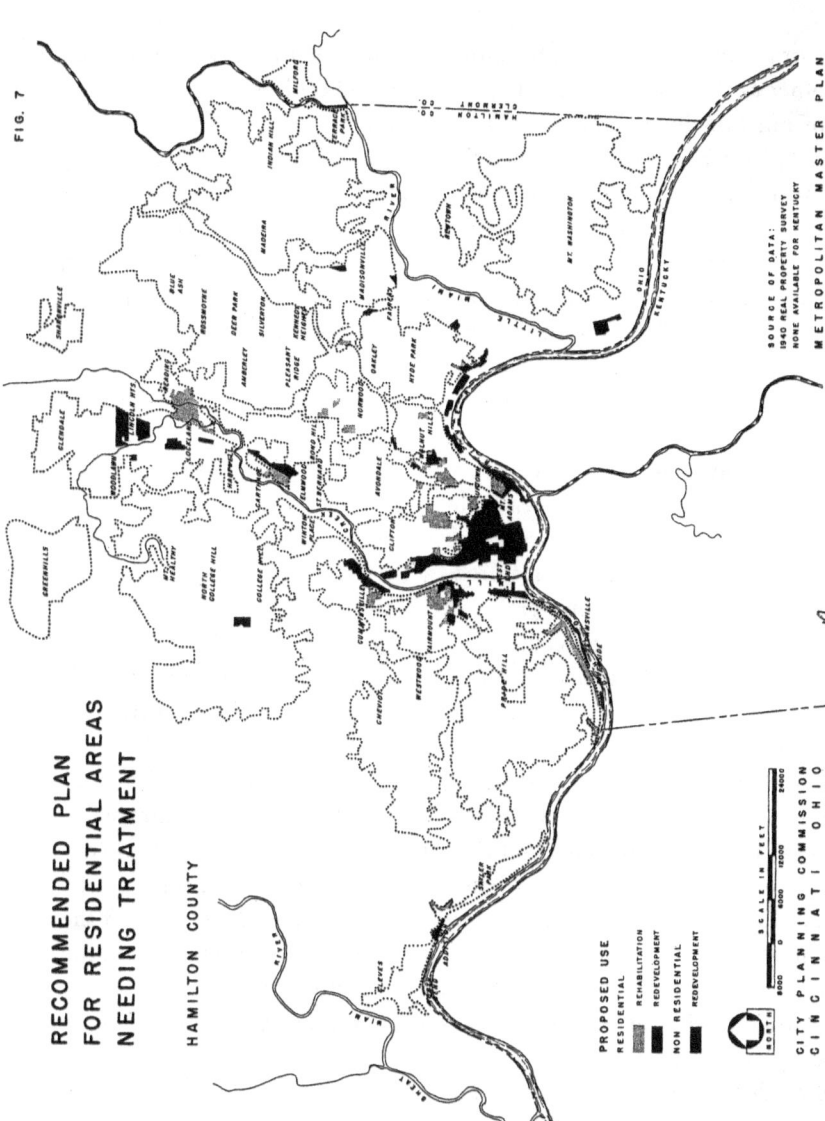

Map 10. Recommended Plan for Residential Areas Needing Treatment, 1946. This map shows the planners' confidence in Clifton's immediate future. The shaded area scheduled for rehabilitation looks small but in fact included all the neighborhoods on the east and south of Clifton (Corryville, Mount Auburn, and University Heights, an area then commonly known as two neighborhoods, Clifton Heights and Fairview). Source: *Residential Areas: An Analysis of Land Requirements for Residential Development, 1945–1970* (Cincinnati: City Planning Commission, 1946), 30.

creation or maintenance of subcommunities connected to and separated from one another as the key to solving that problem, and both prescribed the nurturing of functionally differentiated "neighborhoods." The two plans differed in that the planners of 1948 enunciated these principles more straightforwardly by organizing their research, the planning studies, and the plan itself around these principles, and in that the planners of 1948 sought to clarify the distinction between neighborhoods as places of residence and group social activities, and to view subcommunities of the metropolis as places of civic attachment by designating such "communities" as units for the distribution of public services.

It may be useful to point out here that the planners of this era may be seen as thinking of the city in terms of dynamic equilibrium or homeostasis. They believed that particular localities within the metropolis inevitably changed functions with the growth of the city, but that functions that left one locality would reappear somewhere else. In case this process sometimes failed to occur naturally, homeostasis might be restored by the intervening of the planners, either to restore a lost function, remove an "intruding" function from an improper context, or prepare a locality to receive an appropriate function. Planners, as we shall see most clearly in the plan of 1948, applied this idea to residential land use types as well as to commercial, industrial, and residential land uses generally.

The 1948 plan defined a circular Cincinnati metropolitan *region* with outer limits encompassing Huntington, West Virginia, Lexington and Louisville, Kentucky, Indianapolis, Indiana, and Dayton and Columbus, Ohio. It also defined a circular Cincinnati metropolitan *area* consisting of Hamilton County, Ohio, and Kenton and Campbell Counties in Kentucky, and emphasized the redevelopment of the existing urban structure within this area rather than the creation of a new form. The plan described the metropolitan area as a "mature" metropolis with modest prospects for economic and population growth, but one within which the popularity of the automobile would encourage a continuing drift outward of the population. The plan also divided the metropolitan landscape into two systems, one for "living" (residential) and one for "making a living" (industrial areas, major transportation trunkline centers, and the central business district.)[37]

The plan's "industrial policy" called for "growth on a selective, quality basis." It described such expansion as a "means to an end"—shoring up the existing economy in the face of competition from rapidly growing cities in the southern half of Cincinnati's metropolitan region—"rather than the end objective itself," and ranked "'service activities'—utilities, finance, insurance, real estate, communications, government, etc."—as most desirable from the standpoint of their contribution to the metropolitan economy. The plan also posited a rigid separation of industrial land use areas from both residential areas and the metropolitan downtown, in which residential housing also seemed dysfunctional.[38]

The residential strategy of the 1948 plan addressed Clifton's fate for the next twenty years and in the process divided Cincinnati into three arenas of activity: neighborhood, community, and metropolis. This vision and strategy rested on the premise that "when a city expands beyond a certain size it reaches the point of diminishing returns in terms of the advantages which a city, as a social community, should provide for its inhabitants." To gain maximum advantages, and to secure a sense of community at both metropolitan and submetropolitan levels, the plan proposed to organize Cincinnati's metropolitan residential areas into "communities" of 20,000 to 40,000 people, not self-governed but "self-contained in respect to the everyday life of their inhabitants except for such facilities and services as will continue to be located in or supplied by Cincinnati as the central city, and by institutions serving the Metropolitan Area."[39]

According to the master plan and one of the plan's special studies, entitled *Communities,* the concept of a metropolitan area composed of a central city, which existed chiefly for governance and metropolitan serving purposes, and of a cluster of medium-sized cities, some inside and some outside the jurisdiction of the major municipality of the area, and like "real" small cities in every way except governmentally, seemed to offer several advantages. That volume sketched a history of Cincinnati as the growth of neighborhoods around the original settlement, the annexation of some of them to Cincinnati, their retention of "identities," and the grouping of some of them into "communities" by virtue of Cincinnati's hill and valley topography. This circumstance the study deemed most "fortunate," because it tended "to preserve as the city grew, some of the better qualities of small town life, such as the spirit of neighborliness and the sense of attachment to a locality—qualities so easily lost in the full flood of urban expansion." Specifically, people in "smaller cities . . . participate to a greater degree in community activities; a larger percentage go to the polls; a higher proportion contribute to the Community Chest; more are interested in public affairs." And "here in the Cincinnati Area, to a greater degree than in most large cities, residents enjoy the economic and cultural advantages of a metropolis while living in residential localities small enough to satisfy the urge for intimacy in home surroundings and for a social life in scale with the average family."[40]

In short, the evolution of neighborhood, community, and metropolis had proceeded naturally in Cincinnati. Unfortunately, however, history had not completed adequately the task of community building, and the plan proposed "to strengthen the present rudimentary neighborhood composition of the Metropolitan Area . . . to form an organized 'cluster' of communities, each further divisible into neighborhoods." The boundaries of each community should encompass 20,000 to 40,000 people on 1,000 to 2,000 acres and be drawn with reference to "separators," such as topographic features, industrial belts, railroads, large parks, greenbelts, cemeteries, institutions, and projected expressways, and be connected to the expressways by community thoroughfares and by expressways or intercommunity thoroughfares to the central business district and the larger metropolitan community of work, entertainment, education, social, and cultural activities.[41]

The plan cited four internal elements critical to the viability of the new communities which it proposed to create or acknowledge: school, business, civic, and balanced housing facilities. That is, each community should be served by a high school, or at least by two junior high schools, and a cluster of neighborhood elementary schools. Each should possess a "community business district, a secondary business district in relation to the Metropolitan Area as a whole, but the chief center of commercial activities so far as the community is concerned." Each should contain a community civic center near the business center composed of a branch library, a recreation center, a health center, a branch post office, and in some cases appropriate semipublic buildings. In addition, each community should possess both single-family homes and apartments of various density levels so as to accommodate "young couples, . . . growing families and . . . elderly persons," therefore eliminating the necessity for a family "to move away from friends, neighbors, churches and other associations as it arrives at various stages of the life cycle."[42] And while the plan expected future single-family home construction to predominate outside the central city and apartments inside, the distinction made little difference to the planners, who thought of both locales simply as sites for communities, small towns exhibiting the social and civic characteristics ascribed to such small towns by the planners. In short, apartments in and of themselves seemed "normal" to the planners of 1948, and apparently to Cliftonites as well, who complained neither about the proliferation of apartments in Clifton in the 1940s nor about the 1948 plan's concession of their inevitability in places like Clifton.

The 1948 plan's communities scheme, then, presented each community as equal and in many respects as identical, but also provided a way of permitting and accommodating racial, ethnic, and class heterogeneity within a community without talking in *those* terms about diversity, a classic example of a pluralistic taxonomic and rhetorical system and operational mode which harmonized homogeneity and heterogeneity. The mechanism for doing this was the notion of neighborhood, for in forming each community the planners tried to group "traditional" and therefore discrete neighborhoods on the basis of spatial contiguity without reference to their class, ethnic, or racial profiles. Here, too, compromises had to be made, for history had not completed the task of dividing the metropolis into discrete communities. For the purpose of making these compromises, the planners, as they had for the same purpose with communities, prescribed the ideal spatial and population size and function of "the neighborhood."

Such an ideal neighborhood would contain 400 to 800 acres and a population of 4,000 to 8,000, and would be connected to its community and the metropolis by the thoroughfare and expressway systems and bounded but not entered by major traffic streets. Each neighborhood, moreover, would have all the attributes of a community except a civic center. In other words, each neighborhood would have an elementary school with a playground, as well as additional playgrounds where necessary, one or several neighborhood shopping centers, sometimes additional local shopping centers consisting of a few stores, and, of course, some mix of single family homes and apartments, depending on its proximity (a function of its history in the evolution of core and periphery) to the metropolitan central business district, the symbolic and functional center and central cohesive element of the metropolis.[43]

In practice, the community and neighborhood ideal produced some interesting configurations. The plan of 1948 placed Clifton, which the planners considered a traditional neighborhood, within the community of Clifton Hills, an oval unit composed of the traditional neighborhoods of Clifton, Corryville, Mount Auburn, Camp Washington, and University Heights, the latter of which also included areas known as Clifton Heights and Fairview. Thus defined, the University of Cincinnati and Burnet Woods occupied the geographic center of Clifton Hills, which consisted of 2,200 acres (3.4 square miles) and a population estimated at 43,800.

The component parts of Clifton Hills, except for Camp Washington, an "old and declining settlement" isolated by both "topography and industry" on the floor of the Mill Creek Valley west of Clifton, sat on the high elevation immediately north of the basin. The "separators" of Clifton Hills consisted of abrupt hillsides rising from Reading Road near Highland Avenue, McMicken Avenue and Central Parkway to Mount Storm Park, and, on the east, Vine Street Hill Cemetery, the zoo, General Hospital, and Deer Creek Valley. All of the neighborhoods in Clifton Hills, said the plan, traced their origins as Cincinnati neighborhoods to the mid-nineteenth century, although only Mount Auburn, with its many "original mansions" now "converted to multiple family use," could claim an affluent past like that of Clifton, and none of them in 1948 measured up to Clifton's socioeconomic profile or status as a residential neighborhood. Nonetheless, all but Camp Washington, which struck the planners as sufficiently "deteriorated" to schedule it for industrial redevelopment rather than residential use in the future, seemed viable as component neighborhoods of Clifton Hills until 1970, the date to which the plan claimed validity.

The plan for Clifton Hills treated Clifton more gently while making prescriptions that nonetheless touched on Clifton and its interests. The plan suggested, for example, the widening and straightening of Dixmyth Avenue to give Cliftonites access by thoroughfare to a projected Mill Creek [Valley] Expressway and thence to the central business district, which Cliftonites and residents of other neighborhoods in Clifton Hills could also reach via Clifton Avenue, itself ticketed for widening from Ludlow to Woolper for this thoroughfare purpose. The plan also proposed to improve east-west thoroughfare traffic flows through the community on Ludlow by connecting it to a widened Erkenbrecker Avenue, which approached Clifton Hills from the community of Avondale but in 1948 dead-ended at Vine below Woolper, and by the widening of Woolper to thoroughfare proportions and the realignment of the intersection of Woolper, McAlpin, and Clifton, the site of the Clifton School and Probasco Fountain, a historic center of Clifton itself. The plans for Clifton Avenue and Woolper, in short, projected east-west and north-south intercommunity thoroughfares through and intersecting at the center of what once had been the heart of the village of Clifton, a scheme which might have been but was not at the time construed as a compromise of the integrity of a neighborhood for the sake of the functional integrity of the community of Clifton Hills and the metropolis.[44]

That it was not so construed is not, perhaps, surprising, given the plan's boundaries for the neighborhood of Clifton. Those boundaries formed a circular unit encompassed by a line drawn on the south along Dixmyth, thus relegating Good Samaritan Hospital, the Hebrew Union College, and the crematory to the neighborhood of University Heights. From the corner of Dixmyth and Morrison, the line cut northwest between and parallel with Ludlow Avenue and Central Parkway until it hit the proposed Mill Creek Expressway, then curved around the outer edge of the community "separators" and expressway buffers of Mount Storm Park and the spacious German Methodist

Episcopal Deaconess Home on a line to and around Vine Street Hill Cemetery, thence southward past the zoo, which helped separate Clifton Hills from Avondale, to Erkenbrecker, the proposed extension of which to Ludlow formed Clifton's southern boundary to the corner of Clifton Avenue and Ludlow, where it zagged southward along Clifton Avenue to Dixmyth.[45]

Such a boundary seemed to preserve the integrity of historic Clifton, for it left Clifton School and Probasco Fountain near if not precisely at the geographical center of Clifton, where the neighborhood's two chief streets, forming rectilinear intrusions in an otherwise circular form, intersected. The boundary also placed the Ludlow Avenue/Clifton neighborhood business center south of Clifton neighborhood's symbolic center but within Clifton itself and protected from outside use by a projected bypass linking Ludlow west of the business center to Howell.[46] Thus the critical intersection occurred at the heart of the neighborhood, and the two intersecting thoroughfares served simultaneously as "main streets" of the elementary school–centered neighborhood and as intercommunity thoroughfares in the larger scheme of things, while the neighborhood commercial strip stood separated by residences from the educational-symbolic center of the neighborhood, thereby upholding at the neighborhood level the principle of the spatial separation of functionally differentiated elements.

Other aspects of the Clifton Hills community plan bore less directly on Clifton. The planners found Clifton Hills well supplied with schools, parks, and playfields, though some adjustments would be necessary. Each neighborhood had an elementary school, but the plan proposed the eventual construction of a new elementary school for Clifton just south of the Clifton School site, which site itself eventually would be occupied by a new high school replacing Hughes High School.[47] The plan also noted the university's extension of its campus along University Avenue to Scioto Street, recommended a further eastward expansion south along Scioto to Corry Street, and suggested, in the case of additional growth by the institution, more expansion eastward and "the possibility of utilizing a part of adjacent Burnet Woods" for university purposes.[48]

Finally, the plan noted the absence of a "dominant commercial center" in Clifton Hills, without, however, advocating the creation of such a place. Instead, it pointed to the existence of "important commercial development" along Vine Street in Corryville, at McMillan Street and Clifton Avenue, and, of course, at Clifton Avenue and Ludlow, which it described as a neighborhood shopping center deserving, as noted above, protection with a bypass diverting eastbound Ludlow traffic to Howell Avenue and thence across Clifton Avenue and a corner of Burnet Woods to Jefferson Avenue (the name of Ludlow Avenue east of Clifton Avenue). The plan anticipated no expansion of those commercial centers because of the predicted stability of the Clifton Hills population. But Clifton Hills, like other communities, would need a civic center. The plan placed it along Vine Street between William Howard Taft Road, which the plan designated as a "modified expressway," and St. Clair, an area in which the planners found a nucleus for a grouping of public buildings near University Avenue around a branch public library and an elementary school.[49]

The communities and neighborhoods sections of the metropolitan master plan of 1948 looked backward rather than forward. To be sure, the plan of 1948 proposed to change the social and physical environment of the metropolis in a variety of ways and by a variety of methods. But these changes represented efforts to bring the "reality" of 1948 as perceived by the planners into congruity with an antecedent conception of the metropolis, its parts, their attributes, and the relationships of its parts, a conception that "caught on" in the 1920s. This conception received one of its earliest and most systematic expressions in the Cincinnati master plan of 1925, which included as an integral component the comprehensive zoning ordinance of 1924. In this sense, the plan of 1948 proposed to preserve and perfect the status quo, a given conception of what the metropolis was becoming or might become. That is, since conception precedes perception the planners' conception determined what they saw and did not see (their perception of "reality") as they examined the metropolis. And their concept of the processes of metropolitan growth led them to a perception of reality which contended that the metropolitan social and physical environment would develop along the lines and in the ways they ascribed to it in the past.

As a consequence, the entire plan of 1948 looked backward, and two other aspects of the plan carried consequences in the 1950s that would play a larger role in this history of Clifton than the Clifton Hills scheme. The first involved the concern with separating commercial, industrial, and residential districts. That view appeared in the 1925 plan, but in 1948 the distinction between "areas for living" and "areas in which to make a living" was drawn more sharply than in 1925. Nor did the planners of 1948 rely solely on zoning and the natural tendencies of urban growth to promote the desired segregation of land use patterns. Rather, they contended that residential neighborhoods blighted by too much industry should be destroyed and turned over to commercial and/or industrial uses. And in keeping with the public housing and new suburban towns movement of the late 1920s, 1930s, and 1940s, they recommended the demolition and redevelopment of densely inhabited and seriously deteriorated residential neighborhoods on lower density and "community" principles.

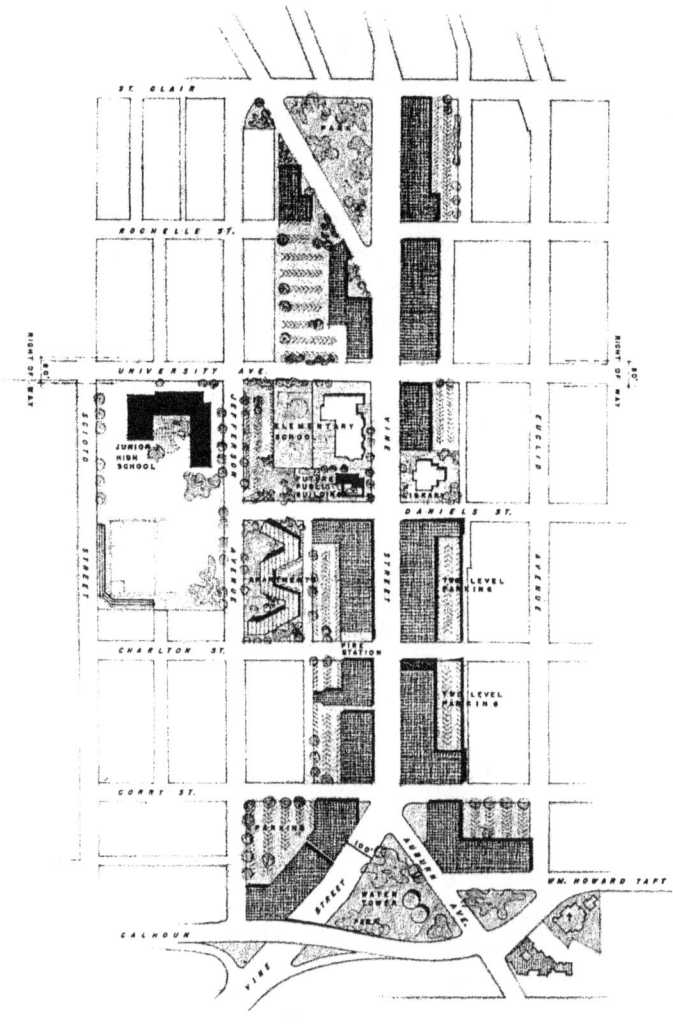

Map 11. The shaded area represented commercial land uses in Clifton Hills. *Source: The Cincinnati Metropolitan Master Plan and the Official City Plan* (Cincinnati: City Planning Commission, 1948).

Most of these blighted and deteriorated neighborhoods lay in the basin or in valleys entering and adjacent to it. The most important of these areas, from Clifton's vantage point, was the valley of the Mill Creek and that portion of the basin known as the West End, then the site of the metropolitan area's black ghetto.

The other portion of the plan which carried serious consequences for this history of Clifton also looked backward but dealt with transportation. The section of the plan on that subject noted that the Federal Interregional Highway Plan (1944) laid out a national network of freeways and expressways designed primarily to connect the principal cities of the country and to relieve traffic congestion within urban areas. Three links in the system came through Cincinnati: U.S. 25 from Detroit via Cincinnati to Atlanta and Florida; an unnumbered route from Cleveland by way of Cincinnati to the Gulf States; and U.S. 52 from Cincinnati to Indianapolis. The 1948 master plan sought to accommodate these highways and laid down guidelines for their location. It suggested, specifically, that they be routed to drain heavy traffic movements from overloaded thoroughfares, to serve concentrations of industrial and commercial activities, and to ensure that the benefits they provided would not sacrifice maximum efficiency or desirable community development. On this last point the plan added that where alternatives existed routes "should be favored which will remove from the tax duplicate the least amount of valuable property, fit in best with the land use, and not involve unjustifiable cost for construction."[50]

Translated onto the map, that recommendation, plus the plans for sharply differentiating industrial from residential areas, meant that Mill Creek Valley, which housed both industry and, in its lower reaches, the bulk of Cincinnati's poor and over half of its black population, would be the site of massive redevelopment and highway construction projects, provided that Congress, the state, and other political bodies took the necessary steps after the war. It also set some planners and city officials to thinking about where in the metropolitan area the population uprooted by urban renewal and expressway construction might resettle.

In the years just after World War II, while the master plan of 1948 remained merely a paper prospectus, Cincinnati's communities and neighborhoods changed slowly. During the 1950s, however, a combination of federal, state, county, and city activity made possible the implementation of much of the master plan's redevelopment and expressway programs. By the late 1950s, various agencies had started to build I-75 and the Queensgate I and Laurel-Richmond redevelopment projects in the Mill Creek Valley and the West End. Each month 210 families lost their homes to the construction of the Mill Creek

Expressway, and one agency estimated that 10,000 families left the Queensgate I area before its completion. Some doubtless left the metropolitan area, but the others, coupled with newcomers from the South, sought out new homes within the city.

Walnut Hills first felt the trauma of the creation of Cincinnati's second black ghetto. Since the mid-nineteenth century, a small but growing enclave of black families lived in that neighborhood, and by 1940 the census listed 2,595 nonwhite families there. Demolition of much of the West End and Mill Creek Valley districts, however, set off a black migration which hit Walnut Hills first, then pressed westward into Mount Auburn and Corryville and through the lower part of Avondale to the north until it washed the bottom edge of Clifton's eastern slope along Vine Street.[51] There, in the mid-1970s, it stopped. But before then, as the new black ghetto took shape, it displaced lower-middle, middle-, and upper-middle-class whites. This produced an angry white backlash and an outburst of violence by blacks infuriated by their removal from the West End and their reimprisonment in yet another ghetto. The era of the long hot summer and the neighborhood organization revolution had reached Cincinnati and Clifton.

No one in the late 1940s and early 1950s foresaw these events, however. Indeed, accounts of Clifton in these years suggested a serenity about the present and future like that attributed to the city by a historian in 1950 who portrayed Cincinnatians as confident in their ability to handle whatever problems might emerge in the short or the long run.[52] In 1949, for example, the *Cincinnati Enquirer* offered its readers a pictorial tour of Lafayette Avenue and its "baronial mansions" and an article on Clifton. The great estates, noted the writer, had been subdivided, but the castles themselves remained "unchanged" and displayed exteriors "unscarred by time" that still sheltered "lavish" interiors. And while "Haughty Clifton isn't 'like it once was,' according to a few remaining contemporaries of the rich suburb's halcyon days, . . . you would scarcely believe it as you drive along Lafayette and see towers" like those on Scarlet Oaks.[53]

Even the auction that year of the antique and historic furnishings (European in origin) of a Clifton mansion evoked no sense of foreboding. The *Cincinnati Enquirer* observed that the auctioneer came from New York City and specialized in liquidating the contents of old mansions located in all parts of the country at the rate of thirty-five per year. He reckoned that such estates changed hands on the average of once every eight years, the time it took for high-income purchasers to raise the children for whose edification and enjoyment they purchased such posh surroundings. As if to emphasize the normality of such property turnovers, the *Enquirer* ran a picture of Dr. Albert B. Sabin, the young director of the Children's Hospital just east of Clifton, and identified him as the new owner of "the Neave mansion on the south side of Lafayette just west of Middleton."[54] In light of Sabin's upfront Jewishness, however, some may have read this picture as a sign of what might happen to a declining neighborhood.

The next year, the *Cincinnati Times-Star* struck a similarly positive tone about the stability of the status quo but noticed three problems, none of them identified in the plan of 1948 or related to intra-urban shifts of population from neighborhood to neighborhood. The first problem, smoke and "dust" wafting over Clifton from "the industrial valley to the west," the *Times-Star* said little about. The second, the installation of a traffic light with a left turn signal at the corner of Ludlow and Clifton and the banning of parking from 4 to 6 p.m. along the Ludlow business strip, received more attention. These steps, said the *Times-Star,* put Mrs. Joseph Sagmaster, a "civic leader," and other members of the community "up in arms" because the left turn signal slowed traffic along the Ludlow business strip and because some merchants feared that the parking ban would deter motorists from stopping to shop on their way home. In response, the planning commission suggested the construction of a parking lot behind the businesses on the south side of Ludlow, a project that would cost $100,000 and require the donation of property to the city. And some thought the slow traffic problem might be handled by cutting a bypass around the corner and through the northern edge of Burnet Woods Park, even though a recent expansion of the University of Cincinnati campus into a small portion of the south end of the park had set off strong objections by park devotees to further encroachments into Burnet Woods.

The third problem consisted of a disagreement over the proper boundaries of Clifton. Some Cliftonites, noted the *Times-Star,* preferred the "old" definition, by which anything south of Howell Avenue lay beyond the pale in a separate entity referred to as "Dutch Clifton." But merchants claimed that Clifton spread as far south as McMillan Street and included (south to north) the University of Cincinnati, Hughes High School, the Hebrew Union College, and Good Samaritan Hospital. Although this view coincided with that of the WPA guide to Cincinnati and many Clifton residents besides merchants, the reporter refused to take sides. Indeed, he proposed that each reader should "take your choice," a position suggesting that this issue, like the parking and traffic problems, would be resolved without disturbing the "quiet" and "dignity" that, according to the reporter, prevailed in "Old Clifton" north of Ludlow Avenue.[55]

By this reference to "Old Clifton," however, the reporter came down on the side of the merchants by implicitly annexing a "new Clifton" south of Ludlow to the old. In doing so, moreover, the reporter endorsed a widely held view of the "new" Clifton. That conception took shape in the early twentieth century and both integrated "south" Clifton between McAlpin and Ludlow with the land of the stately mansions in "north" Clifton and reinforced the legitimacy of a "new" and greater Clifton encompassing also territory on Clifton Avenue south of Ludlow and past the university to McMillan Street. This conception of a "new" and greater Clifton, of course, violated the boundaries in the plan of 1948 for the neighborhood of Clifton and the community of Clifton Hills. But that seemed not to bother anyone at the opening of the last half of the twentieth century as city officials prepared to implement the urban redevelopment, expressway, and other projects designed to perfect the system of neighborhoods and communities that the expert planners regarded as natural developments in the evolution of the metropolis.

3

Establishing Clifton as an "In-town Suburb," 1955–1964

THE 1950s and 1960s may be seen, like the late nineteenth-century annexation era, as another critical period in Clifton's past, a period marked by the sense that its essence might once more be violated. This time, however, the fear produced not only protests but also programs of civic action, including the establishment in 1961 of the Clifton Town Meeting (CTM), a new kind of neighborhood organization that lobbied city hall for neighborhood improvements and also pushed residents themselves to participate in making and implementing plans and projects for their social and physical environment.

But CTM was not unique. Through it Cliftonites joined the neighborhood organization revolution, the metropolitan drive to empower local communities we tend to associate exclusively with inner-city black neighborhoods. To be sure, the dissatisfaction of CTM's founders stemmed from the growth of Cincinnati's central business district and the expansion of blighted areas around it, both of which took place at a much more rapid pace than forecast by the metropolitan plan of 1948. But these phenomena prompted CTM leaders both to acknowledge and to reject the 1948 plan's assumption that the "natural" tendencies of metropolitan growth led inevitably to the blighting of older neighborhoods, a prospect for Clifton that now seemed both imminent and avoidable if residents took the initiative in steering a different course instead of fleeing to a newer neighborhood farther out.

Yet CTM leaders intended more than merely to rescue Clifton from blight. They wanted to abandon the preoccupation of the planners of 1948 with the creation and maintenance of homogenous neighborhoods to engineer social and civic lifestyles for the promotion of metropolitan coherence and community. In this effort CTM leaders took the neighborhood rather than the metropolis as their chief area of concern and reconceived the metropolitan area to make room for the preservation of Clifton's alleged historic character as a particular kind of big city neighborhood, an "in-town suburb." In defining this entity, moreover, CTM leaders asserted their right to design their neighborhood and contended that they preferred a diverse rather than a uniform social and physical environment, one capable of retaining and attracting socioeconomically and geographically mobile individuals regardless of their race, ethnicity, religion, or lifestyle.

City officials and the leaders of other neighborhoods reached similar conclusions, a shift in thinking that yielded a new view of metropolitan life as a process driven by individual choices about neighborhood design and a picture of the metropolis as a divided rather than a united entity.[1] The new view divided the big city into three residential sections: (1) a central business district as lively by night as by day that housed people of all income levels, (2) "inner-city" neighborhoods for the poor and impoverished newcomers to the city, especially African Americans, and (3) "in-town suburbs," more commonly called "outer" city neighborhoods, for a more prosperous population, regardless of race. And the new view of metropolitan life located these entities in a universe of big city and surrounding neighborhoods locked in a competition for the right kind and mix of individuals as defined by the leaders of each neighborhood.

The new thinking also inflated the stakes in the neighborhood sweepstakes, which since the late nineteenth century had pitted one locality against all the others in a race to secure scarce resources. At the turn of the century, the contest focused on acquiring infrastructure improvements. The Federated Improvement Association sought to coordinate competing local claims, a task that planning advocates in the 1910s tried to assign to the city government in the form of a planning commission. Between the 1920s and the 1950s, the nature of the competition shifted once more, and this time it centered on securing for neighborhoods community development facilities laid out in metropolitan master plans.

At midcentury, however, a new focus emerged: citizens redesigning their neighborhoods for the purpose of attracting the right kind of residents. This concept of neighborhood competition and striving for neighborhood autonomy through the maximum feasible participation of citizens in planning and implementing changes in the social and physical environment manifested itself first in Clifton during the summer of 1955, when a group set up Clifton Meadows as "a club to provide recreational facilities," including a swimming pool, tennis courts, and a "'family center'" for "all families in the area." Within a year, the club acquired seven and a half acres on a knoll between Amazon and Egbert Streets overlooking the Mill Creek Valley. The new institution opened in the summer of 1957 and offered its members a clubhouse, pool, tennis and volleyball courts, and space in which to play baseball. The leader in the movement to start the club, and the first president of the corporation, Francis L. Dale, explained in 1955 the need for such an institution: "Clifton had had nothing to keep residents in Clifton. As a consequence, Clifton was slowly developing into a transient community." At that time an *Enquirer* reporter described the venture as "trend-setting" and as "sort of a barrier against the drift to suburbia." Two years later, another *Enquirer* reporter wrote that Clifton Meadows had "been a boon to property owners, helping to preserve property values and changing a lot of minds about leaving Clifton for suburbia." The *Enquirer* noted that the club had "attracted groups from far and near who want to know how to do it too, and it has become one of the selling points for attracting potential home buyers."[2]

Yet Cliftonites could not rest on their laurels because of competition stemming from the contemporaneous growth of interest in the conservation and embellishment of other old neighborhoods close to downtown by retaining and attracting socioeconomically and geographically mobile individuals. In the 1950s, for example, middle- and upper-income individuals began to establish residences in a working-class hilltop neighborhood just east of the central business district called Mount Adams, sometimes building new homes, but more often refurbishing one of the neighborhood's nineteenth-century row houses, which had until then sat forlornly in a compact and crowded milieu built in the last half of the nineteenth century. The planners of 1948 had scheduled this neighborhood for extensive demolition and redevelopment, as well as for "rehabilitation" (bringing some old housing up to building code standards and tearing down the most dilapidated), as part of the scheme to merge it into the community of Walnut Hills.[3] But the newcomers saw it differently, and by 1956 a metropolitan daily newspaper dubbed the Mount Adams revival a "fashionable" movement supported by speculators and those who wanted to live there. When asked why they chose Mount Adams, newcomers noted its closeness to Eden Park, a "traditional" desideratum for a "good" neighborhood, as well as its historic charm, its view of the Ohio River *and* downtown, and the fact that they could walk downtown from their homes within a few minutes.[4]

Yet Clifton faced other competitors as well. Residential developers began moving into the central business district itself, despite the disdain of the planners of 1925 and 1948 for such use of downtown real estate. In 1961, for example, one developer converted an office building on Walnut Street into a twelve-unit apartment house. Another transformed a five-story structure on East Fourth into a multipurpose building that contained several apartments, including one for himself, and a "young sophisticated developer" turned a four-story edifice on the same street into a three-unit dwelling to "show people what can be done downtown," an assertion he supported by saying he received eight to ten rental inquiries a day as proof of the existence of a "definite desire to live downtown."

Even big-time developer Marvin Warner touted downtown's residential potential. In the late 1940s and 1950s, Warner had built large low- and middle-income housing projects, including the new community of Forest Park next to Greenhills in north suburban Hamilton County, on outlying sites across the face of the metropolis. In 1961, he proposed a renovation project at Eighth and Walnut, arguing that increasing numbers of people wanted maintenance-free living so that they could travel to Florida or Europe whenever they pleased, and that people had moved to the suburbs in the 1950s in such numbers because of the absence of an alternative downtown. Now, Warner contended, things were changing and "a few major developments [downtown] could turn the tide."[5]

Worse still, from the perspective of CTM leaders and the boosters of other "in-town suburbs," city planners joined developers in efforts to lure socioeconomically and geographically mobile people into new downtown housing, not only by revising the conventional wisdom about the range and diversity appropriate for downtown but also by changing their approach to planning. In the 1950s, the planners began to utilize for downtown and other urban redevelopment purposes a provision of Title I of the Federal Housing Act of 1949 which provided subsidies for cities or other public agencies to acquire sites for redevelopment by public and private capital, substantial parts but not all of which redevelopment had to be reserved for residential use. As part of the preparation for such undertakings, the planners in the late 1950s abandoned their old technique of comprehensive metropolitan planning in favor of formulating renewal plans for particular parts of the city, including downtown. The first of these appeared in 1957 and presented a conception of downtown quite different from that of 1948 and one which acknowledged the appropriateness of downtown as a site for residential housing.

The 1957 scheme drew the boundaries of downtown to encompass the Music Hall–Washington Park complex in the Over-the-Rhine district and the Lytle Park–Taft Museum area east of the financial district, thereby acknowledging the legitimacy of expanding the number of high culture institutions and parks as parts of the central business district rather than putting new ones outside of downtown in a district with government offices. Also unlike the plan of 1948, the 1957 document defined precisely the boundaries of the downtown "core" and "frame" and noted the existence of low-cost residential sites in the frame, labeling them "residual" and predicting their disappearance in the face of increasing demand for land for "major" and "minor" downtown functions. But the plan of 1957 also dubbed as successful in economic terms more expensive high-rise apartments in the vicinity of Lytle Park and endorsed that sort of residential construction within the central business district by designating that location and Garfield Park as sites appropriate for residential and club as well as office development.

After the release of the downtown plan of 1957, various schemes for housing developments around the central business district reflected the more flexible attitude toward residential buildings in or near downtown and the apparent higher commitment of city planners to "inner-city" areas than to "in-town suburbs." In 1959, for example, the city planning commission issued plans for the redevelopment of cleared land in an area the commission called Queensgate I. Located immediately west of the downtown frame, plans for Queensgate I concentrated on commercial and light industrial uses, but also designated a small part of the area as residential and showed it hemmed in on the west by the Mill Creek Expressway (I-75) and on the east by a proposed civic center on Central Avenue and public low-income housing projects.

The riverfront plan of 1961 displayed a similar disposition toward fostering residential construction adjacent to the central business district. Completed at the time of the outburst of private residential development within downtown itself, this plan explicitly acknowledged what it saw as a national trend toward downtown living, and recommended the construction of high-rise apartments on the central business district waterfront. The 1961 proposal described the riverfront apartment project as desirable not only because of its "accessibility to downtown" but also because it would serve as the southern portion of a ring of residential housing circling the central business district. And the plan saw this kind of housing as ideal both for people who worked downtown and for retirees, who would find living near the central business district "interesting," a clear shift from the 1948 plan, which oriented housing in areas adjacent to downtown, such as Mount Adams and the West End, away from the central business district and toward one of the new communities that formed the heart of the 1948 plan's residential strategy for the metropolitan area.

Three years later, the city planning commission unveiled yet another downtown plan, this one composed in a citizens participation process through a city manager's working review task force consisting of city planners, representatives of downtown business interests, and various elected and appointed officials who would be responsible for approving and carrying out the plan. The 1964 scheme identified the capturing of corporate headquarters and high-technology industries as the key to renewing the vitality of Cincinnati's central business district. This could be done, it contended, not only by providing "tangible" features, such as superior transportation facilities, but also by fostering "intangible" attractions for industrial management personnel, such as creating a central business district as lively by night as by day, a strategy requiring an "intermingling" of downtown land uses, including housing. Specifically, the plan of 1964 proposed by 1970 to increase central business district residential space in thousands of square feet from the 1963 level of 2,315 to 3,620, and to make available not only more but also more varied housing on the downtown "fringe." In particular, the plan stressed the importance of adding West Fourth Street and Block "E" (just west of Lytle Park) to the Lytle Park and Garfield Park areas previously designated for residential and office use. And Block "E" seemed especially significant because it would provide a link in a "broad band of downtown housing" extending from Mount Adams on the east and around Lytle Park to its other end at the central riverfront apartments.

The plan of 1964, then, differed from the metropolitan master plan in ways other than the range of territory covered. Professional planners controlled from start to finish the process that yielded the plan of 1948, while the plan of 1964 came out of a maximum feasible participation scheme through a process that involved not only professional planners but also city officials and citizen representatives of the unit of concern. And the 1964 plan rejected the 1948 plan's separation of downtown from residential land uses by inserting apartments into the central business district, by considering adjacent residential neighborhoods as fringes of downtown, and by arguing that "the fringe supports downtown." Indeed, the plan of 1964 went beyond officially recognizing the benefits for downtown of the residential development of Mount Adams, the central riverfront, and Queensgate I by suggesting that the lower-income Over-the-Rhine neighborhood north of downtown, which consisted of an almost wholly intact late nineteenth-century cityscape, might be turned into a similarly valuable area through a program placing particular emphasis on conservation and rehabilitation. Taken together, the plans and recommendations of 1964 amounted to a virtual endorsement of the view that downtown should be a place of enormous diversity, juxtaposing historic charm with modern architecture, mass with respect for the human scale, big businesses with small entrepreneurs catering to downtown residents as well as visitors to the central business district, money making with pleasure, residence with commerce, and vitality by day with liveliness by night.[6]

Yet the city planners' concern for downtown did not mean that they ignored the anxiety in Clifton about the deterioration of the neighborhood. They sought to allay the nervousness in a way that sparked the founding of CTM and launched its campaign to precisely define and establish the idea of Clifton as an "in-town suburb." In the mid-1950s the city noticed trouble on the hilltops north and east of the basin, trouble stemming from the displacement of blacks in the West End by expressway and urban renewal projects. The trouble consisted of the association with "blight" of the new black ghetto spreading westward from Walnut Hills on a line north of the University of Cincinnati and Burnet Woods and through south Avondale and Corryville toward Vine Street, a thoroughfare traditionally viewed as the "separator" between Avondale and Clifton. City officials assigned the Department of Urban Renewal and the City Planning Department the task of planning an Avondale-Corryville urban renewal project[7] not only to battle blight in those two places but also to preserve from "deterioration" the nearby neighborhoods of North Avondale and Clifton.[8]

But the Avondale-Corryville renewal plan, published in December 1960, also pointed to a revolutionary shift in notions of neighborhood planning and in the relationship of neighborhoods to one another and to the city government, a shift that not only facilitated the founding of CTM but also helped make it a city planning agency. The planners wanted to apply conservation and rehabilitation techniques to Avondale-Corryville, treatments that required the cooperation of property owners. To secure that cooperation, the planners consulted with neighborhood residents and organizations. The city's planners then compiled what they heard into an extraordinary plan, a document that devoted one of its four chapters to promoting individual citizen participation at the household, block, and neighborhood levels in the renewal process. As presented in the plan, moreover, that process required the commitment of each citizen to the definition and realization of economic, architectural, urban design, civic, and social service goals appropriate for each of the two target neighborhoods, a task the plan assigned to the neighborhood organization in each place.[9]

The Avondale-Corryville plan also revised the meaning of rehabilitation in the lexicon of city planning. The document rejected the 1948 plan's notion that rehabilitation should be used only to postpone demolition and reconstruction

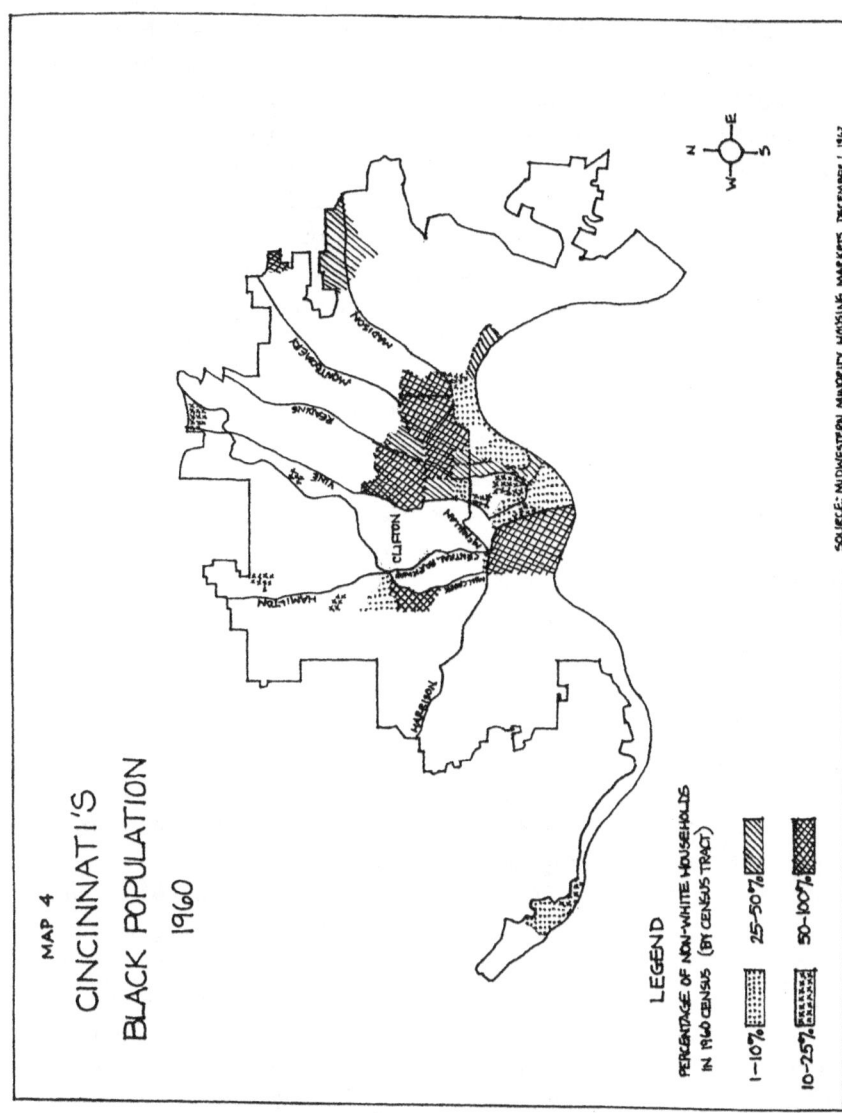

Map 12. Though crude, this map vividly depicted the concern of both city officials and CTM leaders about the spread of "blight" and the city's black ghetto. *Source:* CTM project files.

and came down in favor of rehabilitation as a program of renewal and preservation of old housing stock as an ongoing policy. The Avondale-Corryville plan also rejected the 1948 plan's idea that the neighborhoods should be grouped into communities designed to accommodate a presumptively immobile population throughout the family life cycle. Instead, it favored a strategy to make Avondale-Corryville attractive to people shopping among a variety of neighborhoods for one suitable to their current but presumably changeable tastes. And the Avondale-Corryville scheme also rejected the 1948 plan's implicit assumption of the desirability of intra-neighborhood socioeconomic homogeneity, for in both its physical and citizen participation aspects it proposed to create environments appropriate for each neighborhood to become either racially and socioeconomically integrated (Corryville) or racially segregated but socioeconomically integrated (south Avondale, which was almost entirely black in 1960), but renewed and viable (preserved from deterioration) in either case.

The Avondale-Corryville plan also revised the 1948 plan's recommendations for transportation facilities and business districts. The new plan gave each neighborhood a commercial district, both of them separated from Clifton by residential areas, and introduced a new zoning category for residential neighborhoods, an "office district" in southeastern Corryville "to accommodate primarily professional, management and other similar offices which, in recent years, have shown a trend of seeking locations some distance outside the central business district in [southeastern Corryville and other] favorably located areas," thus legitimizing neighborhoods not only as minicompetitors with downtown but also, given the new emphasis on residential housing downtown, as minidowntowns themselves.

As for transportation, the Avondale-Corryville plan rejected the 1948 proposal to extend Erkenbrecker to Ludlow but endorsed the widening of Forest to handle heavier traffic flowing up Woolper into and through Clifton via McAlpin. Finally, in consultation with University of Cincinnati officials, the planners built into the renewal scheme preparations for the dramatic growth of the university and for its continuing expansion, both north into Burnet Woods to St. Clair (for what became in the 1960s the College of Design, Architecture, and Art) and east into Corryville to Jefferson Avenue to provide room for new athletic facilities for the university's entrance into "big-time" intercollegiate athletics and for faculty and student housing in high-rise apartment dormitory buildings. Officials estimated the cost of the entire project at $24 million in federal and municipal funds.[10]

Such talk about nearby Avondale and Corryville attracted serious attention in Clifton in 1961, when the Clifton branch of the League of Women Voters organized a study group to investigate "the details of the Avondale-Corryville Renewal Project and the university's plans for expansion." Concerned about the consequences for Clifton, the group worried in particular about the university's proposal to build three residence halls with 530 units for faculty and students. They expressed concern that such facilities constituted "competition with free enterprise" and that they would draw a high concentration of people of questionable character and behavior to the very edge of Clifton itself. Members of the group took their questions to the city's director of urban development, Charles Stamm, who encouraged them to form a neighborhood association for Clifton, which he characterized as "one of the most delightful residential suburbs in the country."[11]

The women took that as sound advice, returned to Clifton, and on April 19, 1961, convened a meeting of nineteen interested Cliftonites. This group became the steering committee for an organization first called the Clifton Community Association and then the Clifton Town Meeting, a title resonant with implications of village atmosphere and local civic responsibility in a hallowed American democratic tradition. As they organized, moreover, members of the steering committee considered how to handle the race question so as to avoid panic that might lead to a mass exodus of respectable residents, all of whom were white, and thus to ghettoization, and to prevent the new organization from becoming a vehicle for the exclusion of persons from Clifton because of race or religion. They knew that some Cliftonites supported racial residential integration, while others took "the black cloud that is all set to move in from Vine Street" as Clifton's major problem and segregation as the appropriate solution. But they prevented that latter sentiment from capturing the organization.[12]

Steering committee members chose, however, not to focus their organizational campaign on the issue of race, at least not directly, and only indirectly by opposing ghettoization of Clifton while working quietly for integration.[13] Instead, they selected a ghetto-related question, a proposal by city government to widen Clifton Avenue from Spring Grove Avenue to Woolper and to straighten the awkward corner at the confluence of McAlpin, Clifton Avenue, and Woolper. This became a handy item for CTM exploitation when city council, on June 1, 1961, passed a resolution in favor of securing the necessary rights-of-way for the improvement.[14] At a July strategy meeting, CTM organizers noted that residents of Clifton Avenue had previously objected to the widening of Clifton Avenue from Ludlow north to McAlpin. But the most recent Clifton Avenue proposal, CTM leaders believed, involved all of Clifton north of Ludlow, and they determined "to *preserve* and improve something which exists,

Fig. 2. The north Clifton Avenue hill, looking northward. Photo (1998) courtesy of Jon Hughes.

instead of waiting until it had been destroyed and spending large sums of Federal and local money to bring it back. If Clifton deteriorates," they agreed, "residents will move, possibly out of the city, the tax duplicate will drop— many features of this [Clifton Avenue scheme] are bad for Cincinnati." They decided, therefore, to fight a delaying action by seeking in August a deferral of action by the city until they could bring petitions to city council and present alternative plans for handling the Clifton Avenue problem, a scheme which succeeded.[15]

The delay in August kept the question alive through September, which enabled the leadership to raise it at CTM's first community meeting, which drew a crowd of 550. And while the Clifton Avenue issue and what to do about it dominated the meeting, CTM officers also discussed three other problems: parking and land use in the business district, adequate and attractive street lighting, and additional recreational facilities.[16] In October and November, representatives met with city officials on the Clifton Avenue question, and in January 1962 the city manager, C. A. Harrell, postponed the improvements until 1965, when he expected the completion of the expressway near Clifton (I-75). He did this reluctantly, however, for he regarded the curvy and hilly northern portion of Clifton Avenue as "very dangerous" for motorists.[17]

Fig. 3. The Woolper and McAlpin intersection, looking southward, with Clifton School on the right. Photo (1998) courtesy of Jon Hughes.

By that time, however, CTM had become a strong organization with a constitution, adopted in 1962, that announced its objectives in broad, conservative terms. CTM's object was "to preserve and develop the community of Clifton as a delightful in-town suburb, a fine residential area for all citizens." The document described Clifton as one of "Cincinnati's finest suburbs" possessing a "traditional charm." Its future, CTM's founders declared, "should not be left to chance," as if, indeed, it ever had been, and "its growth and development should be guided by actively interested residents" with a particular interest in "zoning regulations, housing code enforcements, traffic patterns, shopping, school and recreational facilities, attractive appearance, and other measures designed to preserve and upgrade the area known as Clifton," an area defined in the constitution by boundaries virtually identical to those for the neighborhood of Clifton in the city's 1948 metropolitan master plan.[18]

During its early history, CTM devoted considerable time to the issue of establishing those boundaries and the appropriate image of the milieu they encompassed in the consciousness of non-Cliftonites as well as Clifton residents. For example, CTM members seriously considered but did not adopt a proposal to erect on major streets at Clifton boundary points signs reading, "You Are Now Entering Clifton," the traditional welcome accorded travelers approaching municipal corporation limits. And in considering the decision about Clifton's boundaries, CTM members said their territory should be "of limited geographic extent, large enough for a variety of residents and to maintain certain community facilities, . . . but small enough to give a feeling of cohesion" in a place where "all elements are to be subordinated to residential use—no manufacturing—no large-scale shopping or commercial activities— no dominant institution" (such as the University of Cincinnati, for example). Similarly, Cliftonites worried about the "maligning" of Clifton's reputation by the metropolitan daily newspapers, which once reported the arrest of a narcotics suspect in Clifton when the incident occurred in a nearby neighborhood, and which occasionally placed homes and apartments for sale or rent on McMicken or "near" Hughes High School in the list for Clifton, tendencies some Clifton residents thought stemmed from ignorance about Cincinnati on the part of new reporters or from realtors' desire to "glamorize their listings" in declining areas just beyond Clifton's edge by associating them with Clifton itself.[19]

Early in its history, too, CTM monitored property maintenance and the character of the suburb, a campaign which centered on Clifton's peripheral areas. CTM sent letters of reprimand to those deemed responsible for a littered parking lot next to the United Dairy Farmers store in the business district along Ludlow and for items of furniture and bathroom fixtures thrown into a rear parking lot on the other side of Ludlow, and one CTM official conducted a tour of the bars along Ludlow to ascertain the character of their clientele. CTM also sent letters of reprimand to people who failed to keep neatly trimmed lawns and well-ordered premises, especially on Juergens Avenue, a precipitous and curvy little passageway connecting Greendale to Vine, and a street with some residents who stored junk and/or household appliances on front porches and who seemed uninterested in efforts to rehabilitate the condition of their houses. And CTM members worried in the early 1960s about the design, size, and price of apartments being developed on lower McAlpin, about unspecified zoning problems on Senator Place, a crowded cul-de-sac with an apartment complex at the street's dead-end, and on Hosea, both in Clifton's southeast corner, and about traffic noise and the danger of accidents on Woolper, a street which seemed "teetering on the brink of blight and deterioration."[20]

Closely related to these activities to curb deterioration and exclude blight stood CTM efforts in the early 1960s to prevent panic among Cliftonites about Clifton's current condition and future prospects. The concern about the Avondale-Corryville renewal plan and university expansion that prompted

CTM's founding may be seen as part of this effort, but the worry soon centered on the issue of race, and in particular on the threat of ghettoization rather than residential integration. CTM's leaders in the first years stressed that the organization aimed to exclude no one on the grounds of race or religion, just as they tried to make it clear that they hoped to retain and attract residents sharing the vision of Clifton as a historic in-town suburb, which by CTM's definition included a heterogeneous population led by energetic, vigilant, urbane, politically sophisticated, and well-educated citizens.

CTM leaders expressed these views in 1961 and 1962 as they considered the implications of the appearance of the new hilltop black ghetto on Clifton's eastern flank. They concluded that heavy black migration into Clifton, if it began, should be accommodated by block-level organization and the preparation of each block's residents "to accept the possibility of one colored family on the block, with the other residents expressly stating that they will not sell to colored without consulting their other neighbors." Such a strategy aimed to thwart "block-busting," a practice among realtors of moving a black family into an all-white block, warning other whites of the imminence and inevitability of a black "invasion." This practice sparked white flight and temporarily lowered real estate values, which then recovered and rose as blacks moved onto the block to escape the old ghetto. This process operated within the framework of a tightly and historically segregated metropolitan real estate market and thus perpetuated the spread of the ghetto contiguously.

In this context, residential integration, to succeed, had to resist the "invasion" by a form of discrimination: by establishing a de facto quota system to produce and maintain a salt-and-pepper racial residential pattern at the smallest unit of measurement, the block (which CTM leaders assumed to mean a group of houses fronting both sides of a street between its block corners or other boundaries). Here, as in the image campaign, CTM leaders assumed the necessity and possibility of educating each resident, regardless of race (or religion) in the value of diversity as an appropriate characteristic for an in-town suburb with a village atmosphere. Thus defined, the public interest within the suburb justified a quota system, a form of discrimination against those whites who preferred to exclude all blacks and against those blacks whose movement into Clifton would exceed the quota and create an addition to the ghetto, or conditions which might threaten ghettoization.

In pursuit of this goal, CTM leaders walked a fine line. They noted in October 1961 a newspaper report about North Avondale entitled "Negroes Next Door No Cause for Panic," and in 1961 and 1962 they observed the activities of community organizations in three neighborhoods (Kennedy Heights, East Walnut Hills, and North Avondale) then also seeking to cope with racial residential integration.[21] They heard a report from a CTM member on urban renewal that attacked city planners for placing economy and efficiency above the preservation of historic charm and for "moving slums and blight around the city in order to facilitate the clearance of existing slums," and that contended that the removal of Clifton's gas and boulevard lights "could easily become the critical invitation" for blight to enter Clifton.[22] And they remained aloof from Clifton Enterprises, Inc., a for-profit corporation organized in 1962 that fought "panic" in the Clifton real estate market by purchasing distressed properties, including three on Woolper, as a means of excluding blacks from the neighborhood. Instead, they authorized the establishment of antipanic block committees after a black physician bought a house on Warren Avenue "in the center of the best residential district" in Clifton.[23] That same year CTM officers provided information to the assistant minister of Immanuel Presbyterian Church for a special sermon urging the congregation to "prepare for inevitable change," pointing to the dangers of racial violence stemming from a century of discrimination and segregation, counseling racial tolerance and understanding, and warning that fear, not integration, was "our enemy."[24]

CTM leaders also kept tabs on the African American housing market in Cincinnati. They acquired, for example, a Better Housing League report identifying fourteen areas of black residential concentration in the city (and five in the county) and the existence of racial transition neighborhoods in North Avondale, eastern Walnut Hills, and southwest Hyde Park. The report urged the stabilization of the transitional areas and of areas likely to undergo transition by the adoption of "positive, immediate, cooperative steps to prevent a panic switch-over."[25] And in May 1962, CTM went on record in favor of a Cincinnati ordinance to "promote the stability of neighborhoods" by prohibiting realtors from using race, religion, nationality, or neighborhood unrest, tension, and the threat of racial, religious, or nationality change to induce or influence the sale or rental of property.[26]

But that same month a CTM committee chair reprimanded the director of the Mayor's Friendly Relations Committee for publicizing a meeting he scheduled with the residents of Woolper Avenue to advise them not to panic when blacks moved onto their street. CTM had asked him to keep quiet about the meeting "because we believe that any publicity at all increases fear and tension in quarters where there was none before. With respect to whatever problems Clifton may have at this point we believe that much more can be accomplished by working constructively but quietly under cover. The barest mention of Clifton can bring pressure on the Clifton Town Meeting to try and keep Negroes out of Clifton and increase the difficulties of the Board in getting cooperation from the entire membership on this and other problems. Such mention also starts the rumor that 'Clifton is going the way of [South and Central] Avondale.'[27]

Indeed, 1962 proved a harrowing year for CTM. The organization struggled to prepare maps and petitions for zoning changes as the Cincinnati City Planning Commission (CCPC) staff reviewed and revised zoning districts for the entire city. The chair of CTM's zoning committee, Betty Ames, recognized that Clifton would change in the next few years and contended that when "large estates are subdivided and some larger houses are remodeled, we want these changes to take place in an orderly fashion according to comprehensive planning."[28] She labored to keep up with the professionals on the CCPC staff, especially to secure R-1, quarter-acre lot status for much of Clifton, but in November she had to apologize for submitting an incorrect map, explaining that "Clifton Town Meeting is working hard to stabilize a fluid situation because, as you may not be aware, speculators have been active in acquiring property in Clifton."[29] The pressure mounted to the extent that the organization barely found time to notice, let alone to act officially on, the planning and opening of Aiken High School in College Hill, which was intended in part to alleviate "overcrowding" at Hughes, which soon became a predominantly black high school. The assignment to Aiken of students (mostly white) from the Clifton school district north of Dixmyth made Aiken a predominantly white school.[30]

Concern about the question of race persisted. In October 1963, the president of CTM reported to the board that he had met with a delegation of Clifton clergymen who had heard "unfavorable reports of CTM's position on integration." The president told them that "CTM has from the beginning maintained a policy of non-panic."[31] That same fall, CTM leaders jumped at an opportunity to "stabilize" Clifton, an opportunity associated with the problem of what to do with the sale and breaking up of large estates. The possibility arose when the Cincinnati Woman's Club, a prestigious organization established in the 1890s, lost its downtown headquarters to expressway construction. On learning of the club's search for a new site, CTM leaders immediately sought to secure for it two adjacent estate properties on Lafayette Avenue; one had just gone on the market, and the other had been available "for years." The Greek Orthodox Church made inquiries about the land, but CTM opposed this option because the use of the land for school or church purposes "will make Clifton like East Walnut Hills," a "trend" that was "invading" other areas of the city with large estates. CTM also preferred the club to the subdivision of the sites into six or eight residential lots, and argued, after consulting with the club, that the acquisition of the new clubhouse, designed to resemble a Georgian or Colonial style mansion, would add the "prestige and influence" of the club to CTM and "greatly assist in the fight to preserve Clifton." The club, said one proponent of the idea, would be "our anchor."[32]

This proposition, however, faced stiff opposition within Clifton. Indeed, it went through only "after months of meetings, discussions, [and] hearings" at which "no Cliftonite was neutral," and after CTM helped in amending the zoning code for R-1 districts to admit clubs for educational and literary purposes in such districts.[33] Opponents claimed that the club's presence would "downgrade" Lafayette Avenue by generating heavy traffic, including the flashing of headlights at night, and predicted that the club would abandon its "dry" tradition and secure a liquor license. The president of CTM regarded these arguments as specious, but not as cloaks for racial fears. He believed that the opposition stemmed from Catholic physicians who objected to the club because its membership included only two or three Catholic women, fewer even than its Jewish contingent.[34]

Yet CTM leaders in the early 1960s worked hard not only to improve deteriorating conditions and fend off the ghetto but also to preserve and publicize what they regarded as Clifton's positive attributes. They liked, for example, Clifton's convenience, including, as one CTM letter to a Kansan moving to Cincinnati noted, the fact that it took just fifteen minutes to drive downtown from the suburb. Similarly, another CTM member in these years called Clifton "a good residential area convenient for those who work at our hospitals, the University of Cincinnati, and the many other educational and religious institutions of the area," and "convenient also for those who prefer to live near the core area [of Cincinnati]."[35]

CTM founders, in short, thought they could hold and attract socioeconomically mobile residents by touting Clifton as an in-town suburb conceived as a diverse and dynamic entity that contrasted sharply with the homogeneity and serenity of the out-of-town suburbs. They emphasized Clifton's proximity to institutions that served the metropolitan area and its renewed central business district and renewing inner-city. But they also stressed its differences from these localities by touting not only Clifton's "residential" character but also its alleged status as one of the city's "historic" (as opposed to "old") in-town suburbs, a status based in part on a collection of traits they hoped to preserve.

This preservation predisposition also manifested itself in other ways during the early 1960s. CTM opposed, for example, a second proposal by the city to widen the northern part of Clifton Avenue and to connect it directly to the Mill Creek Expressway by building a railway bridge and an expressway traffic interchange at the foot of Clifton Avenue. During city council hearings on the widening proposal, CTM representatives applauded the city's core restoration and expressway construction program but contended that the widening of Clifton Avenue as an urban renewal measure would backfire by destroying the venerable attractiveness of the in-town suburb and drive its residents into the out-of-town suburbs.

CTM used the same arguments (also successfully) against city proposals to eliminate some of Clifton's nineteenth-century village gaslights and to replace the early twentieth-century boulevard-style electric and relatively dim globe lights on ornamented iron posts that lined Clifton Avenue north of Ludlow. One protestor even claimed that the globe lights evoked the ambiance of Paris in an attempt to link the in-town suburb of Clifton with the reputation of Paris as a *real* big city because of its historic reputation for cosmopolitanism and urbanity.

These lighting battles consumed an enormous amount of time and effort, a sign of the intensity of the drive to create an in-town suburban atmosphere that would retain and attract the right kind of resident. The city's proposal in 1962 involved only gaslights on Bryant, Hosea, Middleton, Morrison, Lafayette, Telford, and Brookline (a total of 107), but CTM leaders nonetheless surveyed the views of Cliftonites generally (a minority favored switching to electricity), sought advice from other cities and local specialists in the field, lobbied city hall, and elicited support for gas from Cincinnati's two metropolitan daily newspapers. Three years later, when residents on Senator Place petitioned council to remove their gaslights, CTM leaders organized another gaslight preservation campaign, one that included hiring a consultant to investigate means of protecting all the gaslights in Clifton.[36]

Despite this busyness, CTM proved adept at devising new campaigns to make Clifton desirable for socioeconomically and geographically mobile people. These activities included a successful campaign to retain the branch post office on Telford in an old building half a block south of the business portion of Ludlow and a request to the National Trust for Historic Preservation for a film demonstrating new techniques for "maintaining and improving a neighborhood."[37] In addition, the CTM *Bulletin*, the organization's newsletter, ran articles on aspects of Clifton's history, including pieces on Mount Storm's "Temple of Love," the Probasco Fountain, the Abbe Observatory, and abstracts of Dr. Arthur King's two articles (1951 and 1962) on Clifton's past.[38] The *Bulletin* also applauded the CTM board's endorsement of moving the

Cincinnati Woman's Club to Clifton, claiming that its presence would "maintain the unique quality of Lafayette Avenue, which is truly one of Cincinnati's historic and beautiful spots."[39]

Nor was that all. The Clifton annual house tour, inaugurated in 1964, may also be seen as part of CTM's effort to convince Cliftonites and outsiders that Clifton was not a declining but a durable in-town suburb. The tour organizers selected eight homes designed to display the variety of housing in Clifton, including old mansions, a contemporary "A-frame," and two apartments in a remodeled single-family house, and concluded the tour in St. John's Unitarian Church, a new and modern edifice which had won an architectural prize. Tour organizers publicized the event heavily in Clifton, sending, for example, notices to all the Clifton churches. But they also sought metropolitan coverage by soliciting coverage from the *Cincinnati Enquirer,* the area's most widely read daily newspaper, and from WCPO-TV, a station known for its coverage of similar undertakings. And CTM prepared a tour guide, which sold for fifty cents, the contents of which it directed to an audience of "outsiders" and which boasted of the history, charm, beauty, variety, warmth, and convenience of Clifton as a place in which to live.[40]

But the most important single effort to use preservation to establish the idea of Clifton as a historic in-town suburb consisted of CTM's participation in developing a master plan for Clifton. For this purpose, CTM initially asked for assistance from a professional planner, W. G. Roeseler, who provided advice in a letter dated September 21, 1961. Roeseler described Clifton as a residential neighborhood according to the canons of "contemporary city planning" because Clifton encompassed the "service area" of Clifton School and Annunciation School, public and private elementary facilities, respectively. He also pointed out that Clifton's population in 1961 consisted of 10,000 people occupying 3,000 dwelling units, 15 to 20 percent of whom lived in apartments and the rest in single-family homes. He asserted, too, that Clifton generated little of the Clifton Avenue or McAlpin-Woolper traffic, which consisted mainly of vehicles from surrounding neighborhoods using Clifton streets as shortcuts in the absence of adequate thoroughfares bypassing Clifton (a defect presumably to be remedied by the expressway and by the traffic provisions of the Avondale-Corryville plan, although he did not say so).

Roeseler then set down a "Sketch Plan," the preamble of which stated as the goal of "contemporary city planning" the creation "wherever feasible" of "physical units of relative self-sufficiency." By this he meant not the community scheme of the 1948 plan but the residential neighborhood focused on a school and local shopping area, the "most important single urban planning unit." In such a unit, public facilities should be centrally located, through traffic should be discouraged, and the unit should encompass half a square mile to a square mile, with a central grade school positioned so that students had no more than half a mile to walk. Given these assumptions and rules, he said, the expressway should bypass Clifton as prescribed in the 1948 metropolitan master plan, but Clifton Avenue should not be connected to Winton Road (and presumably improved but not widened, although he did not say so). In addition, wrote Roeseler, McAlpin should be cut off from Woolper, thereby avoiding the "permanent" bisecting of Clifton by Clifton Avenue and McAlpin-Woolper, which "in time" would create "four unrelated quadrants each too small to retain neighborhood identity and long-range stability."[41]

Roeseler also pointed out what he saw as anomalies in the zoning of Clifton property, most notably that the zoning prescribed for some areas did not conform to existing land uses in those areas, as at locations consisting largely of two-family units but zoned for apartments, or consisting largely of single-family houses but zoned for two-family occupancy. These discrepancies, which reflected assumptions dating to the 1948 metropolitan master plan about likely changes in Clifton's residential structure, and which projected for Clifton both a greater population density and larger numbers of "transient" apartment dwellers, now caught the attention of CTM leaders, and correcting them occupied much of their energies in 1962 and 1963.

By July 1963, when the city adopted a new zoning code, several changes in Clifton's zoning regulations had taken place, most of them involving "upgrading." Much of it also occurred piecemeal, a process involving tedious work by CTM volunteers in researching property ownership, preparing petitions requesting zoning changes, drawing maps of proposed changes, and making presentations before the CCPC, city council, and its committees. But CTM's efforts yielded results. For example, apartment and business zoning on Woolper gave way to one- and two-family housing, two-family zoning replaced apartments in the vicinity of Howell and Terrace Avenues, and a total of 302 multiple-dwelling properties ended up in two-family zones on Juergens Avenue, lower Greendale, Lyleburn, Cornell, Whitfield, Middleton, Bryant, Thrall, Telford, Brookline, Bishop, and Ruther. After heated discussions, CTM approved an amendment to the R-1 zoning category (the most restricted residential zoning) enabling the Cincinnati Woman's Club to abandon its downtown site for new and spacious quarters on Lafayette Avenue, the location until then of two large mansions.[42]

Roeseler's sketch of a plan also proved useful in CTM's efforts to prevent the widening of Clifton Avenue, but it did not sate the longing among some of the organization's leaders for a Clifton master plan. That longing produced little activity, however, until 1964, when CTM representatives met with Herbert Stevens, director of Cincinnati's City Planning Department, to discuss the city's efforts to promote citizen participation in planning outside of federally subsidized urban renewal project areas by creating a Neighborhood Planning Service. If adopted, Stevens explained, the Neighborhood Planning Service would not set up goals and objectives as part of creating a vision of the future social and physical environment in particular neighborhoods. Instead, it would assign staff members to neighborhood organizations to assist them in developing their goals and to aid them in such technical matters as identifying population trends, describing the physical aspects of the neighborhood, and determining land use changes and how to make them. He added, too, that the planning service staff could be used to enlist the interest and aid of other city departments in handling problems identified by the neighborhood organization, but he stressed that "the planner in a neighborhood would have no responsibility for community organization or for [dealing with] social problems or situations."[43]

CTM leaders responded to this presentation by requesting assistance, and the next week City Planning Department staff members recommended to the CCPC the use of Clifton as a pilot project for the new Neighborhood Planning Service. They said that the planner would do physical planning exclusively to help produce a general neighborhood plan similar in its level of detail to the community plans contained in the 1948 metropolitan master plan. The staff also suggested that the neighborhood might assume financial responsibility for doing whatever the city could not do. In addition, the staff members listed but did not specify the nature of recurring zoning questions, which fell under the CCPC's jurisdiction, on Hosea, Juergens Avenue, and Senator Place, and concluded by describing Clifton as well organized, capable, and desirous of self-help but in need of assistance in making planning studies.[44]

Three days later, CTM formally accepted what it called a "proposal" to explore its use of the Neighborhood Planning Service, noting that such a service as CTM understood it would "in no way limit the autonomy of CTM." Shortly thereafter, Stevens met with the CTM planning committee, and on June 1, 1964, the committee decided to give the business area top priority in long-range planning. Committee members then met with the Clifton Business Association and Professional Men's Association. The two groups discussed parking problems and noted a 25 percent increase over thirty years in the num-

Fig. 4. The Clifton post office remains a small, plain, but useful building. Photo (1998) courtesy of Jon Hughes.

ber of businesses and an increase in the same period from 1,500 to 2,800 square feet of store frontage on the business strip.[45]

Another part of the planning process for the business district involved CTM volunteers, assisted by the CCPC's Neighborhood Planning Service, in a survey of shopping habits and "needs" of Clifton residents as they related to the Ludlow business strip. The returns suggested that Cliftonites patronized most intensively the grocery stores, banks, and post office in Clifton; that most used the district for "convenience" shopping and went elsewhere for a greater selection of goods; that 72 percent of all Clifton business district shoppers lived in the Clifton postal zone; and that 59 percent drove their own cars and 24 percent walked to the business district.[46]

What turned out to be the last step in the first effort of Cliftonites to plan for themselves consisted of what then was usually one of the first steps in the planning process, the hammering out of an agreement on general goals to serve as guidelines for working out the details of the master plan. CTM reached this stage on July 8, 1964, when the CTM board of trustees adopted fifteen goals (see table 3). These fifteen goals repeated sentiments previously expressed in the CTM constitution and bylaws and others entirely consistent with the various activities of the organization since 1961, but provided no more detailed guidelines for business district planning than for residential, educational, traffic, land use, urban design, cultural, recreational, or community organization planning, despite the top priority assigned by CTM's planning committee to the commercial area.

Yet some parts of the goals statement deserve notice, for they remind us of the discontinuity between planning in the late 1940s and planning in the early 1960s. Among the goals, for example, stood the provision of "suitable residences for [a] wide range of ages, economic levels, taste and family size," a goal assigned to the "community" of 20,000 to 40,000 people in the 1948 metropolitan master plan, not to a "neighborhood" of roughly 10,000 population. Another 1964 goal called for the provision of "adequate spiritual and character-building agencies," such as churches, a youth center, and scout groups, an emphasis on the need for and role of particular institutional experiences in the preparation of young people for individual autonomy alien to the 1948 plan's community orientation, with its emphasis on the way in which the community should mold the aspirations and character of individuals to prepare them for life within the community. And it should be noted, too, that above the fifteen goals stood the goal of CTM itself, "to preserve and develop the community of Clifton as a delightful in-town suburb, a fine residential area for all citizens," a locution suggesting the definition of Clifton as a place chosen by individuals for the development and exercise of their autonomy rather than as a neighborhood as part of a community, the vision of 1948.

The CTM goals statement of 1964, then, assumed that character adheres to and inheres in individuals, not places (such as a neighborhood or a community), which now have ambiance but not personality. The planners of 1948, that is, assumed that they could shape the way people lived (their culture) by locating them in neighborhoods and communities endowed with a personality that would rub off on their residents through their experience of living in artfully designed localities equipped with an appropriate array of citizen-building institutions. The planners of 1948, moreover, aimed above all at developing loyalty among citizens not only to their neighborhoods and communities but also to the metropolis.

The Clifton planners of 1964 ignored the idea of metropolitan community and focused on their own turf. For them, however, the neighborhood functioned not as the determinant of its residents' culture but merely as a setting that might be adjusted to fit the self-defined lifestyle (cultural) aspirations of people who chose to live there. And CTM decided to preserve and embellish Clifton's physical legacy to entice the right kind of residents, which it defined as socioeconomically and geographically mobile individuals.

Table 3

Clifton Town Meeting Planning Goals, Adopted July 8, 1964

The goal of the Clifton Town Meeting is as stated in its Constitution to preserve and develop the community of Clifton as a delightful in-town suburb, a fine residential area for all citizens. This goal must be achieved through cooperation with the city government and other groups, public and private, in order, thus, to benefit all of Cincinnati.

1. Limited geographical extent—large enough to provide variety of residents and to maintain certain community facilities; small enough to give feeling of cohesion.
2. Satisfactory geographical relation between land use components—business area, school area, recreation area appropriately located.
3. All elements subordinated to residential use—no manufacturing, no large-scale shopping or commercial activities, no dominant institution.
4. A significant number of owner-occupied residences for stability; appropriate number of rental units available.
5. Provision of suitable residences for wide range of ages, economic levels, taste, and family size.
6. Adequate schools available at all educational levels.
7. Adequate spiritual and character-building agencies available—churches, youth centers, scout groups, etc., as needed.
8. Suitable cultural and recreational facilities available—parks, playgrounds, libraries, etc.
9. Shopping and professional and personal services primarily to serve the needs of local residents and adequate in diversity and quality to meet those needs.
10. Restricted traffic on all residential streets through traffic routed around suburb on suitable arteries—no high-speed traffic or through trucking on residential streets.
11. Appropriate intra-suburb traffic patterns for autos and pedestrians.
12. Good access to adjoining areas, C.B.D., and to through highways by roads and public transportation.
13. Adequate parking for all land use components—residence, business, institutions.
14. Attractive appearance of all areas as appropriate to their use—in architecture, building, landscaping and maintenance of privately owned areas; good planning, design, and maintenance of public areas.
15. Community organizations to focus interests, desires, and activities of residents.

Source: CTM Papers, box 1, folder 4.

This did not mean, however, that CTM turned its back on the city of Cincinnati. Indeed, the goals statement declared that the overriding aim of preserving and developing Clifton as an in-town suburb "must be achieved through cooperation with the city government and other groups, public and private, in order thus to benefit all of Cincinnati," a position for which the organization had already developed credentials. The CTM board had voted in 1962 to endorse a $16.6 million city of Cincinnati bond issue for central riverfront improvements and for the construction of a new convention-exhibition hall in the heart of the city's central business district.[47] These acts may be seen as an affirmation of the continuing commitment of the in-town suburb of Clifton to the welfare of the big city and an acknowledgment of Clifton's interdependence as a locality in but not of the city. The chair of CTM's zoning committee expressed that spirit in 1964 while explaining the inevitability of apartment development and her determination to make it compatible with ideals set down in the planning goals adopted that same year. Clifton still, she said, "has the possibility of becoming an example, not only to this city but to communities all over the country."[48]

4

Toward Community Control, 1964–1974

CLIFTON headed in the late 1960s and early 1970s toward the fulfillment of one of the neighborhood's chief planning goals of 1964, the diversification of its population, for the neighborhood both attracted and retained socioeconomically and geographically mobile residents, principally because of the rapid growth in the size of the faculty and staff at the University of Cincinnati and nearby hospitals. To be sure, many white newcomers had to look long and hard for housing because of "gentlemen's agreements" prohibiting sales to non-Christians almost everywhere and to non-Protestants in some districts, and because of the reluctance of realtors to breach these informal rules of the game. Blacks faced even more stringent discrimination, and Clifton lost no territory to the expanding second African American ghetto, which stopped at Vine Street on Clifton's western flank and marched to the northeast along Reading Road between the white enclaves of Norwood and St. Bernard, two municipalities within the municipality of Cincinnati, and farther out the same corridor into Paddock Hills and toward Bond Hill and Roselawn on the inner edge of Cincinnati's corporate boundary.

But tensions generated by the arrival of newcomers, especially Jews, an historically underrepresented element in Clifton's population, worried Clifton Town Meeting (CTM) leaders. Jews seeking units to rent in the 1950s had run across "gentlemen's agreements" barring them from multiple dwellings or apartments. That practice faded in the 1950s, but Jews seeking to buy homes continued to encounter difficulties. In 1959, for example, the Jewish Community Relations Committee (JCRC) compiled a report on the high level of Jewish-Gentile residential segregation in Cincinnati generally and on the persisting practice of maintaining "traditionally" Jewish and non-Jewish neighborhoods.

According to JCRC sources, a story circulated that a Catholic priest had urged his parishioners to sell their properties in Clifton only to Catholics, not to incoming Jews, because of the problem of maintaining the parish church and parochial school in the face of a declining Catholic population. This story, said the report, "gave rise to and fanned anti-Semitism in the area," a sentiment that affected Jewish access to the Clifton housing market throughout the 1960s.[1]

CTM leaders also worried about other related problems. These included depressed housing prices in Clifton, which ran about one-fourth of those in Hyde Park and one-half of those in North Avondale, neighborhoods they viewed as prime competitors in the race for the right kind of residents. They also worried about the construction in Clifton of more new apartment units than they preferred, the result of a mistake during the rush to change the area's zoning in 1962 and 1963. The zoning committee, as it turned out, overlooked a large vacant tract of R-5 land, which it thought ranked as an R-1 zone. This tract, bounded on the south by Ludlow Avenue, on the east by the back lot lines of houses on the west side of Lafayette where it turned to go downhill at its western end, and on the north by Mount Storm Park, attracted two developments: first, an apartment complex called Maison Lafayette, and then in the late 1970s, a federally subsidized and very controversial high-rise apartment building for the elderly.

Some Cliftonites worried in the 1960s and early 1970s also about crime, which they attributed to dark streets lit only by gaslights, and drugs, which they attributed to the influence on the neighborhood of university students and faculty. A newspaper reporter who investigated "stress" in Clifton, for example, uncovered rumors "in some circles" about "counter-culturists" and "places where the 'hippies' go on Friday and Saturday night 'to smoke their pot,'" rumors he associated with a disagreement among Cliftonites about whether to include the university and the Ludlow Avenue commercial strip, which contained many older apartment buildings and flats above storefronts, within the boundaries of the "real" Clifton. As the priest at the Church of the Annunciation described the split, "University people don't like conservatives, and vice versa." Nor was that all. He claimed that some professors had said "openly that the university [crowd] is going to take over the running of Clifton."[2]

Professors certainly moved into Clifton as the university expanded in these years. But they did not "take over" Clifton Town Meeting (CTM), which expanded yet remained loyal to its original purpose of defining the nature and extent of Clifton as a community while undertaking new projects and programs and adopting new techniques in its quest for control of its turf. Indeed, by 1964, just three years after its founding, CTM had established itself as an extraordinary community organization. It sought, like political parties, both to define and represent a territorial community. Thus it resembled a quasi-political and governmental entity, one in competition with partisan organizations in the Fifteenth Ward, the state-sanctioned basis for political activity in an area which included not only Clifton but also parts of Northside/Cumminsville on its east and of Avondale on its west. CTM also resembled a corporation, for its members provided working capital through membership dues and elected the board of trustees. The trustees, however, took care of both the affairs of CTM as an organization and the welfare of Clifton as a community, whose varied residents might or might not choose to participate in CTM but in any case shared something in common: their residence in a particular locale. After 1964, moreover, CTM moved farther along the path toward community control as city officials, especially after 1974, encouraged and abetted the drive for neighborhood autonomy within a decentralized polity without relinquishing their responsibilities and without seeking a change in Cincinnati's charter or in the political and governmental structure of local and state relationships.

In making this shift, however, CTM continued many of its early activities and concerns. It monitored building code enforcement, urged property owners and residents to maintain the appearance of their grounds, and fought an occasional zoning battle. Such battles included a successful effort to provide much of Clifton north of McAlpin with lots no smaller than twenty thousand square feet and a contest with a Gulf gas station to prevent it from installing a drive-through carwash by demolishing two buildings (a newspaper and magazine store and a bar) on Ludlow Avenue near its intersection with Clifton Avenue.[3]

But the most controversial land use fight erupted over the fate of an auto repair shop on the Ludlow business strip after its owners sold the building to a developer from Youngstown, Ohio. CTM officials limited the options for the use of the site by preventing the new owner from acquiring a liquor license. They also disliked a proposal from Jim Tarbell, a youth drug counselor. Tarbell and his lawyer, S. Arthur Spiegel, chair of the Cincinnati Human Relations Commission in the mid-1960s and a resident of Clifton, raised $250,000 to refurbish the building for use as a teenage music concert hall in which the use and sale of drugs (and alcohol) would be forbidden but from which drug users would not be banned. Before the club opened, CTM officials met twice with Tarbell and Spiegel and warned them to expect lots of opposition from merchants and older residents of nearby apartments, who would complain about the noise and parking problems the club would create. Nonetheless, the Ludlow Garage opened in 1969, and its first concerts evoked such a flood of complaints that board members called an open meeting on the subject, a session to which they invited Tarbell and Spiegel. Opponents denounced the project and asserted that it brought drugs and drug users into the neighborhood. Tarbell and his supporters, including some Cliftonites who lived near his club, explained the importance of having in Clifton and Cincinnati a drug- and alcohol-free hangout for teenagers, after which Tarbell invited everybody down to the Garage for sandwiches and soft drinks. That muted the protests, but Tarbell's foes won out in 1971 when the club closed for financial reasons.[4]

CTM also continued to worry about the city's plans for widening Clifton Avenue and for facilitating the movement of heavy east-west traffic by taking out the half-block jog on Clifton through which that traffic flowed into Woolper Avenue and on down the hill to Vine Street. The fight against widening Clifton Avenue by this time ranked as the founding myth for CTM, a fact which contributed to the elan with which CTM persisted in trying to eliminate the need for both widening Clifton and straightening out the McAlpin/Woolper jog by making Clifton Avenue a dead-end at Spring Grove, a step that would dramatically reduce the volume of north-south traffic on Clifton and mitigate the snarls at the McAlpin/Woolper jog. But CTM at last dropped the dead-ending proposal after reaching the conclusion, as had the Cincinnati City Planning Commission, that the completion of a four-lane east-west route known as the Dixmyth–St. Clair extension would reduce traffic flowing south along Clifton toward the University of Cincinnati, the hospitals in Clifton, and downtown, and reduce the number of cars cutting through McAlpin from the west toward the hospitals and the university's College of Medicine in neighboring Avondale.[5] And CTM continued to fret about the public's perception of Clifton's boundaries, especially the tendency of outsiders to regard Calhoun Street (south of the university), which earned the reputation as a "hippie haven" during the late 1960s, as part of Clifton.[6]

Yet CTM in the late 1960s also encouraged several new activities to serve or tap a variety of local interests. These included a local artists' exhibit, the organization of an independent senior citizens association, and the sponsorship of a clean-up campaign during which residents could hire local teenagers to help with the chores.[7] And in 1965, CTM launched a major new annual activity: a Memorial Day parade. Although its organizers secured coverage by the city's only morning newspaper and by television, they did not design the event as a meticulously disciplined or dignified occasion.[8] Indeed, they organized it as if

Fig. 5. The Ludlow Garage after its conversion into a retail space and a restaurant. Photo (1998) courtesy of Jon Hughes.

in fear of representing Clifton as a place of conformity and stuffiness. Parade organizers urged parents to mobilize local youth organizations or "the people in your neighborhood" but without prescribing what they might do. Motorized vehicles were banned, but anything "pushed, pulled or driven by childpower can be decorated and used in the parade," said one announcement, which urged all Cliftonites to be inventive and "plan something special" while calling for the participation of anyone who could twirl a baton, juggle, play a band instrument, "or in any way enhance the gala atmosphere."[9] And it worked. Over eight hundred children paraded on foot, on bicycles, and in floats on four-wheeled, hand-pulled wagons. The afternoon ended with a huge picnic in Mount Storm Park on blankets brought by those gathered to salute "our nation, its flag, its heroes, its soldiers, its freedom."[10]

This sense of unity proved momentary, however, for CTM confronted a crisis during the late 1960s, one leading to a reinterpretation of its constitution and bylaws and the forging of a new strategy for community control, one calling for a selective and often formal affiliation and cooperation with other groups and agencies on social policy questions. Once again, race played an important role. But this time the issue was not the fear of "panic" and ghettoization.

It was racial integration—specifically, the problem of how to define it, secure it, and maintain it, a question answered partially in 1968 when Marcus Cummings became the first black person elected as a member of the CTM board of trustees.[11]

But this was, of course, a citywide concern, for the civil rights movement, which then centered on the achievement of integration, gained momentum and strength in Cincinnati during the early 1960s. It focused on the Cincinnati School Board, against which the Cincinnati branch of the NAACP filed suit in 1963 on the grounds that the board had created and maintained a racially segregated system despite the Supreme Court decision in 1954 declaring school segregation unconstitutional. At the same time, the local chapter of the Congress of Racial Equality opened a campaign to persuade the school board to take steps immediately to integrate the schools. After the failure during the fall of 1966 of two school bond levies, moreover, black and white integrationists established the Citizens United for Good Schools to nominate and elect school board members and invited various community groups, including neighborhood organizations, to send representatives to its meetings.[12]

The movement toward racial integration in Cincinnati's public schools came just as the issue of integration (outside the residential arena) first arose in Clifton in the form of a bitter conflict among members of the Clifton Meadows Swim Club, a conflict that took five years and several lawsuits to resolve. The club's regulations did not mention race but opened membership to all residents of Clifton and others interested in promoting its civic, recreational, and social development. Trouble started, however, on July 2, 1965, when the club manager refused to admit a black youngster as a guest of the children of two white members. Two days later, the club's board of trustees overruled the manager, only to reverse its position two weeks afterwards. The issue came up again in 1966, first through a board decision to admit black guests, followed once more by a reversal, after which the club board on a close vote prohibited black guests unless the membership as a whole voted to change the policy. Twice the question was raised in this broader arena and twice it was defeated, each time by a margin of just eleven votes.[13]

In the course of this conflict, several members resigned in protest against this racially discriminatory policy, and in the spring of 1969 forty more threatened to do the same. S. Arthur Spiegel, a Cliftonite already prominent in the city as a civil rights advocate, however, persuaded them to file suit in U.S. district court for southern Ohio to secure the elimination of the restrictive guest rule and to prevent the board from adopting any other racially discriminatory measure (such as barring black members). But the suit also sought an injunction to delay a scheduled membership meeting called by the board to elect four new board members and to review the guest policy. Spiegel claimed in the suit that the once narrow majority on the board in favor of the ban on black guests had been transformed since 1965 into a substantial majority as a consequence of the board's manipulation of its nominating committee, and that the four candidates in the forthcoming election all favored the restrictive guest policy. Their election, wrote Spiegel, would deny a significant minority representation on the board, guarantee continuing conflict over a policy that promoted divisiveness, and thus violate the club's corporate intention of promoting and maintaining the civic, recreational, and social welfare of Clifton.

Spiegel's brief for the injunction laid out the lines of conflict and contended that it threatened to destroy the club. He claimed that the issue had split families, some of whom forbade their children to play with those whose parents opposed the bar on black guests; that it created an undercurrent of ill will toward Jewish families because most of them favored an open guest policy; that it contributed to a "hardening" of anti-Catholic sentiment because so many of those supporting the restrictive rule belonged to Annunciation Church; that it had split the congregations of the Episcopal, Presbyterian, and Methodist churches in Clifton; and that it had sparked opposition to the admission of faculty and administrators from the University of Cincinnati because of their presumably "liberal attitude." As for the forthcoming election of four members of the club's board, Spiegel argued that three belonged to Annunciation Church, that no Jews sat on the board, and that the election of the nominating committee's slate would yield a board "completely dominated by members" of Annunciation and a board without representation from persons opposing the restrictive guest rule.[14]

This case, as it turned out, never came to trial, because the club's board signed a consent decree agreeing to eliminate the controversial rule and to reinstate club members who had resigned in protest. The next day, however, several board members changed their minds and asked the district court to set aside the consent decree. The court refused, after which the dissenters appealed to the Sixth Circuit Court, which upheld the decision of the district court.[15]

Although the CTM *Bulletin* ignored the fight over integration at Clifton Meadows, the *Bulletin* and the CTM board displayed an increasing interest in the Clifton School as blacks enrolled in its classes, a development that made some white Cliftonites uneasy about the quality of the school. The *Bulletin* tried to mitigate these fears, starting in 1966 when it noted the introduction at the school of Operation Head Start, a federally funded program for preschoolers from culturally deprived backgrounds, and in January 1967 the paper called for volunteer tutors to assist the PTA's work with "children who learn more slowly."[16] In February, the *Bulletin* announced the Board of Education's decision to terminate the kindergarten, a step that prompted the CTM board to announce a plan to set up a nonprofit foundation to raise $25,000 to fund a kindergarten program at Clifton School, a plan soon abandoned with the creation of a district foundation for the same purpose.[17] In May 1967, at the CTM annual membership meeting, the principal of Clifton School discussed problems at the school, including "area problems evident in school enrollment, [and] efforts to adjust to changes in the type of enrollment."[18] In September 1966, the *Bulletin* announced a forthcoming meeting in Clifton on "The Cincinnati School System: Its Problems and Prospects" featuring a panel discussion involving representatives of the Clifton and Annunciation School PTAs, the education writer for the *Cincinnati Enquirer*, and the president of the Cincinnati chapter of the NAACP.[19]

Meanwhile, the CTM board invited the principal of Clifton School to deliver a special report on its racial composition, its relation to secondary schools, and its quality. He said that 33 percent of the 982 students enrolled were black, and that three of the students were nonresident from the Burton School (predominantly black) attending Clifton under an open enrollment experiment conducted by the Board of Education. He pointed out that students graduating from the Clifton Elementary district who lived south of Dixmyth went to Merry Junior High and Hughes High, while others passed on to Schwab Junior High and Aiken or, if they had passed the Special College Prep Program exam, could attend Walnut Hills Junior and Senior High, which accepted students from throughout the district. He added that 54 percent of Clifton's students passed that exam and that the school divided its pupils into four groups depending on their achievement in reading and math.[20]

The principal's suggestion that racial integration had not adversely affected the quality of education at Clifton School allayed fears on that score but only temporarily. They reappeared a few months later when the Citizens School Committee (CSC), a new city organization promoting the election of pro-integration candidates in Cincinnati School Board races, asked CTM to name a representative to the CSC board, a proposal twice considered and twice rejected by the CTM board, as if a majority of its members feared that CSC membership would give Clifton a too liberal reputation and attract as residents more blacks and/or other undesirable residents. Many CTM members, however, supported the idea of joining CSC, and in February 1969 the CTM board called for a special meeting of the whole membership to consider the question. The announcement said that the meeting would review CTM policies and precedents established by the board's interpretation of the CTM constitution with reference to the CSC invitation. But the fundamental issue, the board noted, was the question of CTM's role in "city-wide activities in general." At the same time, the board released a copy of the letter rejecting the CSC invitation. In it, the board president argued that concerns about schools "may be more appropriately expressed by CTM's members individually as representative citizens of the city than by this organization becoming a formal part of any association or society for city-wide involvement, no matter how laudable its purposes or how important its goals may be to Clifton as a part of the community at large." He added that, of course, CTM would be happy to offer its views with respect to Clifton's public or parochial schools.[21]

More than one hundred Cliftonites turned out for the special meeting on March 11. They heard two board members explain the reasons for rejecting the invitation and one board member present the minority view. The discussion opened with a motion from the floor that the membership "strongly urge" the board to seek CSC membership. Then various speakers addressed several issues, such as the boundaries of Clifton as defined by CTM, "the reported critical opinion of near-by city residents about the attitude of Cliftonites in general, a need for additional constructive action on school problems, communication between the membership and the CTM board of trustees, and further specific opinions on the role of the Citizens School Committee in relationship to school problems." After the discussion, the motion passed without dissent by voice vote.[22]

With this strong encouragement, the board moved quickly to intervene more broadly and aggressively in school affairs, including their racial integration. The board at the annual meeting in May 1969 announced its endorsement of a 5.3 mil school tax levy, contending that the future of a community such as Clifton depended on the continued excellence of its schools to attract new residents, to keep up property values, and to train future citizens of the community. That spring, too, the board voted to join the CSC and established a committee to study the question of open housing.[23] And within four years, and with the cooperation of CTM, Cliftonites also established a task force to make Clifton School an exemplary institution, transformed the task force into the Clifton School Foundation, and through it helped to select a new principal and raise $5,000 for the school. In 1973, when 43 percent of Clifton School pupils were black, a foundation leader called Clifton a "model integrated school."[24]

Despite the settlement of the CSC question, similar issues proved contentious for the CTM board the next year. As the president put it in his report of 1970 to the annual meeting, "Some of our members would have us adhere to our traditional policy of strictly minding our own business in our own neighborhood. Others see us as too aloof from endeavors which they feel should be shared by many community organizations." In the face of these pressures, and probably "to the total satisfaction of no one," he said, the board "tried to play the diplomat and tread a middle course." Thus the board met with school board candidates, sent representatives to an organization setting up a proposed Community Mental Health program to treat and prevent drug addiction within a portion of the county including Clifton, and joined the Community Chest's new Social Planning Council. But the board dropped its own study of open housing in favor of maintaining liaison with Clifton Citizens for Open Housing.[25]

As it turned out, these new citywide initiatives of 1970 did not lead to much. The activities of the Community Chest's Social Planning Council went unrecorded in CTM's records and in the CTM *Bulletin*. Clifton Citizens for Open Housing, after a brief fit of zeal yielding a half-page newspaper ad signed by 347 Cliftonites for open housing and three lawsuits charging racial discrimination in apartment rentals, faded from view within a year of its founding.[26] The Community Mental Health drug treatment program remained a regular item on the CTM agenda for two years, but Clifton's participation ended after the program's governing committee decided against the establishment of a drop-in treatment center in Clifton because of the existence of such centers on Calhoun Street and in Mount Adams.[27]

As CTM interest in citywide issues waned, Cliftonites enthusiastic about improving the neighborhood's leisure facilities gained the support of the Cincinnati Recreation Commission to secure CTM's first major bricks and mortar accomplishment. Movement in this direction began during November 1969, when the CTM *Bulletin* announced that the Clifton Summer Activities Organization, established in the spring of 1969, had arranged for various recreational events in the basement of the Clifton School Annex, secured permission for Cliftonites to swim at the Hebrew Union College pool, and proposed a survey of all the neighborhood's indoor recreational facilities. This report, prepared by the CTM recreation committee, appeared the following month and featured a criticism of a Cincinnati Health and Welfare Council study (1967) which assigned recreation the lowest priority among Clifton's needs. This study, claimed the CTM report, rested on false premises, namely, that Cliftonites did not want an indoor center and pool, and failed to note that many younger people had moved to Clifton since 1960, in part as a result of apartment construction. The report also asserted that Clifton Meadows cost too much for the people most in need of recreation, namely, those living in the "high density" area from Dixmyth through McAlpin to Woolper and Vine.[28]

Interest in a recreation facility increased in the spring of 1970 as rumors circulated about the impending sale of the Sacred Heart Academy, which included spacious grounds next to Mount Storm Park as well as buildings. Clifton recreationists asked the CTM board to urge the Recreation Commission to acquire the property as an extension of Mount Storm Park and to equip it with recreational facilities. The board refused to do that, and doubted that it could do much for the recreation drive, but agreed to sponsor an open forum to bring together those who wanted to discuss recreation in Clifton and to invite the superintendent of the Cincinnati Recreation Commission. The forum was well attended and made it clear that Clifton residents wanted more recreational facilities for children and teenagers. But those present heard discouraging news from the superintendent, who said a Recreation Commission survey in 1967 gave Clifton the lowest priority among areas of the city in line for recreational facilities.[29]

The next month, when Sacred Heart went on the market, the board changed its position on its role in the disposition of the property and on the acquisition of recreation facilities. In June and July, the CTM president sent the city manager a request that the city acquire the land for park and recreational purposes. He acknowledged the area's zoning as a premier low-density residential district, and the city's financial plight, but argued that CTM worried about what developers might do with the site and that the city could not afford to lose this chance to help preserve Clifton. Neither the city manager, the Recreation Commission, nor the Park Board agreed, however. The CTM board's anxiety intensified in November 1970 when the realtor handling the sale of Sacred Heart reported that he was not optimistic about finding a buyer who would use the property without seeking a zoning change. Failing that, the realtor thought an apartment would be one of the best uses for the land.[30]

The Park Board and Recreation Commission remained uninterested in Sacred Heart until 1973, but developers did not, and they approached CTM for approval as they hatched their proposals. One, who wanted to use the property for a school, a hospital, and a home for autistic children, never got beyond the inquiry stage.[31] But in 1972 and 1973, CTM and a new group, the Citizens Association for the Preservation of Sacred Heart, opposed a proposal for an apartment development for eleven hundred persons in three hundred dwelling units, including seven acres for federally subsidized units for the elderly, and took a position against any change in zoning for Sacred Heart while standing ready to entertain another proposal at a lower density. The board also opposed a revision of the proposal, which would have omitted the housing for the elderly and switched from a rental to a condominium plan, on the grounds once more of high density.³² The same developer nonetheless sought a zoning change, despite CTM's objections to the plans, and the CTM board implored city hall to turn down the request, arguing that the multifamily development would ruin Lafayette Avenue, create drainage and traffic problems, and undermine Clifton, "a fine residential area in the inner city, . . . necessarily a fragile thing," as an asset to the city of Cincinnati.³³

Meanwhile, the board pursued various schemes for nonresidential development of the property. In 1971, it encouraged the idea of establishing a Cincinnati Woodlands Fund to raise $500,000 to buy and "preserve" the parcel, a scheme which did not work out, although CTM loaned out its membership list as a part of the fund-raising effort.³⁴ It also secured the aid of the Cincinnati Institute, a citywide organization established in 1971 by a small group of citizens interested in open space projects to "enhance the quality of life in urban communities." The two groups sent a proposal to the Max C. Fleischmann Foundation for funds to establish a Hillsides Landmark for Cincinnati, with Sacred Heart as the first acquisition, and for the orderly disposition of the land in accordance with an intensive study of the best uses of the land.³⁵ This, too, failed.

At the same time, the board, pushed by two more local advocacy associations, "Clifton Is a Neighborhood for Children" (CLINCH, established in 1970 and defunct after 1974), and the Clifton Recreation Commission (established in May 1973), kept after the Cincinnati Recreation Commission, which in May 1973 indicated an interest in Clifton if CTM would establish priorities on what kind of recreational facilities it wanted, and where.³⁶ The Recreation Commission was even willing to help solve this problem, for in November 1973 it hired a consultant to survey the needs and prepare a recreation master plan for Clifton and three adjacent neighborhoods (Clifton–University Heights, Fairview–Clifton Heights, and Corryville), in part by seeking the "input" of the communities involved.³⁷

The recreation survey and master plan, published in September 1974, must have satisfied Clifton's most ardent recreational enthusiasts, though it did little to help resolve the Sacred Heart problem. The report noted the absence in Clifton of a public indoor recreation center, pool, playfields for team sports and tennis courts, and pointed out that Clifton Meadows served just 254 families and required of each a $450 initiation fee and annual dues of $125. It called for tennis courts, a baseball diamond, a soccer field, and a citywide Arts Education Facility on the Sacred Heart property, a baseball diamond and children's play apparatus on Juergens Avenue, and tennis courts, a baseball diamond, a soccer field, and bike trails in the Dixmyth-Lowell area. But the top priority went to the development of a recreational complex at Clifton School and on the privately owned land behind the school. According to the plan, the complex should consist of a soccer field, two baseball diamonds, a deep water pool, a children's play area, and the renovation of the coach houses on the property as an environmental education center.[38]

The Recreation Commission did not carry out this expensive scheme, but before the publication of the survey and master plan it joined with the Board of Education to propose a recreation center as an extension of Clifton School, a $700,000 building housing a gym, an arts and crafts and performing arts facility, a teen center, and sauna baths. CTM vetoed the saunas in favor of extra lockers, then lobbied hard and successfully with city council to fund the project. These pleas emphasized Clifton's distress; its 86 juvenile offenders, its families with incomes below the poverty level (12 percent), the high proportion of black children in Clifton School (50 percent, said one letter), the high proportion of children at the school provided with free lunches, Clifton's problems with vandalism and purse snatching, and Clifton's lack of public recreation facilities—"no tot lots, no swimming pool, no nothing."[39]

In the midst of this concern with Sacred Heart and recreation, CTM confronted what it thought was another crisis involving Clifton Avenue. In the winter of 1972, CTM learned that the Ohio-Kentucky-Indiana Regional Council of Governments (OKI), a federally mandated regional planning agency, had prepared a regional transportation study calling for the improvement of Clifton Avenue between Ludlow and Spring Grove by expanding the section south of Lafayette into a ninety-foot right-of-way and by turning Spring Grove into a four-lane undivided highway. The OKI held no power to effectuate such a plan, but the proposal set off a furor. CTM gathered petitions, fired off a letter of protest to the OKI, and invited the OKI director first to a board meeting and then to a special meeting open to all Clifton residents, not just CTM members. At the meeting the OKI director explained that his agency existed to assist in developing regional plans for highways, water, sewerage, and mass transit and that it could only plan. A representative from the city's Public Works Department confirmed this, adding that only the city could carry out such a plan, and that OKI had to exist for Cincinnati to share in federal funds for projects within the scope of OKI's planning authority. The meeting then voted unanimously to oppose the widening of Clifton Avenue and Spring Grove, and the proposal and the issue of widening Clifton Avenue (but not Spring Grove) subsequently disappeared.[40]

All this talk about planning as the Sacred Heart problem festered raised doubts about Clifton's planning goals of 1964 as guidelines in CTM's efforts to control the pace and direction of the neighborhood's growth. A CTM board member raised those doubts in 1972 when he noticed that the development of comprehensive community plans that not only set down goals but also prioritized objectives for achieving them and strategies for fulfilling the objectives had become "big" in other Cincinnati neighborhoods. Another board member endorsed such planning as particularly useful for the business district and in the area of recreation.[41] The discussion ended there, however, and the notion of comprehensive neighborhood planning as the key element in community control languished in Clifton until the city government persuaded CTM to take up the process.

Comprehensive community planning by neighborhood organizations had in fact become "big" in other communities, though not on the initiative of neighborhood organizations. As we have seen, the city in the late 1950s and early 1960s began to encourage neighborhood participation in planning, most notably for the downtown and in the Avondale-Corryville area. In the mid- and late 1960s, several other neighborhoods, all of them inner-city and distressed areas, came into the planning game through federal programs associated with President Lyndon Johnson's war on poverty, especially after the city applied for and received a Model Cities planning grant. By this time, too, business leaders and city officials had become concerned about the city's declining population and its apparent decline in economic viability. Results of the 1960 census showed a decrease in the city's population, and the 1970 figures showed a decrease in the population of both Cincinnati and surrounding Hamilton County. With the decline in population came a decline in available tax revenue for local government purposes, and to some degree a shock to local pride.[42] From these concerns emerged a continuing campaign to improve Cincinnati's attractiveness as a place to live and work and as a place to locate or maintain business activities. This campaign did not center exclusively on downtown or distressed neighborhoods, however. This campaign intended to preserve and improve the attractiveness of *all* of Cincinnati's neighborhoods.[43]

The prime impetus for moves in this direction came after 1971, when a coalition of Democrats and Charterites, playing in part to the growing neighborhood organizational movement,[44] wrested control of city council from the Republicans, who had presided over the city's urban redevelopment and renewal activities. This included massive expressway construction, slum clearance, and, of course, the creation of the city's second ghetto, which had contributed so much to the creation of CTM. The new council soon selected a new city manager, one sympathetic to its own political and administrative commitment to neighborhood participation in city governance, including the maximum feasible participation of the poor and not so poor in both planning and zoning and in the construction of biennial city budgets.

An early sign of the city's new strategy came in the form of a study, begun before the fall 1971 council elections, by the city's Department of Urban Development. *From Housing Rehabilitation to Neighborhood Development* centered on deteriorated housing and evaluated the various programs, beginning with the Avondale-Corryville project, to rehabilitate such housing for low- and moderate income occupancy. It pronounced those programs a failure, for despite them the city faced "the paradox of continuing low income housing demand coincident with continued withdrawal of low cost housing from the market." The study also surveyed the entire city, not just distressed areas, to locate housing that failed to meet the city's minimum building code standards. The document contained a color-coded map identifying those deteriorating areas, including parts of Clifton, and indicating the estimated unit cost of rehabilitation. It stressed, too, that the problem possessed social as well as economic dimensions, and argued that rehabilitated housing units "will have no lasting impact if residents do not develop faith in the future of their neighborhoods" and that "deteriorated neighborhoods will not be transformed into desirable places to live unless rehabilitation efforts are directed at the broader goal of neighborhood development!"[45] As a solution the study offered a proposal for a complicated citywide process of city and neighborhood cooperation in comprehensive local community planning involving maximum feasible participation of neighborhood residents through community organizations. It suggested, too, that if community organizations would not or could not do such planning, the city should do it for them.[46]

The city manager took the first step in pushing this proposal during his response to a council resolution expressing concern about the location, in the summer of 1971, of two large public housing projects in neighborhoods that objected to their presence, including North Avondale, where the struggle to maintain racial residential integration persisted. Council called for the development of "a comprehensive strategy for the development and maintenance of housing resources for all income groups, and household sizes, in and out of established neighborhoods," but expressed special concern for the "location, design, community impact and quantity of low and moderate income housing." The city manager responded to this request by establishing a broadly based working review committee on housing, composed of representatives from the private and public sectors engaged in housing activities, and by expanding council's request. He charged the committee with developing a strategy to address "the quality of residential living in Cincinnati," not just the issue of controlling low and moderate income housing and its impact on communities. The committee engaged as a consultant Anthony Downs, whose Chicago-based Real Estate Research Corporation's proposal called for a "truly comprehensive housing strategy," not a single plan but "an effective planning/decision-making action/evaluation process."[47]

In 1973 the direction of Downs's thinking became clear. By that time he had prepared and discussed with the committee and with community organizations a series of position papers. Among other things, these documents divided Cincinnati into forty-four statistical areas, or neighborhoods, and ranked them first into five categories for purposes of analysis. The criteria for these rankings included neighborhood age, location (center to periphery), housing conditions, and the race and income levels of their residents. He also tried, because he had been hired to do it, to define "balance" regarding housing and ways in which the concept might be applied practically to secure more "balanced" neighborhoods. He noted that this had never been done in any large American city, because it was complicated and difficult and because the results "might be politically controversial."[48] What he meant, of course, was that "balance" required the racial and economic integration of both black and white and low- and middle-income neighborhoods, something which, given the racial and class biases of most Americans as etched on the social geography of American cities, would require the imposition of quotas of some sort or another, among other things.[49]

CTM kept its eye on the progress of the working review committee on housing, and the board eventually voted to endorse what the committee said in its final report about housing in the city and in Clifton.[50] The report's strategy for balance focused on low-income and racially transitional neighborhoods and treated others as problems of lower priority. It also ranked Clifton among the city's most solid eleven neighborhoods (Clifton, Roselawn [though Roselawn carried an asterisk, indicating it had probably dropped in the ratings after the 1970 census], Hyde Park, Pleasant Ridge, Fernbank, Saylor Park, Hartwell, College Hill, Mount Airy, Westwood, and Mount Washington), ones with the highest income and home ownership levels and with a predominantly white population not undergoing rapid racial transition. Those neighborhoods contained 125,143 persons in 1970, or 27.7 percent of the city's population, and the working review committee thought they should be preserved.[51]

Before city council considered the working review committee's comprehensive housing strategy, it and the city manager had moved aggressively to develop new tools through which such a policy, or parts of it, might flow. These included the preparation of two new categories of overlay zoning for environmental protection and historic districts. The first of these became law in 1976 and provided council the authority to establish by ordinance environmental quality districts (EQD) with guidelines to control and regulate development on the city's hillsides, in areas of high public investment, such as Fountain Square in the city's central business district, or in areas for which an urban design plan had been adopted, such as a neighborhood business district, by city council. The local historic district legislation did not pass until 1980, but it established a procedure by which council might act to preserve historic sites, buildings, and districts by so designating them and, in the case of historic districts, by designating and adopting guidelines to regulate demolition, renovation, rehabilitation, and new construction in such districts. The CTM board endorsed both measures in principle when first presented with the idea.[52]

At the same time, the city manager took steps to encourage the community organization movement and to goad community organizations in all forty-four of Cincinnati's neighborhoods into planning and budgeting. Complaining that the established procedure produced budgets reflecting the desires of the city's departmental bureaucracy rather than those of citizens, and acting with the assistance of the League of Women Voters through its Metropolitan Project for 1973, he called on community councils to draw up priorities for improvement projects in their areas and to select delegates to serve on task forces that would meet with city departments to evaluate city and other social services and to determine city budget priorities and recommendations for city council. He called these Community Organization Planning and Evaluation (COPE) task forces. To participate in the budget and evaluation process, a community council had to be "certified" by city hall by demonstrating that it represented a broad spectrum of neighborhood residents and that it commanded sufficient organizational skills and procedures to operate with continuity and responsibility.[53] By June 1973, CTM, claiming 840 family memberships and representation of some 2,000 households, had registered as a legitimate community organization.[54]

The city's initiative with respect to housing strategy and the budget and service evaluation implied, of course, real community planning, and in 1973 CTM began to move, albeit slowly and uncertainly, in that direction. In April 1973, the CTM board decided to pursue the possibility of working with the University of Cincinnati's Graduate Department of Community Planning to draw up a long-range plan for Clifton.[55] In June, CTM's newly elected president, Mrs. Betty Ames, challenged the organization to move further toward taking more responsibility for Clifton's future by working with other entities, especially the city of Cincinnati.

Ames, a founder of CTM, began her acceptance talk by noting that CTM in the beginning "wanted to take care of Clifton—period." Now, she said, we must look to what goes on in other neighborhoods, and when we do we find that "the City's problems are Clifton's problems." She pointed to the new housing strategy, and the contemporary concern for new kinds of rehabilitation programs for the mentally ill, drug addicts, and criminals which would probably place "half-way houses in every neighborhood." North Avondale, she added, could teach CTM how to maintain a racially integrated neighborhood. Then she issued a rousing call for "neighborhood power" and an endorsement of "the New Populism" by urging broader citizen participation at the local level. She urged CTM to be both "responsible and innovative" and to involve "a great many more people" through devices like the open meeting. "The more responsibility CTM takes," she concluded, "the more the City will give us. The time will come, no doubt, when funds are allocated to communities to spend as they might see fit. The wave of the future is participatory democracy."[56]

The wave of the future, as it turned out, was not in the direction of letting neighborhoods participate in planning both for their own welfare and the welfare of other neighborhoods, and the welfare of the city as a whole. Nor did it point to allowing neighborhoods to spend tax dollars as they saw fit, a prospect the CTM board itself considered but dropped. In October 1974, for example, it heard a proposal from City Councilman Tom Brush that would have provided just that on the grounds that the power to make budgets would render community councils more democratic, more responsible, and more efficient. Brush said he was impressed with community councils, but he regarded only eight as effective, worried about the unrepresentativeness of all of them, about jurisdictional disputes among organizations, about their tendency to act only in the negative, to obstruct things they did not want in their community. As a remedy, he proposed the creation of an Office of Community Affairs under the city manager to assist communities in setting up councils and defining boundaries. But he also proposed to give taxing and budget authority to the councils, citing as precedent the established procedure of permitting residents to vote on tax assessments for certain improvements, such as sidewalks. The board listened and discussed the idea, but neither endorsed it then nor pursued it later.[57]

The city rejected this course, too, but kept up the pressure on communities to participate jointly with the city in planning, in preparing budgets, and in the budget and service evaluation process. CTM managed in June 1973 to put together its priorities for the budget in 1973, but city officials deferred all its requests, including street improvements and the repair of "derelict houses" along Juergens Avenue, and a recreation proposal.[58] CTM also tried to start a local planning effort. In June 1973, the board met with planning students from the University of Cincinnati who indicated an interest in doing a planning study of Clifton.[59] This effort faltered, too, but in May 1974 Betty Ames said bluntly that all the city's neighborhoods "must make a plan or one will be made for them." She confessed that CTM had been slow in getting started, but in the summer of 1974 she announced progress, in part because Kenneth Corey, a resident of Clifton and head of the Department of Graduate Community Planning at the University of Cincinnati, had taken over supervision of the effort and enlisted the aid of planning students. Mrs. Ames indicated that the board gave high priority to the work on land use, including open space, recreation, and education, on housing and on the business district, and assigned a "medium priority" to "Attitudes and Racial Concerns." She added, too, that only neighborhoods with representative community councils and completed neighborhood plans would be eligible to receive funds from a proposed federal program that would grant money to states and local governments for use on projects of their own devising.[60]

The endorsement by Ames and the CTM board of comprehensive neighborhood planning put CTM in an aggressive stance. In the early 1960s CTM began to broaden its activities and to work now and then more closely with "outside" organizations and entities, including most consistently the Cincinnati School Board and various branches of the city government. This broadening of CTM's scope of action suggested to some that Cliftonites might not merely influence but actually control the fate of the neighborhood. By 1974, CTM seemed intent on becoming Clifton's agency of community control through the exercise of neighborhood power by developing a comprehensive plan for the future of Clifton and by participating in ways not yet clearly defined in the implementation of that plan. City hall had already recognized CTM as the legitimate representative of Clifton, and the development of a comprehensive plan under the auspices of CTM seemed the appropriate next step on the way to neighborhood self-determination.

It remained to be seen, however, the direction that Clifton might take as it moved toward self-determination through comprehensive neighborhood planning. Ames in her first address as president of CTM laid out one vision when she took as Clifton's problems the city's problems, which she defined as residential segregation by race and class and the unwillingness of neighborhoods to accept "half-way houses" for the rehabilitation of drug addicts, criminals, and the mentally ill. But that vision was just one of several alternative visions, as the recent unpleasantness over the integration of Clifton Meadows suggested. And her vision might be abandoned or significantly altered in a planning process that Ames herself saw as an exercise in "the New Populism," the broader participation of Clifton's varied citizens in defining the nature and extent of Clifton and the problems for which Cliftonites might seek solutions.

5

Making a Comprehensive Neighborhood Plan, 1974–1982

City officials pushed Clifton Town Meeting (CTM) in the mid-1970s into participation in Clifton's neighborhood planning process as part of a larger effort to create a new plan for all of the city's neighborhoods and for its government. To accomplish this, the city government sought to engage every city neighborhood in participatory planning for the production of plans regarded by city officials as appropriate for each neighborhood, plans that neighborhood residents would presumably help implement because of their authorship stake in the plan. The city government based this planning process on several premises that set basic rules of the game that neighborhood organizations had to accept to become players. The rules stipulated that each neighborhood's plan would focus on its own welfare rather than on the welfare of other neighborhoods or the city as a whole, the concept on which the metropolitan master plan of 1948 had rested. The rules also stipulated that planning for each neighborhood would start with the city government's analysis of each neighborhood's economic structure, population, and residential character, measures that suggested significant changes for troubled and semitroubled neighborhoods and almost none for those in the top bracket.

These rules carried several implications for Clifton's plan. They proscribed any concern for feebly supported efforts by a few Cliftonites in the 1960s and 1970s to take on some of the problems of other neighborhoods or the city as a whole. They also suggested that the process would yield a conservationist Clifton plan, for city officials started the work by providing Clifton's resident planners with a very favorable picture of the neighborhood's population and its residential character. But the rules of the game left more room for resident initiative on other matters, for they possessed a freer and broader range of choices with respect to land use and design controls so long as those choices comported with the conservationist structural aims of the city administration and city council.

The completion of the Clifton comprehensive neighborhood plan took five years and involved an irregular and messy planning process that helped precipitate a crisis of public confidence in the leadership of CTM, a crisis to which the board responded by opening its deliberations, in the spirit of citizen participation, to broader public scrutiny. The length and messiness of the planning process stemmed in part from its heavy reliance on amateurs, people by definition unschooled in planning, but more importantly on the large number of players involved in the maximum feasible participation in planning of all parties concerned, including parties inside and outside Clifton. And the intrusion of other problems contributed not only to the delay in the completion of the plan but also to a crisis of confidence in the city's comprehensive neighborhood planning processes and in CTM as the guardian of Clifton's welfare and the interests of its varied residents.

In September 1974, the city administration gave CTM the decisive nudge. At the CTM board meeting, city officials explained the Total Neighborhood Assistance Process, which encompassed both planning and budgeting. Under this process, each of the city's communities would develop a plan for itself, either through a consultant or with the assistance of a team of city planners organized in four to six teams, each of which would work with one neighborhood per year over a five-year span. Plans thus devised would form the basis of and be integrated into a new document to replace the metropolitan master plan of 1948. Called a "coordinated" city plan, it listed guidelines for programs, projects, and land use statements from the plans of particular neighborhoods and entities of city government.[1]

The planning process embodied in the Total Neighborhood Assistance Process made explicit several tendencies apparent since the early 1960s, mostly in the budget evaluation and the housing strategy projects. Under it, city government would assemble a plan for the city, not the metropolitan region, as in 1925 and 1948. It would treat neighborhoods as fundamental urban units of analysis and action. And under it, the city would set down rules by which to plan with neighborhoods rather than for them, or more precisely with individuals in neighborhoods who would decide what their neighborhoods needed and did not need with respect to land uses and design controls. This arrangement put the city in the role of the coordinator, first of the planning activities and then of the budgeting and carrying out of the activities dictated by the various local community plans.[2]

This local community planning scheme flowed immediately, however, from the passage in 1974 of the federal Community Development Act. That legislation became effective in January 1975, and it merged six programs from the federal Department of Housing and Urban Development (HUD) into a single block grant program that would dispense $90 million over six years to cities, which would then decide where to spend their share of the funds to eliminate or prevent blight most effectively. Cincinnati officials decided to divide its neighborhoods into three groups based on the stability of the composition of their population and the condition of their housing stock, a process which categorized Clifton as a stable residential community. The city envisioned using the money in this class of neighborhoods for housing loans and for improving business areas and recreational facilities, and promised priority consideration for projects attracting matching dollars. The city also offered the possibility of technical assistance in drawing up a comprehensive community plan and funding to aid in carrying out some part of it, such as improving Clifton's business area.[3]

Under these circumstances, comprehensive planning activities in Clifton intensified. In January 1974, the CTM board sent a list of provisional goals, objectives, and priorities to the director of city planning, Herbert Stevens. His staff found them internally inconsistent and reflective of the views of only those living north of Ludlow Avenue. Stevens then announced that the city had no funds with which to revise the objectives and publish a final plan. He suggested that CTM hire a student from the University of Cincinnati Graduate Community Planning Department to work six months on this task under his staff's supervision. The draft of the plan would be prepared by a CTM planning committee assisted by a faculty member and graduate students and by John Sheblessey, the assistant director of the Cincinnati City Planning Division, who also happened to reside in Clifton.[4]

The goals and objectives aspect of the comprehensive plan took shape quickly. By January 1975, the planning committee had established three task forces and acquired graduate student consultants. CTM's new historic preservation committee reported that it had met with staff members from the Miami Purchase Association (MPA), a historic preservation organization for the advocacy of that cause in southwestern Ohio. MPA had signed a contract with the Cincinnati City Planning Commission (CCPC) to do a preservation survey of Cincinnati's forty-four neighborhoods, and wanted to cover first those properties, such as Sacred Heart Academy, in immediate danger of demolition. The MPA staff also recommended nominating a Lafayette Circle historic district to a place on the National Register of Historic Places.[5]

In the process of developing the goals and objectives, the planning committee gathered statistics comparing Clifton with the city as a whole. It learned that Clifton came out better in every category: it had a lower violent crime and infant mortality rate, a higher mean income and median house value figure, a greater percentage (73 percent) of persons with high school or higher education, a lower share of housing units rated overcrowded or lacking plumbing, a lower proportion of families living in poverty and households headed by women. In addition, Clifton's population had increased by 12 percent between 1960 and 1970, rising from 9,635 to 10,750, and blacks made up 9 percent of Clifton's residents in 1970, compared with 27 percent for the city. Planning committee members also learned to define Clifton in an unaccustomed way, as composed of census tracts 70, 71, and 72, and as Cincinnati Statistical Neighborhood #7.[6]

The planning committee presented its goals to CTM members for review in April 1975, and a few weeks later the Clifton community plan appeared in print. The booklet included a picture of a gas streetlamp as a frontispiece, a map with Clifton in the center of a field covering the most densely inhabited parts of Hamilton County and northern Kentucky, a map of early Clifton (undated, ca. 1817), and a map showing streets, lot lines, steep hillsides, open spaces, churches, schools, the Woman's Club, the Scarlet Oaks Bethesda (retirement) Home, and cemeteries. The section on "image" called Clifton a "unique community" and stressed the large number of medical and educational institutions within or near the area, the services they afforded Clifton residents, and their influence in attracting single people and small families, thus contributing to Clifton's low person-per-household figure of 2.53. The section on "Historic Clifton" told a story beginning in 1790 with the establishment of "Ludlow's station," a blockhouse on the western edge of Mill Creek at the foot of what became Ludlow Avenue, and ending in 1896, the moment of annexation to Cincinnati. It did not refer to other neighborhoods, the city of Cincinnati, or the metropolis of which Clifton might be seen a part except to note briefly that Cincinnati created Burnet Woods Park and Dixmyth Avenue, the southern boundaries of Clifton as defined in 1961. Three appendixes described several organizations in Clifton that CTM viewed as "community resources," including CTM itself, the Kiwanis Club, the Clifton Business and Professional Association, the Cincinnati Woman's Club (with ninety members from Clifton), the Clifton Senior Center, and two residential institutions for the elderly, the Bethesda Scarlet Oaks Home for "middle-income professional people" and St. Peter's Home at 476 Riddle Road for "110 low-income persons." The appendixes also listed names and addresses of people who attended the review and critique meeting, and added supplemental goals for business areas and institutions approved by the board after the review meeting, leaving some doubt about their legitimacy as part of the planning report proper. Another section described the planning process and defined terms used in the report.[7]

The goals and objectives themselves, including those in the appendixes, suggested that the planning committee agreed with city officials, who wanted to preserve Clifton essentially as it was. The housing goals, for example, aimed to strengthen and maintain "the residential quality unique to Clifton," ratify the existing mix and distribution pattern of single-family homes and small and large apartments, set down a policy of no population growth, encourage historic preservation, protect private housing for the elderly by upgrading the zoning for houses already converted to apartments so as to obstruct their demolition and replacement by new construction, and acknowledge the desirability of nondiscrimination on the basis of race, religion, nationality, ethnic origin, or sex without proposing affirmative action to alter the mix or distribution of these elements of the population (11–13). The plan took a similarly status quo stance on parks and open space, but called for more recreational facilities, specifically the completion of the recreation complex at Clifton School as recommended by the Glaser and Myers consultants' report to the recreation commission, the development of a Juergens Avenue playground, and additional facilities for senior citizens (16–17). The Clifton community plan also made clear that the "central neighborhood business district" should remain modest in size and be developed according to a theme stressing historic preservation and Clifton's "village atmosphere." This part of the report called for more parking space, deplored drive-in and fast-food restaurants (except along Central Parkway), and requested a CCPC study of two business areas near Clifton's borders, one at Vine and Woolper and the other at Jefferson and Ruther, to determine what steps might be taken in those apparently troubling spots. It also advocated the location of offices providing service to Cliftonites on the periphery of the neighborhood's central business district (18–19, 32–33).

The goals and objectives also covered environmental quality, education, transportation, and education and human services. These aims generally held with established CTM traditions, although the report came down forthrightly for racial and cultural diversity among participants and programs in educational institutions, expressed a distaste for the addition in or near Clifton of any new "citywide" institutions of any kind, and condemned air pollution (16–17, 19, 26). Perhaps the expression of a concern for the psychological well-being of Clifton's residents ranked as the most novel feature of the report. This occurred most explicitly in "the broad education goal" of Clifton as a community, which aimed "to encourage the transmittal to and acquisition by *individuals* throughout the entire life span, of adequate knowledge and skills so that they may *achieve optimal personal and social development*" (22, emphases in original). This goal, given its breadth, might have served as the centerpiece of this effort by Cliftonites to define their community, except that its explicit commitment to the accommodation of the desires and tastes of an extraordinarily broad range of diverse individuals contradicted the general tendency of the report, which aimed to uphold the status quo (for example, by excluding "citywide" institutions, most if not all of which assisted individuals in acquiring knowledge and skills useful for personal and social development).

Nonetheless, the completion of the goals and objectives statement fulfilled the first step in the comprehensive neighborhood planning process. After that, according to recommended but not inviolable CCPC procedures, should have come the preparation of an existing conditions study, followed by the writing of a comprehensive neighborhood plan itself and the creation of a neighborhood business district urban design plan. Progress through this sequence was impeded by a crisis, however: a threat to tear down the grand old Roanoke apartment building near the western end of the central business district and to replace it with either a Burger Chef restaurant or a Kroger supermarket. This threat created a furor involving the intervention of city council and forced CTM to develop a neighborhood business district plan while struggling to finish the existing conditions report and to prepare the comprehensive community plan itself.

The threat of an assault on the Roanoke materialized in the summer of 1975, after the preparation of the goals and objectives planning report. News that a Burger Chef restaurant might occupy the Roanoke site broke first. Residents of the Roanoke established a Concerned Clifton Citizens Committee to protest the proposal, and CTM soon joined the fray. CTM strategy centered on persuading city council to designate the site as part of an Interim Development Control (IDC) zoning district for the Ludlow business corridor, a step which would have prevented the issuance of demolition permits in the area for three months, renewable by council action for an additional nine months, to permit the drawing up of alternative planning and zoning for the area. CTM found Burger Chef objectionable because it thought fast-food chains brought "traffic congestion, littering and loitering," a complaint CTM repeated when Kroger expressed interest in opening on the Roanoke site a "mini-super store" for Clifton residents as a supplement to its other store next door to the Roanoke building. The crisis abated after Kroger dropped its plans for the site in August 1975 and the city council established an IDC for the Ludlow business strip, including the Roanoke lot, and persuaded Burger Chef officials to drop their proposal.[8]

The imposition of an IDC on the business district intensified the pressure on CTM to step up its planning activities, but also created some confusion within CTM. In April 1975, the director of city planning had reminded community council representatives that all communities must make comprehensive plans or allow the city to make plans for them, and that funding would go to those who finished their comprehensive plans first.[9] Yet the writing of a neighborhood business district design plan not only ranked as the last rather than the next step in Clifton's planning sequence as prescribed by the planning commission but also fell under the jurisdiction of the Cincinnati Department of Urban Development, which funded and prepared urban design plans for and with neighborhoods. Unsure of where to turn or how to proceed, CTM accomplished nothing during the three months of the IDC, and when it sought an extension, CTM had to overcome CCPC objections on the grounds that CTM lacked a comprehensive community plan and had not applied for a zoning change. City council chose to disregard these procedural niceties and granted the extension, at the same time requesting funding for the project but urging swift action so that an Environmental Quality District could replace the IDC district after its expiration as a control measure to regulate development and design in the business district. By January 1976, with the use of Community Development funds for the Clifton business district plan, both the business district plan and the existing conditions study for the comprehensive plan went forward.[10]

HUD did the business district urban design plan, but with CTM as a full and occasionally troubled partner. Both parties spent some time working out preliminary proposals, and in early 1977 they arrived at the point where diverse decisions had to be made, although the securing of a Community Development grant, matched in part with private funds, eased the way by making possible the addition of parking space near the IGA supermarket. Nonetheless, parking remained a point of contention, for the First National Bank wanted to tear down several residences so that a parking "corridor" could be pushed through at midblock behind the bank on Ludlow and Whitfield to the Kroger store at Ludlow and Middleton. That created resentment in Clifton,[11] but not nearly so vocal as a CTM proposal to expand commercial land uses onto the streets of Telford, Shiloh, Middleton, and Hosea, streets regarded as essentially residential by their inhabitants, who protested loudly. One of them called it "creeping commercialism" imposed by "Upper Clifton" on "Lower Clifton." "Upper Clifton," claimed the protester, "fronts on fancy streets [north of McAlpin] and houses most members of the Clifton Town Meeting. Lower Clifton exists more as a series of tributaries to Ludlow, breathing the exhaust from congested streets and fighting to preserve what little peace it has. Lower Cliftonites, stand up and be counted!"[12]

This vision, of course, was not that of the CTM and HUD planners. They saw Clifton as a mini-metropolis. They saw it, that is, in core and periphery terms, with the core consisting of a business district encompassing multifamily residential units, apartments which would provide clientele for shops, stores, the movie theater, library, post office branch, and bars and restaurants, and apartments which would also limit the expansion of the business strip proper, acting thereby as a buffer protecting peripheral low-density residential areas from nonresidential and high-density intrusions. Thus, as part of the business district urban design scheme, the CTM also proposed an urban design environmental quality district (EQD) with a boundary larger than that for the business district proper as a means of controlling development and preventing deterioration within both the business district and the "buffer" apartment zone. And just as the city's planners assigned the metropolitan central business district a core (Fountain Square and the immediate surrounding blocks), so Clifton's planners designated a core for Clifton's central business district. They put its center not at Ludlow and Clifton Avenue, however, but at Telford and Ludlow, and proposed for the northeast corner of that intersection a quarter-block new commercial and residential development. They devoted all the rest of the block except the side facing Middleton to parking, a proposal which would displace the occupants of businesses along Ludlow and of residential units along Telford, including those residents of an apartment notorious to CTM leaders during the 1970s for its slovenly upkeep by a landlord indifferent to CTM standards of decorum. To carry out this part of the plan, as well as to reinforce the proposed EQD, the planners considered forming a nonprofit Urban Development Corporation to purchase, demolish, rehabilitate, or sell deteriorated buildings as well as stimulate new development projects.[13]

Nor did the CTM planners feel they had deviously imposed their plan on lower Cliftonites or anyone else. Prior to board consideration and action on the plan, they took the proposal to open hearings in five areas throughout Clifton to seek reactions, pro and con. Indeed, the CTM president sought to facilitate an informed discussion of the proposal by explaining in her letter of invitation to the hearings that CTM had to engage in planning to qualify for city, state, and federal fundings, by reminding Cliftonites that one such grant of $150,000 had assisted in the construction of a new parking lot near the IGA store, by informing them that the Cincinnati City Planning Commission had allotted $25,000 for professional planning assistance in the business district planning project, and by suggesting that "Clifton has many of the problems other communities have, and we are in competition with those communities. The key for us is to be informed and organized," she contended, through such activities as participating in the development of a plan for the business district.[14]

Despite the CTM president's reassurances and cheerleading, bitter opposition to the plan persisted and enlivened the meeting at which the board finally approved the document. On May 2, 1977, fifty residents from homes close to the business district showed up to protest that they had received no notification that the board would vote on the plan at the meeting and to present a petition with 165 signatures against the plan. The CTM *Bulletin*'s account of the session noted that the board had to vote then because the city's funding for the project expired at the end of May, and reported soberly that a "significant and negative confrontation" had occurred, and that the board adopted the plan by a vote of 17 to 3 "under a cloud of contention and ill feeling." The board president defended the action, nonetheless, claiming that it marked a shift in board policy "from a posture of responding to crisis and sometimes fighting proposed solutions imposed by the City to actively planning and proposing alternatives and developing long-term guidelines for the time when future changes will inevitably occur in Clifton."[15] In that spirit, the board did little to placate those who opposed the plan, except to amend the plan by recommendations calling for the finding of acceptable locations within Clifton for persons and businesses displaced by the implementation of the plan and, where possible, the moving rather than the demolition of houses which might have to make way for progress under the plan.[16] The CCPC, however, ultimately imposed a compromise on the combatants by reducing the size of the EQD recommended by CTM while retaining the idea of an apartment buffer between the business district and the low-density residential periphery of the neighborhood.[17]

The board now pushed ahead with comprehensive community planning. In the fall of 1977, and with no furor, CTM took the next step, the completion of an existing conditions study. As we have seen, CTM planners had already enlisted the aid of UC students and faculty and "experts" from the city's Planning Department. In 1976, they received additional help from one of the city's Community Assistance Teams (CAT), a new service offered by the city to every neighborhood as city officials sought to replace the metropolitan master plan of 1948 with a coordinated city plan. This new city "plan" was not in fact a plan but a process for coordinating and drawing priorities from particular projects and programs drawn up by the city departments, city council, and communities. In part, the process aimed to secure control by the city of the orgy of plans flowing from neighborhood-by-neighborhood and department-by-department planning, and it emerged amid concern in city hall about declining revenues and shrinking municipal budgets and the prospect of having to plan for less rather than more.[18]

The coordinated city plan and CAT program dictated the process and form of CTM planning from this point forward. CAT teams worked out of the new Division of Community Assistance in the city manager's office, which "absorbed" various community planning programs developed by the CCPC between 1969 and 1976. All CAT teams consisted of a physical planner, a human services planner, a technician for research and graphical aid, a part-time draftsman, and a secretary. Their charge was to assist each community in maintaining and improving its environment, its organization, and its sense of identity, that is, to help communities "to organize, to plan, to participate and to act" in partnership with the city. The teams were expected to help each community devise a written concept of what it wanted to become, a work program of projects to realize the concept, and a means to focus resources on issues in the work program. In return, the city would get a structured set of realistic budget requests from each community, elements for inclusion in the coordinated city plan process, knowledge of communities from which to design new city and departmental programs, and documentation for use in federal grant applications. And the CAT team took to each community a process for planning that ideally began with the establishment of the community concept, then moved through the development of goals, a work program of objectives and priorities by phases, a land use plan for projects involving the city, and the preparation of an existing conditions study. Finally, if the community wanted a written history, "the community as part of the team/community partnership" would undertake the writing and publication of such a document for inclusion in the comprehensive plan.[19]

Thus CTM planners could be seen as out of step with the ideal configuration of the planning process, as defined by the city government in 1976 when it established the CAT teams program, for they had prepared a goals and objectives statement that could be taken as the writing of a community concept (and history) but had not established a work program of objectives, a land use plan, or plans for projects involving the city. Instead, they produced the existing conditions study in the fall of 1977, and with some fanfare (a special meeting) but no furor, CTM approved its existing conditions study. This was a lengthy document crammed with maps and statistical tables interspersed with a text and divided into sections covering land use and zoning; socioeconomic characteristics; housing characteristics; community facilities, institutions, and services; transportation and circulation; and the neighborhood business district. Besides this inventory, the study also contained a history of planning in Clifton, a history that began in 1961 and featured CTM in the starring role in a story designed to explain "how the community has come to be the unique urban neighborhood that it is." This history did not, however, examine the question of whether or to what extent Clifton really was unique, but accepted its uniqueness as a given, and ignored the issue of race in its analysis of CTM as planning agent.[20]

The existing conditions study also offered two very ambitious recommendations that would have made CTM a perpetual planning body. The first urged that CTM adopt a "plan of action" involving the creation of an annual report similar to the existing conditions study, conducting an annual opinion survey of the views of Cliftonites on desirable community goals and objectives, and developing an archive and appointing a "community historian" to keep track of events in the history of Clifton planning and of changes in the community as part of a continuous planning program. Such a program, the study noted, would provide information annually as a basis for budget requests to the city, and in format should be compatible with a similar process at city hall, the coordinated city plan.[21]

This recommendation saw CTM as an analogue to the city's planning commission and prescribed its function as that of the coordinator adapting and synthesizing proposals produced by a myriad of planning agents in Clifton, including individuals through the opinion survey. As in city hall, the Clifton existing conditions study sought to move away from the planning principles associated with the city master plans of 1925 and 1948. It wanted to shift the emphasis from the plan to planning itself as a meritorious activity somehow good for the community and individuals residing in the community, to place the focus on the process, not the product, perhaps because of the absence of a clear and widely shared vision of what the product might become or should be. Planning thus would become a perpetual huddle in which the heterogeneous participants on one side in an endless game gathered repeatedly to establish sequential solutions to problems which, because of the eternal flux of circumstances, never seemed the same and always looked perplexing. As the CCPC put it, the coordinated city plan would not be a plan at all, but a "process . . . , open-ended, dynamic, and on-going," just as the Clifton existing conditions study called for Cliftonites to engage in a "continuous evolving community plan process."[22]

The second recommendation occurred almost as an afterthought in the last of five appendixes. Entitled "Toward the Concept of the Clifton Community," this section gently chided the city government and CTM for parochialism in their planning, for their failure to view Clifton in the context of its relationship with other neighborhoods and the city and metropolis of which it might be seen as a part, for their failure to adopt plans for Clifton's welfare designed also to serve the welfare of other neighborhoods, of the city, and of the metropolis. This recommendation capped its criticism by suggesting as one of the "major tasks facing Clifton planners" the preparation of "a 'concept of the Clifton Community' that incorporates both the values and strengths from the community's past planning concepts, and also incorporates tomorrow's urban needs." After all, the study concluded, "Clifton is an integral part of urban Cincinnati, and as such, it must have a future community concept that is realistically reflective of its past and desired future."[23] There the second recommendation ended. It neither proposed techniques for de-parochializing Cincinnati's neighborhood planning process nor acknowledged the tension between the second recommendation and the first's call for a plan of action, which by its emphasis on planning as a continuing activity implied the absence of notions which might be crystallized into a concept of Clifton so widely shared by individuals and institutions that it could be used as a goal to guide and direct all the community planners within Clifton.

CTM adopted neither of these recommendations. Instead, aided by the city's Community Assistance Team #4, it pushed ahead with the development of a comprehensive community plan for submission to the CCPC as part of the coordinated city plan. This took two more years, in part because of CTM's tendency to crowd its agenda with other pressing items. During the summer of 1977, for example, after the CTM board's endorsement of the neighborhood business district plan, rumors spread of the proposal to develop a subsidized high-rise apartment for the elderly on the Rue de la Paix, a hillside location on the undeveloped land behind the houses along the west side of Lafayette Avenue where it turned downhill toward Ludlow, a site that some CTM members worried about because CTM had overlooked it during its rezoning efforts in the early 1960s. The rumors proved true. In December a developer appeared before the board with such a project and asked for CTM support in his efforts to persuade the Cincinnati Metropolitan Housing Authority to float tax-exempt bonds to help finance the project. By this time, however, Lafayette Avenue residents were incensed, lest the building destabilize the hill and endanger their property, while others protested the isolation of the site from the business district, the plan for which envisioned elderly housing in or near the district, close to shopping facilities, the library, public transit, and the Senior Citizens Center.

The board voted no on the proposal, but the developer persisted, relying on HUD for aid. In the summer of 1978, representatives of the Clifton Senior Center urged the board to reconsider its objection to the project. By this time the board had secured from the city an environmental quality hillside district zone for the location, a district with guidelines prohibiting such a development. City council concurred in all this, and the issue seemed moot until the developer took his case to court, which determined that the project's inception antedated the EQD and could go forward under the old zoning. It did, and the project opened in 1980, having overcome the isolation problem by securing two vans to meet the transportation needs of the elderly residents and having provided space for the Senior Center rent free, although requiring the organization to pay $600 per month for utilities.[24]

At the same time, the board fretted over the future of Sacred Heart Academy, an issue which remained unresolved but which appeared in the late 1970s in a rather different form. In 1976, the city, using a combination of federal recreation funds and local revenues, acquired the property and began to work with CTM on a development for the site. By March 1977, several alternatives existed, including its use as a continuing education and conference center by the University of Cincinnati, as a citywide arts center, as a hotel and restaurant, as a recreation complex, as a site for commercial development, as a place for housing in a variety of configurations, including housing and recreation, and as a location for a public elementary school for handicapped as well as normal students. At its March meeting, the board considered the school, noting fears among some that Clifton might become overly institutionalized, citing the goals and objectives statement (1975) about preserving open space and the need for recreation, and observing that additional single-family housing would be good for the city's tax base. By the end of the summer, the board decided to reject the school and started a process to determine exactly what it preferred to do with the location and the buildings.[25]

By this time, the possibility of the University of Cincinnati saving the buildings had passed, evaporating apparently with the resignation of the president who had proposed it,[26] but university faculty and students in the College of Design, Art, Architecture and Planning, after an open meeting on the issue, worked up a plan to preserve the buildings, secure additional recreation facilities for Clifton, and retain open spaces. The scheme did not involve single-family homes, however, but the conversion of the large Sacred Heart building into apartments (14–16 in the first proposal, 22–26 in the second one). This group also pressed for and finally persuaded CTM to take the lead in establishing a Clifton Urban Redevelopment Corporation to spark the preservation effort, incorporation papers for which were filed early in 1979, and assisted in the designation of the property as historic. CTM did not succeed, however, in finding a developer who could secure enough assistance from the city to make the project financially feasible under the plans laid down by CTM, although one developer, a Clifton resident himself, attracted CTM and city interest during 1980. When those negotiations collapsed, CTM put the Sacred Heart project on "hold" as it sought other developers, reaffirming at the same time, however, its top priority of housing and recreation for the site.[27]

This emphasis on recreation at the Sacred Heart location stemmed in part from a bitter fight in 1977 over the use of vacant land behind Clifton School. In 1975, the owners of the property, including one with a parcel on the north side of McAlpin that contained the undeveloped part of the historic Rawson estate, began to talk about selling or donating the land to the city's Park Commission or the Cincinnati Zoo. In that same year, the city appropriated $125,000 to buy the land behind the school to build soccer and baseball facilities as recommended in the consultants' report of 1974 on recreation in Clifton. The money could not be used on another project, such as Sacred Heart, but the owners could not decide to whom the land should go or whether restrictions as to the use of the land should be included in the donation or sale.

Frustrated with the delay of the project, and concerned that the land might ultimately be sold for apartment development, the CTM board in 1977 urged the city to use its power of eminent domain to force the sale. This step cheered the recreationists but angered those who opposed soccer and baseball facilities on that site. Both sides of the fray now organized, one as the Committee for the Children of Clifton, the other as the Committee to Keep Clifton Green and Preserve Trees. The former, citing the absence of facilities for structured recreation in Clifton, praised the site because of its central location and its accessibility to physical education classes at the school and because of the existence of established traffic regulations and routes to get to it. The opposition complained that soccer and baseball fields would create traffic congestion and litter, worried about an adverse effect on property values, disliked the use of eminent domain to acquire private property, fretted about the loss of green space, and expressed concern about the possible use of the fields by people who did not reside in Clifton, a concern annoying to some other Cliftonites who wondered if the drive to keep this part of Clifton green might be driven by a fear that the facility would attract black youngsters from the ghetto on Clifton's eastern border.[28]

By September 1977, the CTM board knew it held a hot potato, for a public opinion survey of Clifton residents showed not only a preference for the school over Sacred Heart as the site for soccer and baseball fields but also that 50 percent of those polled who held an opinion on the question believed Clifton's recreation facilities to be adequate. Thus the board decided to hold an open meeting on the issue and invited people from both sides to express their views while tabling a motion to withdraw CTM's request for the use of eminent domain.[29] At the October meeting, the CTM president reviewed the history of the issue and reported that the owners were still considering donating the land for zoo and park or recreational purposes. Representatives of the two opposing committees made brief presentations, and the board then considered and passed a resolution on the question. It stated CTM's commitment to the preservation of the undeveloped part of the historic Rawson estate and urged the park board and zoo to accept the donation without restrictions regarding its use for recreation but to review its use with CTM after the owners died. The resolution also stated that "at this time" the city should set aside proceedings of eminent domain to acquire any land in the proposed gift.[30]

The intracommunity dissension over the Clifton School recreation complex and the neighborhood business district plan clearly had a chastening effect on the CTM board. In October 1977, after the recreation fight, the board president issued a carefully worded and rather defensive report emphasizing that until 1974 the board met in private residences, and that for the first time the board that year advertised its meetings, held them in places of public access, and allowed CTM members to attend as "observers," although without permitting them to speak on nonagenda items. In 1976, he noted, the board made "resident concerns" a standing agenda item for floor discussion, and in 1976 and 1977 the board made earnest attempts to secure participation on CTM committees by nonboard members and began to hold advertised public meetings on specific issues, of which there had been nine in 1977. Thus, he concluded, CTM had been "moving towards an open manageable forum."[31]

That process also led, as we have seen, to a defeat for those board members seeking aggressive action, such as the use of eminent domain to acquire land. For several years thereafter, the board took a more passive stance. To be sure, it continued to support the Coalition of Neighborhood Groups (CONG), which it joined in 1977 and which sought cooperation among Cincinnati community councils for their common good and promoted legislation beneficial to community councils.[32] But the board did not make CTM a leader in CONG, which proved ineffective and soon disappeared. Similarly, the board expressed interest in finding a new site for a larger library, but emphasized

Fig. 6. The Clifton branch of the Public Library of Cincinnati and Hamilton County, one of the smallest in the county. Photo (1998) courtesy of Jon Hughes.

when it considered the southwest corner of Burnet Woods that it had not endorsed such a location and recommended merely a feasibility study, one which ultimately proved useless because the park board refused to permit that use on its land.[33] The board then proposed the use of some space in the Ludlow Garage, then being refurbished as a shopping mall and pizza restaurant, but did not press when the library board rejected the idea.[34]

Fig. 7. The Clifton community kiosk on Ludlow Avenue, with the Roanoke apartment building in the left background. Photo (1998) courtesy of Jon Hughes.

The board handled other issues in this passive way as well. A proposal for brighter lights along Clifton Avenue north of Ludlow aroused concern, but the board accepted as "modest" the increased assessment demanded by the city to retain boulevard lights along with the new system.[35] In connection with that issue, the board considered but rejected expanding the boundary of its jurisdiction so as to encompass much if not all of Clifton Avenue as far south as Deaconess Hospital and Hughes High School,[36] and took an identical anti-annexation stance after backing residents in the Bishop and Jefferson Avenue area who fought an extensive but losing battle against the granting of a liquor license for the Corinthian Restaurant in a converted garage just beyond Clifton's eastern border and then suggested adding themselves and Burnet Woods to CTM's turf.[37] In that same period the board also ignored a serious expression of concern by a Clifton resident and city hall employee about areas of transition and vacancy rates in the neighborhood business district, perhaps because it did not want to discredit the city's progress in carrying out the design plan, including planting trees, installing ramps for the handicapped at intersections and a "sitting area" at the firehouse, and widening sidewalks and locating a community kiosk near Telford.[38]

By this time, CTM had completed its community plan, which received board and membership approval without a murmur of protest in October 1979.³⁹ The CTM board then sent the plan to the Cincinnati Department of Neighborhood Housing and Conservation for shepherding through city hall and for negotiating revisions with G. Franklin Miller, the head of CTM's planning committee.⁴⁰ On March 2, 1981, a staff member sent out copies of the plan for review by ten departments and divisions of city government, all of which responded by April 20, 1981, and none of which raised significant objections or proposed significant revisions.⁴¹ Miller submitted one set of revisions (five pages of typed text, double spaced) on October 28, 1980, and another (two pages of typed text, double spaced) on July 6, 1981, after his review of the responses from the various city departments and divisions.⁴² The corrected version went to the planning commission on December 9, 1981, and thirty days later the commission accepted the plan "as a guide for making planning decisions" and adopted "from the plan, appropriate Goals and Policies, Projects and Programs for Clifton as part of the Coordinated City Plan." ⁴³

The Clifton community plan contained lots of maps and thirty-two pages of text but did not depict an ideal social and physical environment for realization in twenty or thirty years, as Cincinnati's metropolitan master plans of 1925 and 1948 had done. Instead, it laid out policies, objectives, projects, and programs for adoption into the city's coordinated plan as "guidelines" for making decisions on developments that might be advocated by city government, private institutions, businesses, individual property owners, and CTM itself. The Clifton community plan drew this information, moreover, from the recreation study of 1974, the goals and objectives statement of 1975, the neighborhood business district plan, and the existing conditions study. The only major deviations from these documents occurred in the section on recreation, which explicitly deleted the idea of putting soccer and baseball fields and a deep water swimming pool behind Clifton School, and which did not mention the recreation proposal in the Dixmyth Avenue area.⁴⁴

That section of the coordinated city plan dealing with Clifton consisted of five pages with two columns per page: one listing goals and policies, and one listing projects and programs. The latter, representing priority items for action by one or another branch of city government, called for just four changes in Clifton: the completion of an economic analysis as a supplement to the neighborhood business district urban design plan, the installation of tennis courts and ballfields at Sacred Heart, the addition of more parking spaces at the Clifton School Recreation Center, and the development of a Juergens Avenue playfield.⁴⁵

Both the city and CTM, then, wanted to keep Clifton essentially as it was.

The plan called for no alteration in Clifton's demographic, socioeconomic, physical, land use, or zoning structure, and it remained silent on the issue of "balance," the possibility of securing a thorough residential integration of races and economic groups, even though blacks constituted one-quarter of Clifton's population but remained largely confined in one census tract (70), indeed largely within a narrow corridor along Vine Street, the western boundary of the city's second ghetto. For reasons unstated in the Clifton community plan and related documents, affirmative action on this question seemed more appropriate for some other neighborhoods, or somebody else's problem, or a problem to whose solution CTM could not or would not contribute. The CTM and city planners seemed content to maintain Clifton as one of the city's and county's few biracial communities, communities with a black population between 10 and 30 percent that faced the familiar problem of stabilization, of how to avoid ghettoization while adhering to a policy of "open housing," of simple nondiscrimination. To some, however, this approach seemed fruitless, for in the early 1980s other local organizations began to argue that real racial residential integration required a metropolitan strategy that intervened in the housing market by adopting and enforcing formal or informal racial quotas in large apartments and in lower-density housing.[46]

6

Implementing the Plan:

The Politics of Neighborhood Autonomy

After approving the Clifton community plan, the Clifton Town Meeting (CTM), as before, sought to defend its turf. But it now seemed more confident and aggressive, both in its willingness to expand its territorial reach and in its stance on public and private development proposals for the improvement of Clifton. These tendencies stemmed in part from the interpretation by CTM activists of the status of the comprehensive neighborhood plan and the urban design plan for the neighborhood business district. Both of these laid down "guidelines" for decision making by CTM, potential developers, and government agencies. CTM regarded these guidelines as legally sanctioned rules that controlled city government and developers and that therefore settled land use questions, but which did not prevent CTM from altering these rules of the game. Some city officials and developers regarded these guidelines as negotiable, however, and some Clifton residents occasionally challenged CTM's proposals to change the rules of the game. These circumstances yielded for CTM some accomplishments and some frustrations, sometimes because of opposition to CTM within Clifton, sometimes because of opposition outside of Clifton, and sometimes because of both, all of which may be seen not only as signs of ambiguity about the status of the plans and the role of city government and community councils in the age of coordinated planning but also as emblems of ambiguity on the issue of what Clifton and CTM might be and might become.

In the first four years after CTM approved the Clifton community plan, the CTM board exercised its new aggressiveness without inciting a determined opposition. Rumors in the late 1970s that Concordia Lutheran Church in the southwest corner of Clifton might build a school or high-rise apartment led the CTM board to initiate and secure in 1980, over the objections of Concordia representatives, the adoption of an environmental quality hillside district for that part of Clifton between Central Parkway and Morrison Avenue and between Clifton Hills Terrace and Dixmyth.[1] In 1982, moreover, CTM joined with other Cincinnati neighborhood organizations in raising funds to create an endowment for the permanent funding of community council activities, funding unfettered by city, state, or federal regulations and conditions.[2] And that same year, with city money from a new neighborhood support program, CTM undertook an ultimately unproductive "in-fill study," an exploration of unused or underused land in Clifton and the sorts of developments that might increase Clifton's population and, of course, the city's tax base without violating the neighborhood's planning guidelines.[3]

More striking still, CTM in the early 1980s proposed its first annexation. The initiative for this came from residents on Bishop Street who had lost their long battle to deny the Corinthian Restaurant a liquor license. Bishop Street was technically a part of Corryville. The Bishop Street leaders felt cut off from that community council, yet desired the clout that affiliation with such a council might provide. After noting that these residents shopped on Ludlow and that their children attended Clifton School, the CTM board appointed a committee to explore the possibility of annexing both sides of Bishop Street, which ran along an erratic line from Vine Street southward across Jefferson Avenue and along the eastern edge of Burnet Woods to St. Clair, and of annexing other "peripheral areas" as well.[4]

With this expansive charge, the committee quickly drew up a plan for CTM's first act of neighborhood imperialism. The committee recommended redefining Clifton's boundaries to include not only all of Bishop Street but also the area encompassed by the Dixmyth–St. Clair extension. This, of course, was the new four-lane road running behind Good Samaritan Hospital and Hebrew Union College across Clifton Avenue and eastward between Burnet Woods (on the road's north side) and the University of Cincinnati. Despite the Clifton community plan's policy objective of excluding institutions from Clifton, this proposal called for the addition of both a part of Burnet Woods and two major institutions to CTM's territory, a recommendation carried out by an amendment to the CTM constitution. Thus CTM took a step toward conceptualizing Clifton as "outsiders" tended to see it, namely, as the whole of the ridge extending from Central Parkway on the west to Vine Street on the east, a view which violated the idea of historical Clifton and the anti-institutional expansionism of the Clifton plan.[5]

At the same time, and in cooperation with the city government, CTM took another step toward the ridge concept. In the late 1950s, when the city adopted the Avondale-Corryville renewal plan to save the University of Cincinnati main campus and the hospital complex immediately east of it from blight and engulfment by Cincinnati's second ghetto, the city tended to focus its interest on that part of the ridge containing the university, the hospitals to its east, and the residential area between and immediately around these institutions. In 1981, however, on the initiative of a staff member of the university's Division of Metropolitan Services, the city broadened its area of concern to encompass the entire ridge. It did so by establishing through the Department of Neighborhood Housing and Conservation an Uptown Task Force involving representatives of the university, all the hospitals on the ridge, and all of the community councils on the ridge. Clifton appointed a representative to the Uptown Task Force in 1982 under the impression that traffic was the major problem. In fact, the city's agenda emphasized the protection of the institutions in Clifton and Avondale, especially the hospitals, which had to compete for patients with suburban hospitals and which worried about the "image" of the area. In response to that problem of image, the task force launched a project in 1984 to develop placards for display in each of the neighborhoods and around each of the institutions, placards which in a brief and compelling way would present aspects of the history of the neighborhoods and institutions to promote their venerability, durability, attractiveness, and excellence.[6]

Within two years, the Cincinnati Department of Neighborhood Housing and Conservation and the City Planning Department had transformed the Uptown Task Force into an instrument for the development of a plan for the six neighborhoods around the University of Cincinnati and hospital complex. This represented an attempt to reduce the city's budget by planning for "districts" rather than for each neighborhood and to create for Clifton (and the other neighborhoods) another level of civic identity and loyalty, one between CTM and city council and therefore one that might unintentionally undermine the liveliness and authority of CTM. Instead of objecting to this step as a threat to its autonomy, however, the CTM board regarded the task force's planning effort as an opportunity to advance Clifton's interests and to protect them from damage by the plans of others. The board sent representatives to task force meetings, but did little more to promote the idea of Uptown as important to Cliftonites.[7]

Indeed, the CTM board spent most of its time in the decade after the adoption of the Clifton community plan in pushing for the implementation of that plan, an effort that included persistent attempts to secure a larger public library branch in the neighborhood business district. The drive for the new library

Planning Issues and Priorities

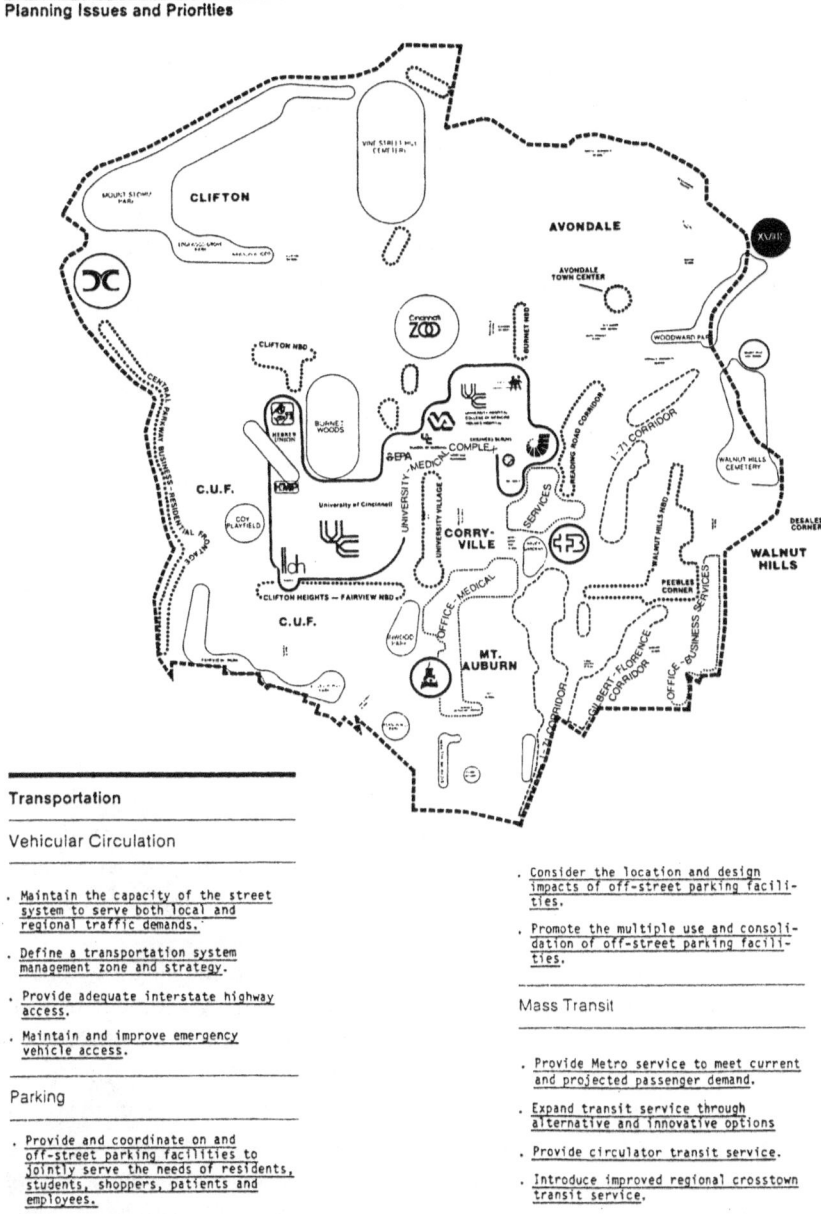

Transportation

Vehicular Circulation

- Maintain the capacity of the street system to serve both local and regional traffic demands.
- Define a transportation system management zone and strategy.
- Provide adequate interstate highway access.
- Maintain and improve emergency vehicle access.

Parking

- Provide and coordinate on and off-street parking facilities to jointly serve the needs of residents, students, shoppers, patients and employees.
- Consider the location and design impacts of off-street parking facilities.
- Promote the multiple use and consolidation of off-street parking facilities.

Mass Transit

- Provide Metro service to meet current and projected passenger demand.
- Expand transit service through alternative and innovative options.
- Provide circulator transit service.
- Introduce improved regional crosstown transit service.

Map 13. The city's Uptown planners saw Clifton and four other residential neighborhoods as the periphery of a newly defined community centered on a core of institutions and one residential neighborhood, Corryville. *Source: Uptown: Planning Program and Priorities* (Cincinnati: Department of City Planning and Department of Neighborhood Housing and Conservation, 1986).

took shape in 1979 shortly after the public library board failed to persuade the park board to approve the construction of a new facility for Clifton in Burnet Woods Park. As a consequence, this proposal never reached the CTM board, which nonetheless expressed in May 1980 its continuing commitment to securing a new branch by urging the director of the public library to search for a site within the Clifton business district. The director responded unenthusiastically to the business district proposal, which presented, he said, "almost insurmountable [site] problems," while at the same time restating his interest in establishing a new branch somewhere else in Clifton.[8]

Nothing came of this interest until 1983, when the CTM board learned that the library board intended to close the Clifton branch in 1985, when its lease expired on the Ormond Avenue building, and that it wanted to replace it with 6,000 to 8,000 square feet of space in a new or rehabilitated structure. In response to this news, the CTM board conducted a "preference vote" on potential sites, which proved negative on Burnet Woods (twelve nays and six ayes) but yielded unanimous support for the Ludlow Garage building, then vacant, and lesser majorities for the firehouse and the Esquire cinema. The board then explored other possibilities both inside and outside the business district and ruled out several, including the Ludlow Garage, the Esquire, a carriage house behind Clifton School, and several houses and vacant parcels of land. In the summer of 1984, the library board once more floated the idea of a new library in Burnet Woods at the corner of Ludlow and Clifton Avenue, a proposal the CTM board this time considered and endorsed. But the park board balked again, after which the library board renewed its lease on the Ormond Avenue facility. This seemed to settle the matter, although two women organized in November 1985 a Friends of the Library Committee (not affiliated with CTM) to pressure CTM and the library board to establish a new and larger branch library somewhere in Clifton.[9]

Meanwhile, the manager of the Esquire had stopped showing movies and the owner of the building approached the CTM board in 1983 for help in finding a new tenant, one that would not, he hoped, "incur the wrath of CTM."[10] He and the board spent a year in search of a new movie operator but found none willing to pay $3,500 per month in rent or $350,000 to purchase the property, the prices set by the owner. In the spring of 1984, however, the owner abandoned the search for a movie operator because, he argued, the advent of cable television and video cassette recorders had rendered "second-run" movies a marginal business proposition. But he also announced that he had found another type of tenant, a Wendy's Old-Fashioned Hamburger Restaurant franchisee, an African American woman regarded (incorrectly) by some Cliftonites as a potent force in city hall. She sought to win popular support for this project by pledging to rehabilitate the structure as a non-drive-through "urban deluxe" facility with a separate room in which to hold community meetings and a litter pick-up service that would clean the premises hourly, or every fifteen minutes, if necessary. Despite these promises, a few CTM board members immediately expressed reservations about this proposal. One noted the existence of a dozen restaurants in the neighborhood business district, and others raised concerns that a Wendy's would compound parking and traffic problems and attract similar restaurants that would spark a "dramatic rise" in property values to the detriment of the many small businesses in the district. Nonetheless, the board appointed three members to explore the proposition and report back in a month "with their sense of things."[11]

Clifton residents quickly gathered more than three thousand signatures on petitions protesting the proposed Wendy's and vowing to "keep the movies." Two hundred of these protesters appeared at the CTM board meeting on May 7, 1984, delivered the petitions, and announced that more would be forthcoming. The ensuing discussion lasted for an hour and a half, during which one opponent contended that the presence of Wendy's would disrupt "the village atmosphere" of Clifton, and others complained about more specific problems, such as traffic, parking, litter, and the tendency for one such restaurant to attract others, as along Calhoun Street on the south edge of the university campus. Some board members doubted that CTM could stop the deal, but a board majority recommended continuing public protests by residents and writing letters urging the theater owner and Wendy's to change their minds. The board then adopted a resolution pledging "to do everything in its power to keep movies in the Esquire" and "to affirm the Clifton Community Plan, which says that fast-food restaurants are not appropriate along Ludlow Avenue," despite the fear of some that this clause in the plan could not be enforced by the city government, for the Cincinnati City Planning Commission (CCPC) had "accepted" the comprehensive community plan and incorporated some of its provisions (including the fast-food franchise ban) into the coordinated city plan, but city council had not adopted in a city ordinance the comprehensive plan or any of its provisions.[12]

This protest, however, did not deter Wendy's and its franchisee, who next went to city hall to secure a permit for remodeling the building by contending that their plans conformed both with the underlying zoning for the area and the overlay environmental urban design zoning regulations for the business district, both of which had been approved by city council in an ordinance and both of which carried the force of law. Enforcement of these regulations fell to a hearing examiner, in this case the head of the Cincinnati Division of Buildings and Inspections. He set May 17, 1984, as the date of the hearing, a session which attracted some one hundred Cliftonites, twenty of whom recited the now familiar litany of objections to the fast-food restaurant. But the hearing examiner ruled that the proposed business conformed to the underlying zoning for the area, and he found nothing in the environmental urban design regulations, which in his view applied merely to aesthetic issues in the design of buildings, that might ban the remodeling of the theater as a restaurant.[13]

The CTM board responded to this decision by hiring a lawyer, Sidney Weil, a resident of Clifton, who filed an appeal of the examiner's decision to city council.[14] Weil based his appeal on a peculiarity of the Clifton environmental quality district regulations, a vague clause which stipulated that new businesses should contribute to the "desired mix of commercial activities" in the district, a clause that could be seen as a land use regulation, and one that carried the force of law, even though the ordinance referred to this regulation as a "guideline." Weil also noted that the administrative rules under which the examiner acted required him to consider not only zoning but also "other official policies, guidelines or objectives of the city of Cincinnati," a stipulation Weil used to dispel the vagueness around the term "desired mix." The meaning of "desired mix" seemed clear to Weil, for he pointed out that the Clifton community plan, which had been accepted by the CCPC, specifically banned the establishment of fast-food restaurants on Ludlow Avenue, a stipulation moreover that the CCPC had adopted in the Clifton section of the city's coordinated city plan.[15]

In June 1984, city council agreed with Weil and overruled the hearing examiner, a decision appealed by the owner of the Esquire and the Wendy's franchisee to the Hamilton County Common Pleas Court, which upheld council's decision. In the meantime, CTM tried to settle out of court by establishing the Clifton Theater Corporation on a nonprofit basis as an entity to raise money for the purchase of the theater and for its rehabilitation as a movie house. In this effort CTM first negotiated with the building's owner, and when that failed petitioned the city government to acquire the property, using eminent domain if necessary to force a sale, and to turn it over to the Theater Corporation.[16]

But the owner and Wendy's franchisee refused to relent, and on February 22, 1985, they appealed the common pleas court decision to the First District Court of Ohio. While awaiting this decision, CTM continued to seek an out-of-court settlement (unsuccessfully) and the movie theater advocates continued to raise money for the theater redevelopment project. But in January

1986 the appeals court upheld the hearing examiner's decision to issue a permit for refurbishing the theater as a Wendy's restaurant. The court held that the Cincinnati municipal code forbade the regulation of land uses by means other than "underlying zoning," that environmental quality regulations applied only to physical and aesthetic matters, not land uses, and that the "desired mix" phrase in the development guidelines for the Clifton environmental quality urban design district was "unconstitutionally vague."[17]

Not surprisingly, the CTM board immediately asked the city to take the case to the Supreme Court of Ohio, a request supported by the city solicitor, city council, and representatives of CTM and other neighborhood organizations, who worried that the decision significantly reduced the city's ability to respond to neighborhood councils in the regulation of land uses and removed a key incentive for citizens to engage in neighborhood planning.[18] The city made the appeal in a brief filed by the city solicitor's office in August 1986. The brief elaborated on arguments already developed by Weil and the city solicitor's office, in part by a more thorough review of precedents regarded as helpful to the appellants. As part of this procedure, the brief virtually invited the courts to stay out of zoning conflicts. "This Court," claimed the brief, "has effectively left zoning decisions in the hands of the people and their elected representatives, where such decisions belong. City councils, not the courts, must confront and solve the problems of declining tax bases, flight to the suburbs, instability of city neighborhoods and their business districts, and declining tax revenues." And if, "as in this case, both citizens and the City agree that the preservation of a neighborhood requires protection from the proliferation of fast-food restaurants and traffic-congested streets, that protection should not be disturbed by the courts."[19]

The state supreme court decided to hear the case, and in April 1987 it reversed the district court's decision. It decided that the district court erred by not interpreting the "desired mix" phrase in the context of the entire environmental quality urban design ordinance and the Clifton section of the coordinated city plan. In addition, the court ruled that the "unconstitutionally vague" argument usually applied to criminal ordinances that neglected to specify prohibited conduct, and that in the Wendy's case the zoning legislation by its nature notified the property owner that the property lay within an overlay zoning district. And the court interpreted the underlying and overlay zoning scheme as a sign that council *intended* to permit flexibility in environmental quality districts and to prohibit certain land uses otherwise permitted under "conventional land use regulations," language which the court found in the environmental quality district enabling ordinance and which, said the court, legitimized the banning of certain land uses in an environmental quality district.

But the Supreme Court of Ohio did not stop there. It not only reaffirmed a previous decision (1984) that "aesthetic considerations may be taken into account by the legislative body in enacting zoning legislation" but also lectured the district courts on the importance of judicial restraint in dealing with zoning and similar cases because of the superior knowledge "of the situation" by municipal governing bodies. As the court put it, the "power of a municipality to establish zones . . . and to determine land-use policy is a legislative function which will not be interfered with by the courts unless such power is exercised in such an arbitrary, confiscatory or unreasonable manner as to be in violation of constitutional guarantees."[20]

Before the court rendered this decision, however, the Wendy's case took another turn. The building owner decided to donate the Esquire to the city to avoid the cost of further litigation and to secure tax breaks in 1986 for giving the structure to a nonprofit entity. The city then deeded the property to the Clifton Theater Corporation, hastily amended the zoning code to specifically and unambiguously authorize land use regulations in environmental quality overlay districts, and altered the Clifton environmental quality–urban design guidelines to clarify the definition of and to ban fast-food establishments within the district, steps necessary in case the state supreme court upheld the district court decision. Shortly thereafter, the city completed the deal by loaning $100,000 at 4 percent interest to the Clifton Theater Corporation, which continued its fund-raising efforts to pay for the cinema's rehabilitation and to repay the debt and interest to the city government. This scheme held up, and the new Esquire opened as a cinema in April 1990 in a festive atmosphere of self-congratulations among the anti-Wendy's/pro-movies forces.[21]

The hoopla over this triumphant localism, however, obscured another step by council that revealed the depth of its deference to the wishes of neighborhood organizations. The staff of the CCPC had opposed in November 1986 the hasty amendment of the zoning code and the revision of Clifton's urban design environmental quality legislation on two grounds: the impossibility of adequately and fairly defining "fast-food restaurant" in the rapidly changing food service business and the inadvisability of giving neighborhoods and other interest groups the ability to "petition" or write plans containing overlay land use regulations that overrode the underlying and citywide land use rules. By this means, the director of planning noted, a neighborhood might ban from its environmental quality district or districts such uses as multifamily buildings, bars, group homes, low-income housing, religious meeting places, single-

Fig. 8. The rehabilitated Esquire cinema with a view of the traffic moving westward on Ludlow on a gray winter day. Photo (1998) courtesy of Jon Hughes.

room occupancy housing, and parking lots, a process that might yield "forty-eight zoning codes in . . . Cincinnati, one per neighborhood." The CCPC followed the lead of its staff and opposed these changes, but city council mustered the two-thirds majority necessary to overrule a negative recommendation from the commission.[22]

The victory over Wendy's represented but one of CTM's major accomplishments in implementing the Clifton community plan. CTM also managed in the late 1980s to carry out the plan's proposals to use Sacred Heart buildings and grounds for residential and recreational purposes, although in this instance, unlike the Wendy's imbroglio, it had to compromise and faced organized opposition within Clifton. The idea for the preservation of Sacred Heart in this way took shape after 1970, when the Sacred Heart Academy closed and after CTM fought off efforts by several developers to change the tract's R-1A zoning to permit high-density residential development on the site. CTM obtained a stronger hand in controlling the property in 1976, when the city government, the park board, and Cliftonites pooled their resources to purchase the 24.4-acre plot for the purpose of creating a greenbelt around the hill and reserved 15 acres on top of the hill for residential and recreational uses. The CCPC bolstered these arrangements a year later when it included the Sacred Heart property in a Clifton hillsides environmental quality district designed to protect "distinctive environmental characteristics, such as . . . hillside slopes, . . . streams, . . . natural wooded areas, . . . trees and lawns around buildings, and . . . the view over valleys" by setting seventeen guidelines for consideration by potential developers on the site.[23]

Two years later, the CTM board approved a redevelopment program for the hilltop mandating the preservation of the Sacred Heart buildings, the environmentally and aesthetically sensitive treatment of the surrounding landscape, the creation of a "community-oriented" soccer field on some of the vacant land in the fifteen-acre plot, and the retention of the R-1A low-density zoning district. At the same time, the CTM board established the Clifton Community Urban Redevelopment Corporation (CCURC) to implement the program, and the city government shortly thereafter recognized CCURC as the prime developer for the site. CCURC then located a "preferred developer," the Pinwood Development Corporation, the president of which, a Cliftonite, unveiled plans in 1980 to redevelop the Sacred Heart buildings as thirty-two luxury residential units. This proposition looked even better after the passage in 1981 of the federal Economic Recovery Act, which qualified the mansion for tax benefits because of its listing (in 1973) on the National Register of Historic Places, and better still after the city's newly established Historic Conservation Board (HCB) created in the same year a local Sacred Heart/Mount Storm Historic District, a step which qualified for tax benefits the rehabilitation of the other Sacred Heart buildings (federal preservation authorities had "certified" the local office to determine the eligibility of preservation projects for the tax benefits).[24]

Nonetheless, Pinwood failed to secure financing for its plan, and after the expiration of CCURC's term as prime developer, the Cincinnati Department of Neighborhood Housing and Conservation, which owned the fifteen-acre plot, issued a call for proposals from other developers willing to meet the terms for redevelopment previously stipulated by the CTM board. This call yielded three bids, from among which a committee of city and CTM representatives selected Lafayette Investments, Ltd. (LIL), a partnership of two Cliftonites. LIL's plans called for thirty-five rental units in the rehabilitated historic buildings at a cost of $4 million, a proposal supported and strengthened by the Recreation Commission, which reviewed and approved the scheme in 1984 and also acceded to CTM's request to make a soccer field the top priority for recreational facilities on the site.[25]

The project cleared another hurdle in March 1985 when the Department of Neighborhood Housing and Conservation agreed to sell LIL the property for $15,000 down and $350,000 in installments payable on the completion of each phase of the project. The agreement also pledged the proceeds from the sale to the Recreation Commission for the construction and maintenance of the soccer field and obligated the developer to start and complete the project on a prescribed schedule of dates, a breach of which gave the city the option of repossessing the land. The department estimated that the project when completed would yield $50,000 annually in property taxes to the city, county, and school board.[26]

LIL, however, failed to secure financing for this scheme, principally because its projected profit of 15 percent fell well below the 25–35 percent range required by lenders interested in making a deal, but also because of the city's option to reclaim the property if LIL failed to maintain the prescribed development schedule. So LIL amended its proposal in ways making it possible for LIL to purchase the property at the outset, but also in ways that violated some of the CTM board's criteria for reusing the site. LIL decided to retain the R-1A zoning for the tract but to loosen those rules by applying PUD (planned unit development) regulations, a zoning mechanism adopted by the city in 1974 to provide deviations from conventional zoning and subdivision regulations. The PUD legislation specified some of these deviations, such as increasing the residential density in an R-1A district by mixing single- and multifamily units, and left others to the director of city planning, who could waive conventional zoning and subdivision controls. LIL also proposed to create condominiums rather than rental units and to rehabilitate the original mansion, the chapel, and the connecting building. But LIL wanted to demolish a school building and part of a cafeteria/gymnasium structure, both erected between 1920 and

1930, to make room for the construction of twenty-seven new condominium units.[27]

LIL took these changes in December 1986 to a special meeting of the CTM board, where the development partnership explained its plans. LIL indicated first that the HCB staff did not object to razing the twentieth-century structures in the nineteenth-century Academy complex and indicated too that the new condominiums would consist of sixteen scattered buildings, five single-family units and eleven duplexes, including some two- and three-bedroom units for "empty nesters" and some three-bedroom townhouses. After some discussion and a few expressions of concern about the changes, a board member pronounced the concept "interesting" but moved to defer action on the proposal until the next regular board meeting, a suggestion adopted unanimously.[28]

At that session, in January 1987, the CTM board approved the concept and urged LIL to hew as closely as possible to its original criteria. But opposition to this amended proposal soon emerged, some of it from individual residents and some of it in the form of an organization called the Citizens Association for the Preservation of Sacred Heart (CAPSH), which complained, among other things, about the destruction of trees, the possibility that the new construction might cause a landslide, and about allegedly inadequate provisions for storm water drainage. These opponents of the new scheme proved persistent, for they raised the issue at the next three CTM board meetings and twice moved to rescind the CTM board's approval of the concept. Both motions failed, one by a margin of a single vote.[29]

LIL next took its proposal to the HCB, the agency designated by the zoning code as the review authority for projects subject to PUD regulations and environmental quality guidelines in instances when these two zoning mechanisms operated within a historic district. Before the HCB's preliminary hearing on the project, however, the Citizens Association for the Preservation of Sacred Heart (CAPSH) obtained a copy of both LIL's plan and the report on it by the HCB staff. The day before the hearing, CAPSH submitted to HCB a nine-page critique which complained that the last CTM vote to abandon the project yielded a seven to seven deadlock broken in favor of the development partnership by the vote of the president, scarcely a ringing endorsement of the project, according to CAPSH. But the rest of the document elaborated on CAPSH's major objections to LIL's scheme. These included the absence of plans for the soccer field and its parking lot, the alleged disruption of the landscape by new construction, the alleged disruption of the view of the mansion, the density of the housing development, and the assertion that LIL's current proposal represented a new plan, not a continuation of the old one, a situation that in the view of CAPSH obligated the city to let others compete for development rights.³⁰

Despite this blast, the HCB staff did not alter its report, which dealt in one way or another with all of CAPSH's objections, except the complaint about the absence of plans for the soccer field, a project scheduled for construction by the Recreation Commission, not LIL. The HCB approved the revised LIL proposal on April 13, and later granted LIL a certificate of appropriateness authorizing the building demolitions and approving the design of the rehabilitated and new structures. HCB then passed the whole package on to the CCPC, which endorsed it and forwarded it to city council. Opponents of the scheme protested all along the way, and at one point they invited city council members to visit the site as the proper location for hearing and understanding their complaints about storm water run-off, hillside erosion, and marred scenery. Two council members accepted the invitation, but after the tour one noted that council in such cases usually deferred to the wishes of the relevant neighborhood organization, and the other observed that in such cases opponents often "really wanted . . . no project at all" rather than modifications of the scheme. City council gave this project its stamp of approval in June 1987.³¹

The Sacred Heart and Wendy's episodes demonstrated the commitment of the CTM board to the use of a variety of governmental tools for the preservation of the special ambiance attributed to Clifton by the Clifton community plan. These tools included the use of historic preservation techniques, especially the listing of historic structures and districts on the National Register of Historic Places under the federal Historic Preservation Act of 1966, which established criteria of historical significance that dramatically increased the range of resources eligible for nomination to the National Register. A burst of nominations from the Cincinnati area followed the passage of this act, and by 1982 Clifton's National Register historic resources consisted of its gaslights, eighteen buildings, and the Clifton/Greendale/Lafayette Circle Historic District, the tight boundaries of which excluded a host of properties eligible for historic designation, in either local or national historic districts.³²

Some Cliftonites recognized that National Register listing did not effectively discourage the radical alteration or demolition of historic buildings, and that local designation involved more effective controls of both rehabilitation and demolition proposals, a factor that had encouraged support by the CTM board for the establishment by the Historic Conservation Board of the Sacred Heart/Mount Storm Park Historic District. In the mid-1980s, several residents worried about potential institutional encroachments on large residential properties along Clifton Avenue north of Ludlow. Their concerns led the CTM historic preservation committee to commission in 1985 a study of that part of the neighborhood by an historic preservation consultant, who suggested that the CTM board should discuss with the city's urban conservator (the head of the Historic Conservation Office) the possibility of designating a local district larger than the Clifton/Greendale/Lafayette Circle district on the National Register of Historic Places.[33]

On this suggestion the CTM historic preservation committee in the fall of 1985 approached the urban conservator, who promised to start work with the committee and the community in general as soon as she could clear a staff member from other projects. This took time, but by late spring of 1989 a Historic Conservation Office (HCO) staff member had worked out tentative boundaries for a potential district that covered several blocks on both sides of Clifton Avenue from Ludlow Avenue to Lafayette Avenue. He discussed these boundaries on June 26 in a meeting with about sixty residents of Clifton, a session he called the first step in "a lengthy process" that might result in a recommendation from the HCB for the designation of a local historic district in Clifton.[34]

The process took longer than the HCO anticipated, however, because of complaints from Cliftonites who lived outside the proposed boundaries who wanted their property and that of their neighbors covered by historic regulations. The CTM historic preservation committee as a consequence called in the HCO staff member and suggested that he expand the boundaries to correspond with the boundaries of Clifton at the time of its incorporation as a village in the mid-nineteenth century. The staff member agreed to see if he could justify such boundaries on the basis of the architectural and historic criteria spelled out in the city's historic preservation legislation, and in the winter of 1990 held his fourth informational meeting with residents, at which time he solicited volunteers to assist in the historical research, especially for the period from the time of Clifton's incorporation as a village to the moment of its annexation to Cincinnati in the 1890s.[35]

Before the HCO completed this work, however, the board of the Public Library of Cincinnati and Hamilton County warmed up the issue of establishing a new branch library in the Clifton neighborhood business district and precipitated a conflict that divided even more deeply than the Sacred Heart controversy the CTM board and the residents of Clifton. In February 1990, the CTM board learned of the renewal of the consideration of the northeastern corner of Burnet Woods Park as the site for a new branch library by the library and park boards. In March, the library director invited the CTM board to become part of the process, and the board discussed the matter in April without taking a position on the idea. Shortly thereafter, the library board commissioned a study of the environmental consequences of building and operating a library (partially underground) in the park, and the Clifton Library Committee, not a CTM affiliate, endorsed the proposition in a landslide vote. But opposition also developed because of environmental, traffic, and parking concerns and sparked a "lengthy and lively" discussion during the board meeting on May 7. At that session, too, a motion to "express concern" about the idea failed by one vote.[36]

Both sides now marshaled support for their positions, efforts that intensified with the approach of the CTM annual meeting of all members. At that session, proponents of the library in the park presented a petition bearing over one thousand signatures, which opponents tried to counter by stressing that the park should not contain institutions of any sort and should be preserved for grass, plants, trees, and wildlife. (The Friends of the Library and Burnet Woods, which opposed the library in the park, depicted Burnet Woods as the home of over seventy species of birds plus squirrels, raccoons, opossums, and rabbits.) A reporter characterized the discussion at the annual meeting as "heated at times," and the library director assured Cliftonites that the proposed library ranked as a "concept" under consideration by the library board and "not a done deal."[37]

On June 4, the CTM board finally acted on the question by defeating (eleven to eight) a motion of its library committee to recommend the continued consideration of the park site, including the completion of an environmental impact study, and by urging the library board to explore alternative sites. This outraged the Clifton Library Committee, which listed as its allies the Clifton Business and Professional Association, the Clifton Coalition on Aging, and the faculty of the Annunciation School. The committee claimed that petitions contained more signatures than the number of members of CTM, and contended that 75 percent of those members supported the idea. Nonetheless, the library board voted to table the proposal indefinitely.[38] The CTM board kept pushing both for alternative sites and for a reconsideration by the library board of its square footage (10,000–12,000) and 1.5-acre site requirements, but nothing came of these efforts, and a new park plan for Cincinnati adopted in the spring of 1993 proposed to put ponds or a lake in the corner of the park at Clifton Avenue and Ludlow.[39]

By this time the proposal for the establishment of a local historic district in Clifton had reemerged and, like the library in the park, stalled because of opposition to the idea within Clifton. The HCO worked for a year with volunteers from Clifton before revealing the proposed boundaries for a larger district than originally suggested. The district did not conform to the boundaries of Clifton Village in the mid-nineteenth century, as some Cliftonites had hoped, but it started in north Clifton, jumped across McAlpin, and ended on a jagged line which ran along the south edge of Ludlow to a point just east of Dunore Park and the Jewish cemetery, then cut to the north along another irregular line. The proposed district ranked as the largest ever considered by the Historic Conservation Office and contained an estimated 740 buildings, most of them constructed between 1850 and 1930.[40]

The CTM board approved these boundaries in February 1991. The HCO then announced the circulation among Clifton residents of a draft of design review guidelines for use by the HCB in considering the facades of structures on both new construction and rehabilitation projects, and stressed that the guidelines did not cover paint colors and would come into play only when property owners undertook work requiring an application for a building permit, not for items of routine maintenance.[41] Mr. and Mrs. Jack Brand, who favored historic preservation but deeply resented the idea that government functionaries should prescribe its practice, wrote the HCO a long letter objecting to the proposed design regulations for three reasons. The couple contended that the guidelines contained "numerous ambiguities" and seemed more related to someone's view of "architectural correctness" than to the character of the neighborhood. The Brands also complained that the guidelines sought "to substitute the opinions of unelected people who are not Clifton residents for the opinions of the individual Clifton residents and property owners who are the ones most affected by the architecture of the area." But most important, wrote the couple, the guidelines threatened the "central" distinguishing feature of Clifton, its broad range of "diversity in every aspect of life, including its architecture." That diversity, they added, stemmed from "the strong current of individualism" among Clifton residents, "a spirit which existed far longer than our lifetimes." In this perspective, the guidelines loomed as an attempt to stifle "the freedom of expression which has always existed in Clifton . . . , a neighborhood which derives its strength from highly individualistic but public minded people and not from architectural uniformity."[42]

At its April 1991 meeting, the CTM board heard these libertarian and other objections to the guidelines, including a complaint that CTM played no role in the appointment of members to the city's HCB, the agency that recommended to the CCPC the designation of local historic districts and the agency that administered historic regulations within districts after their designation. A small number of historic district opponents repeated these objections to historic preservation at public hearings on the measure before both the HCB and the

CCPC, but both bodies approved the proposed designation. Throughout this process, the CTM historic preservation committee kept the CTM board apprised of the progress of the proposal, which the CTM president spoke for during the hearings and to the press, and which seemed likely to clear city council.[43]

The measure recommended to city council by the CCPC included a designation report and a set of conservation guidelines prepared by the urban conservator. The designation report described the process of creating the proposal (it included six neighborhood meetings and several more with a CTM committee and volunteer researchers composed of Clifton residents), noted that the boundaries of the district stemmed from the identification of three distinctive periods covering ninety years of Clifton's history (1840–1930), and depicted each period as characterized by a distinctive mix of architectural styles. The design review guidelines covered rehabilitation, additions, new construction (exteriors only), and subdivision regulations. These guidelines also emphasized the negotiability of the rehabilitation and other guidelines, including the possibility of their waiver when appropriate or necessary, and stressed the issue of design "compatibility" with respect to additions and new buildings instead of advocating the duplication of the architectural styles of buildings contributing to the historic/architectural character of the district (the guidelines said that additions and new construction adjacent to "non-contributing" buildings should "respond" compatibly to them and in a more general way than to "contributing" buildings).[44]

By the time these documents reached city council, however, the opposition within Clifton to the historic district had spread and intensified, and opponents of it lashed out at the CTM board on the eve of the consideration of the proposal by city council's community development, housing, and zoning committee. This raucous session opened with a plea from one resident, who claimed she had been "pressured" to sign a petition objecting to historic designation, urging "those on both sides to respect the opinions of others." Several speakers then not only repeated the standard complaints about the guidelines but also attacked the board for its alleged failure to secure and accurately represent the views of Cliftonites. These dissidents contended that the board neglected to seek out opponents of historic designation, responded with "hostility" to those it heard, and depicted the opposition as emanating exclusively from a small group of developers and architects. The CTM board, claimed the dissidents, should "conduct a poll of residents" on the issue. Instead, board members defended the process from which emerged the historic district proposal by reminding the audience that the process involved "two years of mailings and public meetings" which yielded only requests for "inclusion" within the district, "not exclusion."[45]

This situation, a community council board sticking resolutely to a proposal strongly and loudly opposed on procedural, substantive, and ideological grounds by a large number of its constituents, proved discomfiting to city council, which handled the issue delicately and with finesse. The day before its first public hearing on the matter, council's committee on community development, housing, and zoning received from fifty opponents of the district in Clifton an appeal to turn it down. But the committee did not reject the proposal. Instead, it deadlocked (two to two) on a vote to recommend the measure for passage by city council, which then took up the measure but decided to send it back to committee for more study. The committee responded with a four to two vote in favor of sending the proposal back to the HCB for a reconsideration of the boundaries and guidelines of the proposed district.[46]

The HCB agreed to such a reconsideration, and the urban conservator set up a public meeting in Clifton to correct misrepresentations about historic districts and to see if a consensus might be reached on boundary and guideline adjustments. The urban conservator told a newspaper reporter that he hoped to make clear to Cliftonites that guidelines did not apply to ordinary repairs or maintenance, or to interior work, such as plumbing, wiring, and plastering, and did not require property owners either to make improvements or to restore their properties to their original states. He also stressed that the guidelines served as the basis for negotiations over proposed improvements, and that the HCB might simply approve a proposal, place conditions on it, request an alteration of it, or in some cases simply waive particular guidelines in the course of such negotiations. The urban conservator added, too, that property owners who disagreed with a decision of the HCB could appeal to city council for relief, and that the HCB had approved every proposal it received to provide access for handicapped persons to buildings in historic districts around the city.[47]

In preparation for this public meeting, the CTM president also sought to educate Cliftonites about historic preservation by listing and correcting common "false" statements circulating in the neighborhood about historic preservation. He, too, said that historic preservation guidelines did not require property owners to make changes in their properties, did not prohibit the making of changes for handicapped persons, and did not represent rigid "rules of law" but stood as "expressions of ideals to be followed to the extent possible and practical and to be deviated from when necessary." He also added that the historic preservation regulations did not require the disclosure of private finances to justify a preference for a cheaper mode of construction or rehabilitation, did not ban new construction within the district (he cited Sacred Heart as an example of new construction in a historic district), did not cover paint colors, did not reduce property values and make houses in a historic district more difficult to sell, and did not make all home improvements more expensive. He noted the city's eighteen years of successful experience in administering eighteen historic districts and suggested that this made it unnecessary for opponents of a Clifton district to "imagine the worst in order to frighten the neighbors."[48]

The public meeting took place on a rainy night in January but attracted a packed house to Calvary Episcopal Church. It also produced lots of wrangling, no consensus, and evidence of continued misunderstanding if not calculated misrepresentation of historic district regulations. Some district opponents reiterated the familiar fears about historic preservation under government auspices. Others accused the HCB and its staff of creating guidelines on the basis of "opinion" rather than "fact," some worried about widespread arrests for noncompliance with guidelines, and others wondered how all buildings in such a large district could be regarded as "historic." And some urged the HCB to submit the district proposition to a vote of all 1,700 property owners in the proposed district,[49] another sign of dissatisfaction with the CTM as a representative body.

This outcome perplexed the HCB, which decided to reconsider the process of designating local historic districts generally as a way of finding a solution to the Clifton impasse. Among other things, that reconsideration yielded in August 1992 a proposal to hire a professional mediator to bring both sides together to work out a solution to the stalemate, a suggestion accepted by both the CTM board and the opponents of the district.[50] The mediator, paid for by CTM and the city government, established a committee of eight Cliftonites—three of whom opposed the proposed district, three of whom supported the proposed district, and two of whom had not registered strong views in either direction—to work with the mediator on recommendations for consideration by CTM members and its board. This committee met nine times between March and October 1993 and came up with one recommendation acceptable to all eight members and two on which the committee split. All eight accepted the idea of disseminating historic preservation techniques as advice to people who wished to use them in rehabilitation and new construction projects. Four members supported the designation of a "large area, mostly north of Ludlow Avenue," with guidelines covering only demolition and new construction, and a fifth member supported this scheme for a smaller area. Finally, four members supported the designation of a smaller district around Lafayette Avenue covered by conventional guidelines if a "substantial" number of residents in the district approved of it, and three other committee members found this satisfactory only if it received "virtually unanimous support from the affected residents."[51]

This outcome killed the local historic district idea, but during this feud another one erupted over an attempt to implement an additional feature of the Clifton community plan. This imbroglio stemmed from a proposal to create part of the "buffer" between the business district and residential areas by making a cul-de-sac on Hosea Avenue near the intersection with Clifton Avenue. The impetus for the call to build this cul-de-sac came from a failed effort to prevent Skyline Chili from installing a parking lot behind its business on the corner of Clifton and Ludlow, a lot that, like several others, exited onto Hosea, a narrow avenue with twenty-two houses and an on-street parking problem generally attributed to the thriving of business at the Clifton Auto Repair shop on Hosea. To make matters worse, southbound autos on Clifton Avenue confronted a No Left Turn sign at the corner of Clifton and Ludlow, which prompted many of them to turn left on Hosea and use it as a cut-through to Brookline and from thence to its juncture with Ludlow.[52]

To remedy these traffic and parking difficulties, a group of Hosea residents and the CTM board presented to city council in the fall of 1988 a petition with sixty signatures calling for the construction of the cul-de-sac, and the CTM board stepped up the pressure in June 1989 by making the Hosea Avenue closure its top priority in its annual budget request to the city government.[53] City council responded by authorizing and funding the construction of a temporary barrier some 150 feet east of Clifton Avenue and by commissioning a study of its effectiveness in mitigating the Hosea traffic and parking problems and its consequences for traffic on nearby streets and in Clifton generally. If the experiment proved satisfactory on these counts, the city intended to create a permanent cul-de-sac consisting of low walls, curbs, screen fencing, landscaping, and an auto turn-around.[54]

The city government erected the temporary barricade on Hosea and conducted the traffic study, which proved favorable to the project, and city council appropriated $160,000 to acquire land for the cul-de-sac. But in September 1990 fifty residents on Loraine, the first street north of Hosea that connected Clifton Avenue to Brookline, presented the CTM board with a petition protesting a permanent barricade on Hosea. A representative of the group contended that the city should have assessed traffic conditions on Loraine before as well as after the closure, and complained that the city took its traffic count

Fig. 9. One merchant boasts in 1999 of Clifton's "historic" ambiance. Photo (1999) courtesy of Janet A. Miller.

during the summer school vacation period. By December, moreover, Bishop Street residents had also registered complaints about increased traffic on their street stemming from the closure of Hosea, and the Loraine Avenue protesters had attracted the attention of the *Cincinnati Enquirer*.[55]

Opponents of the project continued to protest both to the CTM board and city council as the city government worked on the final plans, financing, and property acquisition for the cul-de-sac, a process which stretched into 1992.

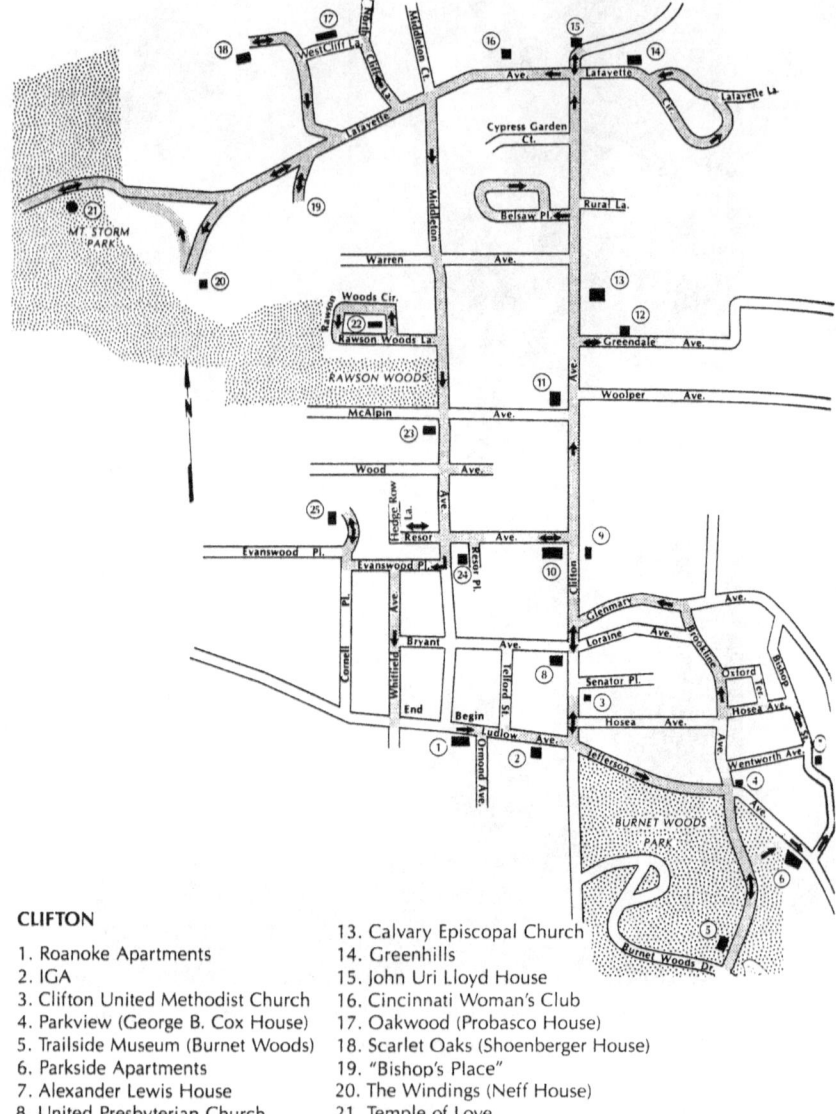

CLIFTON

1. Roanoke Apartments
2. IGA
3. Clifton United Methodist Church
4. Parkview (George B. Cox House)
5. Trailside Museum (Burnet Woods)
6. Parkside Apartments
7. Alexander Lewis House
8. United Presbyterian Church
9. Alfred T. Goshorn House
10. Church of the Annunciation
11. Clifton Public School
12. Greendale (William Resor House)
13. Calvary Episcopal Church
14. Greenhills
15. John Uri Lloyd House
16. Cincinnati Woman's Club
17. Oakwood (Probasco House)
18. Scarlet Oaks (Shoenberger House)
19. "Bishop's Place"
20. The Windings (Neff House)
21. Temple of Love
22. 1 Rawson Woods Circle (Boulter House)
23. 3655 Middleton
24. Battenberry
25. Reuben P. Resor House

Map 14. Clifton as place remained an object of interest and admiration to outsiders, including John Clubbe, the author of an elegant guide to Cincinnati. *Source:* John Clubbe, *Cincinnati Observed: Architecture and History* (Columbus: Ohio State University Press, 1992), 290.

The dissenters disputed the CTM board's and the city's interpretation of a second traffic study of the effect of the closure on nearby streets, especially Loraine. They contended that the urban design plan for the business district called for the closing of Hosea merely for the purpose of creating a new parking lot, a step now unnecessary in their view because of the establishment of private lots in the vicinity since the adoption of the plan. They insisted that the closing of Clifton Auto Repair had eliminated the major cause of traffic and parking problems on Hosea. Indeed, the persistence of these charges and pro-barrier responses raised tension to the point that at least one shouting match took place at the site of the temporary barricade. And at one meeting of CTM two residents exchanged blows during a debate of the project.[56]

Despite these clashes, the CTM board stuck to its position, in part because it feared that a reversal would undermine the credibility of the organization and the Clifton community plan with city council,[57] and city council in turn deferred to the wishes of the CTM board. Finally, three residents took the CTM board and the city government to court in August 1992 in an effort to stop the project. The suit depicted the cul-de-sac as unnecessary because the closing of the auto repair shop relieved the street of the clutter of vehicles created by customers at the garage. It also described the barrier as a public nuisance that lowered property values on streets "victimized by the diverted traffic," deprived property owners on such streets of their rights under the Fifth and Fourteenth Amendments to the U.S. Constitution, and violated city and community plans for the area.[58]

Before the resolution of this lawsuit, the CTM board split over a proposed amendment to the organization's bylaws suggested by residents opposed to the Hosea Avenue closure and to the idea of creating a local historic district in Clifton. The constitutional question surfaced early in September 1992 when a former board member offered a resolution asking the board to submit to a vote of the full membership any issue "involving public or private property or public safety," and to hold the vote fifteen days after notifying all residents of Clifton about the issue. Some board members called this resolution too vague and complained that the notification feature would be too expensive, while another threatened to organize a campaign against the proposal if the board decided to recommend it to the full membership as a bylaw amendment. "What are you afraid of?" responded a proponent of the resolution, who noted that some other neighborhood organizations permitted their members to vote on "important" issues.[59]

The president of the board handled this question by appointing a special constitutional review committee to reconsider bylaw provisions for "methods of decision making, citizen input and representation and the role of elected trustees," and to make recommendations for consideration by a meeting of all CTM members, who could adopt proposed changes by a two-thirds vote of those present. He also reminded Cliftonites that the current bylaws allowed members to vote only for the election of trustees, for amendments to the constitution, and on decisions involving the expenditure of city funds under the Neighborhood Support Program. He also described the CTM's current form of government as a "representative democracy" as opposed to a "pure democracy" under which all members voted on everything, and indicated the existence of "many alternatives" in "the continuum" between these two forms.[60]

The appointment of the constitutional review committee, however, did not cool tempers, especially on the question of the lawsuit over the Hosea Avenue disagreement. The editor of the CTM *Bulletin*, for example, tried to "set the record straight" by describing the events leading to the lawsuit from the perspective of those favoring the cul-de-sac. But the editorial also impugned the motives of the plaintiffs. Some, said the editor, wanted to "destroy the effectiveness of CTM" because of their "disappointment" with the board's position while others "would like to render CTM ineffective in order to develop property in Clifton" and "realize substantial financial gains . . . when allowed to proceed without neighborhood intervention. We should remind ourselves," the editorial concluded, "that CTM's vigorous defense of the same Clifton Community Plan . . . kept developers from putting fast-food restaurants on Ludlow and returned the movies to the Esquire."[61]

This editorial prompted two responses from the leaders of the opposition to the Hosea closure, one of whom sat as a member of the CTM board. They sent a letter to the editor setting out their view of the events leading to the lawsuit in which they contended that the board's refusal to change its decision on the cul-de-sac and city council's policy of deferring to the wishes of CTM left them no choice except to go to court. But they also attacked the editor for using the *Bulletin* as a "personal propaganda machine" and for covering up certain important facts in the case, including the fact that a board member who lived on Hosea voted on the Hosea question, creating "the appearance of impropriety if not being an outright conflict of interest." The same letter also lauded the board for publishing a disclaimer depicting the September editorial as the view of the editor which "may not necessarily reflect the views" of the CTM board or CTM members, and closed by offering an alternative to the closure involving "numerous changes in signage, traffic lights, and the addition of some speed humps."[62]

There the matter simmered until February 1993, when the plaintiffs agreed to drop CTM (but not the city government) from the suit and to refrain from bringing against CTM any additional legal action related to the original suit. That struck the editor of the CTM *Bulletin* as a "victory" that helped preserve the integrity of CTM and by implication the viability of the neighborhood organization revolution. CTM's lawyers, who served for a modest fee of $1,000, explained that they took the case to "preserve the right of neighborhood associations to take positions" without being "intimidated by frivolous lawsuits that must be defended at high cost," lawsuits that also threatened "the willingness of residents to continue to participate in the democratic process. The proper arena to determine issues of public concern is that of the neighborhood [association] and city council—not the courtroom."[63]

This marked the last major intra-community conflict after the adoption of the Clifton community plan and the last of several major victories in efforts to implement the plan,[64] which focused on the protection and enhancement of the historic ambiance of Clifton. These included the rehabilitation of the Sacred Heart property as a residential complex, the banning of fast-food outlets in the business district, and the resurrection of the Esquire as a cinema. Major losses included the failure to secure a new library and the attempt to establish a local historic district in Clifton.

In the longer view, however, this history of the CTM years suggests changes of more significance than lists of victories and losses might indicate. In the thirty-five years after its founding (1964), CTM underwent a drastic transformation in its view of itself and grew more flexible in its view of Clifton. In those years it adopted comprehensive community planning by and for itself, and strove for the financial autonomy to act independently in its struggle to become a liberated entity. Of necessity, this process turned it into a proto-governmental unit within the city government and a quasi-political agency. As such it sought power, including the power that might flow from jurisdictional and territorial aggrandizement. After 1980, its sense of realm tended to encompass the Clifton Ridge, the newly contrived community of Uptown, without submerging its identity in the larger whole.

At the same time, CTM also increasingly resembled a corporation, one rather different from the not-for-profit corporation established in January 1981.[65] That step, of course, gave CTM lower mailing rates and made it eligible to solicit and receive tax-deductible gifts. But the behavior of CTM in other areas looked more like those of a commercial corporation, one competing with others for resources, including population as well as revenues, a competition requiring it to change itself, its community, and its definition of Clifton as a community engaged in a survival contest that defined growth and adaptability as the only available strategy.

The pursuit of growth and adaptability of necessity produced uncertainty and anxiety, which enhanced the lure of history, both as a marketing device and as a source of solace for those who had chosen participation in the delights of planning and power politics and in the dilemmas of creating a stable identity in the face of conflicting views about changing realities. This reconciling of old and new may help account for an attempt to erase the memory of Cincinnati's annexation of Clifton in 1896. In 1992, CTM erected signs that said, "Welcome to Clifton Village, Incorporated 1850," a symbol of the organization's tendency to deny change rhetorically while embracing it in practice.[66]

This process of looking backward while moving forward yielded ironically a shift to isolationism. CTM in its first years considered and occasionally joined other civic and political organizations in attacks on citywide problems intended to promote the welfare of other neighborhoods as well as Clifton. The writers of the community plan eschewed that objective, however, and attempts at its implementation reinforced the turning inward tendency.

It seems unlikely that the process of looking backward while moving forward might lead CTM in the future to identify itself with the city and metropolis of which Clifton is irrevocably a part. The welcome sign reinforced the idea of neighborhood autonomy and the dissociation of CTM with any concept of the public interest that embraced a local entity larger than Clifton. And the attack by some Cliftonites on CTM as a tyrannical governmental unit during the historic conservation and Hosea Avenue hassles demonstrated that some residents defined the public interest as the welfare of their street or household rather than of Clifton as a whole.

Isolationism in Clifton may not hold, however. Cincinnati's and Clifton's attacks on problems first defined in the 1950s have diminished the severity of some, including fears that neighborhoods like Clifton might deteriorate, succumb to blight, and sink to inner-city status. But these attacks have not mitigated other problems. And some of the most corrosive have worsened, including the size of the gap in wealth and power that separates the wealthy from the poor and middle-income strata, and conditions in the African American ghetto, the growth and persistence of which promotes racial stereotyping and interracial fear, misunderstanding, intolerance, and conflicts that promote violence and frustrate attempts to deal with other issues.[67] In addition, the reduction during the 1990s in the size and scope of hospital operations in the vicinity of Clifton and the stabilization of the number of university faculty and staff members raised fears of a stagnating real estate market stemming from factors beyond the reach of CTM and Clifton residents, problems that might freeze or diminish the neighborhood's middle-class residential base.

This frustrating situation—the persisting sense of something profoundly wrong combined with an inability to remedy it—has provoked attempts to revive the idea of the public interest (the welfare of the whole) as the basis for prompting public and private efforts to deal with these and related issues, and on a metropolitan scale.[68] Whether that tactic works, what policy directions it might yield, and their consequences for Clifton and similar neighborhoods remain uncertain and virtually unexamined. But such questions might be worth asking in CTM, in city hall, in the county courthouse, in Columbus, and in Washington, D.C., as well as on the last page of this volume about the changing meaning of neighborhood and community in America with special reference to Cincinnati's Clifton.

Epilogue: CTM, Race, and the Future

Clifton Town Meeting began amid concerns about the spread of the city's central ghetto, an area involuntarily occupied by people of one race who differed individually in every imaginable way, including religion, occupation, income, ideology, sexual orientation, recreational interests, and architectural and landscape taste. The expansion of the ghetto persisted after the 1960s, so much so that blacks constituted almost 40 percent of Cincinnati's population in 1990, and the central ghetto stretched for six miles from the West End across the adjacent Over-the-Rhine neighborhood and from there northeasterly to the city's corporation limits. On either side of the central ghetto, moreover, stood two smaller ones, and together these districts contained 68 percent of the black residents of the metropolitan area.

The tendency of ghettos to expand contiguously posed a threat to CTM's policy of promoting Clifton as a racially diverse neighborhood. But it struck integrationists as a problem on other counts as well, and not only for Cliftonites but for all residents of the metropolis. Residential apartheid seemed particularly repulsive and dangerous because it mocked the American ideal of freedom of association by denying both blacks and whites a full free choice of a home in a neighborhood of their preference. That situation contributed especially to the stark alienation of the so-called black underclass, the most impoverished group in the city. But it also embittered the black middle class, for residential apartheid discriminated against successful adults and reminded them and their children of a grim reality. Even those who secured a good education, acquired a promising job, built a cohesive family, and lived responsible lives stood little chance of escaping the confines of ghetto neighborhoods, including the few gilded ones in outlying and suburban precincts.[1]

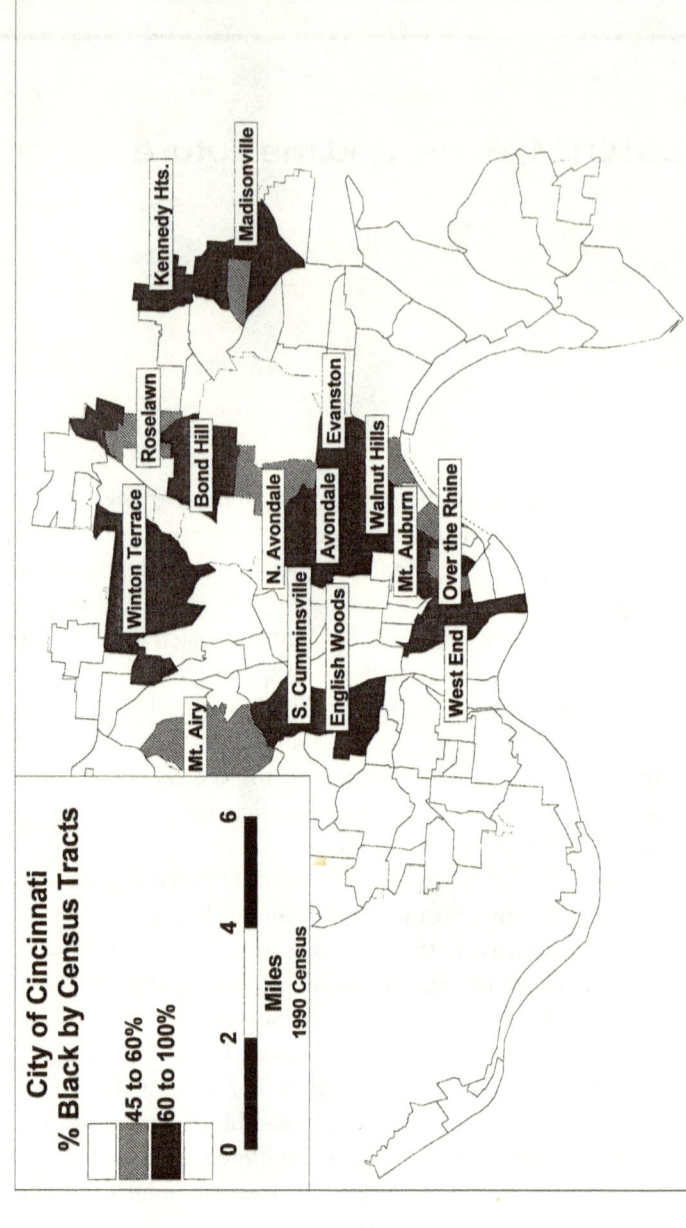

Map 15. City of Cincinnati, Percentage Black by Census Tracts (1990). *Source:* Housing Opportunities Made Equal, 1990.

Table 4
Black Population by County in the Cincinnati Metropolitcan Area, 1900

County	Population	Black Population	% Black
Boone, Ky.	57,589	361	0.6
Butler, Ohio	291,479	13,134	4.5
Campbell, Ky.	83,866	851	1.0
Kenton, Ky.	142,031	4,158	2.9
Clermont, Ohio	150,187	1,291	0.8
Warren, Ohio	113,909	2,415	2.1
Dearborn, Ind.	38,835	252	0.6
Hamilton, Ohio (Cincinnati)	866,228	181,145	20.9

Source: Table prepared by Bill Berger, Housing Opportunities Made Equal.

Note: Blacks living in the city of Cincinnati made up 68 percent (138,110) of all black residents in the metropolitan area, and 38 percent (340,000) of the population of the city.

This view makes the persistence of the ghetto the most pressing public interest problem for Cincinnati and the CTM. The enduring ghetto encourages social and civic alienation among African Americans of all ages and classes. It tempts middle-class youngsters to drop out of school and enter the underclass. It helps explain the continuing gap in test scores between middle-class blacks and middle-class whites. It fosters fear, misunderstanding, mistrust, and resentment that erode faith on both sides of the color line in the city's political system and social and economic prospects. It threatens the viability of the city as an agency for the nurturing of cultural pluralism. And it frustrates attempts to solve other problems because concerns about public education, affordable housing, poverty, sexism, homophobia, and the enrichment of the wealthy at the expense of the middle class and poor get caught up in an interracial crossfire that distorts or deflects attention from these important issues.

Finally, the enduring ghetto raises serious questions about the wisdom and utility of planning neighborhood by neighborhood without reference to the welfare of the whole and about the antigovernment animus that drives the quest for neighborhood autonomy. It points particularly to the importance of retrieving the idea of the public interest defined as the welfare of the whole. This strategy would help us measure the importance of our particular interests against such broader public ideals as those inscribed in the Declaration of Independence and the Constitution, an exercise that in this case makes clear the necessity of guaranteeing to blacks and whites alike the full and free choice of neighborhoods in which to live, especially integrated ones. As one widely respected and eminently sensible social critic, Orlando Patterson, recently put it,

"The greatest problem now facing African Americans is their isolation from the tacit norms of the dominant culture, and this is true of all classes." So let us "do the right thing by working toward the integration of our neighborhoods . . . not only to solve the educational problems of our minorities and greatly enhance their network of cultural resources" but also to "make for a more tolerant and genuinely multi-ethnic nation."[2]

The revival of the public interest involves, of course, an exaltation of our sense of civic identity, the cultivation of our willingness to make sacrifices for the welfare of the whole, and the restoration of our trust in the efficacy of government. This may strike some as impossible in an age of cultural individualism, when few of us would quietly relinquish our liberation, our right to lifestyle choices. But we need not go that far in our pursuit of civic virtue and the recovery of the idea of the public interest. We need only relax our quest for self-actualization and more deeply engage in the struggle to reinvigorate our human capacity for empathy, our ability to walk in someone else's shoes, the ability which facilitates compromise based on the high moral and ubiquitous ideal of the golden rule, a major tenet not only of Christianity but of every one of the world's great religions.

THE GOLDEN RULE

Hinduism	Everything you should do you will find in this: Do nothing to others that would hurt you if it were done to you. —*Mahabharata* 5:1517
Buddhism	Do not offend others, as you would not want to be offended. —Udanavarga 5:18
Taoism	The successes of your neighbor and their losses will be to you as if they were your own. —T'ai-Shang Kan-Ying P'ien
Confucianism	Is there any rule that one should follow all of one's life? Yes! The rule of gentle goodness: That which we do not wish to be done to us, we do not do to others. —Analects 15:23
Judaism	That which you do not wish for yourself you shall not wish for your neighbor. This is the whole law: the rest is only commentary. —Talmud Shabbat 31

Christianity   In everything, do unto others what you would have them do unto you. For this sums up the law and the prophets.
—Matthew 7:12

Islam   None of you shall be true believers unless you wish for your brother the same that you wish for yourself.
—Sunnah

Having restored our moral equilibrium, what other steps can we take to provide more people with a full and free choice of a neighborhood in which to live? Since racial residential segregation ranks as a regional problem, its resolution demands a regional strategy, one preferably worked out by a well-funded regional civic group composed of the area's top business, religious, academic, sports, and cultural leaders. Such a group could produce radio and television ads defining the problem and promoting solutions. It could meet with representatives of suburban municipalities, townships, and white Cincinnati neighborhoods and persuade them to advertise themselves as equal opportunity residential communities. It could establish in integrating places racial Welcome Wagon organizations to make sure that everyone handles the situation civilly. It could start a regional nonprofit organization that would gather the names of people seeking an integrated neighborhood and the names of places looking for such people. It could persuade real estate agents to subscribe to this service and to ask all their clients if they would consider integrated living and show a variety of such neighborhoods to those who say yes. And it could persuade financial institutions to set aside funds to loan to people making integrative moves.

This brief list, of course, does not begin to exhaust the possible approaches to the resolution of this problem, and representatives of concerned organizations should organize a regional conference to seek out other suggestions. The initiative ought to come from a variety of concerned agencies, such as the National Association for the Advancement of Colored People, Housing Opportunities Made Equal, CTM, the North Avondale Neighborhood Association, and the Over-the-Rhine Chamber of Commerce.[3] But conference proponents should also include some unlikely suspects, such as the Cincinnati Preservation Association, the Chamber of Commerce of Greater Cincinnati, the Chamber of Commerce of Northern Kentucky, the Cincinnati Business Committee, and other civic organizations with a regional focus.

Appendix:
Methodological Note on "Liberation" History

The approach I've used in preparing this history of Clifton as a place stems from my long association with Henry D. Shapiro. This involved, among other things, an extended conversation over about thirty years on the doing of history. Out of those conversations came for me several propositions that may be seen as constituting a methodology for doing what I call "liberation" history.[1]

1. The past is past.
2. History is what people say/write about the past.
3. It is through history that the past influences the present and infringes on the future.
4. Some historians do history by consulting evidence of past ideas and activities, and by examining what people said and did not say and what they did and did not do.
5. Some historians (including this one) use this approach to the past for the purpose of establishing a sequence of time periods, each of them characterized by a taxonomy of social reality peculiar to that period but not to a particular place.
6. From each taxonomy people create a dominant conception of what society is, is becoming, or ought to be.
7. Conceptions of reality determine what people look for when they examine reality, and their conceptual "bias" determines what they see and what they don't see in their examinations.
8. Such examinations yield more or less systematic visions of reality that might be described as perceptions of reality.
9. Perceptions of reality often clash with dominant conceptions of reality, a situation of dissonance.
10. Some people discomfited by this dissonance seek to relieve it by bringing their perception of reality into conformity with their conception of reality.
11. Such efforts invariably fail (so far as I know) and lead eventually to another solution to the problems of dissonance, the establishment of a new taxonomy of reality and a new dominant conception of what society is, is becoming, or ought to be.
12. The shift from one taxonomic/conceptual framework to another creates a new period radically discontinuous from the previous one.

13. Radical discontinuity tells us two things (at least) about the utility of studying the past.
    A. We can learn from the study of past periods useful lessons about human imagination and human capacities but nothing of immediately practical use in our period, for people in past periods shared our humanity but thought and acted differently than we because they lived in different conceptual and perceptual worlds.
    B. However, the study of that recent past in which we yet live (since the 1940s) can produce lessons immediately practical for everyday life because we inhabit the same conceptual and perceptual worlds as all of our contemporaries in "our time" (we have been and are playing the game of life by the same basic rules).
14. This approach to the past may be called "liberation" history, for it suggests that we, like our predecessors, possess the capacity to reject the legacies of the past and to think and act anew.

Notes

Preface

1. Zane L. Miller and Henry D. Shapiro, "Learning History by Doing: The Laboratory in American Civilization," *History Teacher* 11, no. 4 (spring 1978): 483–95.

Introduction

1. Before the mid-nineteenth century, suburbs ranked as disreputable places inhabited by disreputable people and disreputable nonresidential land uses. Kenneth T. Jackson, *Crabgrass Frontier: The Suburbanization of the United States* (New York: Oxford University Press, 1985), ch. 1, "Suburbs as Slums."

2. While a sense of intracity territoriality appeared in the mid-nineteenth century, it centered on nonresidential units, such as the identification of the business portion(s) of the city, of concentrations of noxious manufactures, and of the ward as an administrative unit and as a locus for organized political and civic activity, not merely as a district for governmental representation. To the extent that people in the mid-nineteenth century thought of areas of the city as the typical habitat of one or another class of humans, they focused on the behavior (or misbehavior) of individuals within groups and classes and attributed this behavior to factors other than social and physical environments, such as an individual's defective moral character and/or defective training and experience in civilized living. In other words, the mid-nineteenth-century conception of the city did not suggest the existence of distinct and differential residential neighborhoods defined as social and physical environments (rather than as locational identifiers) that significantly influenced or determined the behavior of residents, nor did that conception suggest the existence of distinct and differentiated residential neighborhoods as functional units that interacted within an urban system of functionally specialized groups and parts. City governments and social and civic agencies, as a consequence, did not develop programs for the improvement of residential neighborhoods (defined as social and physical environments) as a means of reforming "problem" groups or classes or of satisfying the distinctive cultural tastes of "normal" groups or classes. Extensive and persuasive writing in this vein about mid-nineteenth-century American cities may be found in Alan I Marcus, "Back to the Present: Historians' Treatment of the City as a Social System During the Reign of the Idea of Community," in *American Urbanism: A Historiographical Review*, ed. Howard Gillette Jr. and Zane L. Miller (New York: Greenwood Press, 1987), 11–13; and in Marcus's *Plague of Strangers: Social Groups and the Origins of City Services in Cincinnati, 1819–1870* (Columbus: Ohio State University Press, 1991). But see also Henry D. Shapiro's essay on the changing role of place in social theory, "The Place of Culture and the Problem of Identity," in *Appa-

lachia and America: Autonomy and Regional Dependence, ed. Allen Batteau (Lexington: University Press of Kentucky, 1983), esp. 116–17. Mid-nineteenth-century writers on the city said that misbehaving people wrecked the social and physical environment, not the other way around. See George C. Foster, *New York by Gas-Light and Other Sketches*, ed. Stuart M. Blumin (Berkeley: University of California Press, 1990) [a reprint of Foster's writing about New York in the mid-nineteenth century], not only Blumin's commentary, especially 26, 50, 57–58, but also Foster's prose, particularly his sketch of Broadway, 69–76, which argues that a lack of character marks both victims (prostitutes in this case) and their exploiters. For another good example of this mid-nineteenth-century talk about character and social problems in cities, see the Rev. E. H. Chapin, *Humanity in the City* (1854; reprint, New York: Arno Press, 1974), esp. 66, 89–90, 162, 207, 209 (on a "true home"), 211.

3. This "of but not in" conception of the suburb-city relationship sounds odd now. But some historians and geographers have long known that the word *suburb* indicated in the nineteenth and early twentieth century "the *connection* of the surrounding population to the city; only in more recent times has the word come to connote the *difference* between those who live in the city and those who reside in adjacent areas." Harold M. Mayer and Richard C. Wade, *Chicago: The Growth of a Metropolis* (Chicago: University of Chicago Press, 1969), 24.

4. The northern portion of Clifton of the nineteenth century apparently looked parklike and attracted visitors to admire its elegant ambiance. But accounts of parklike Clifton as the whole of Clifton necessarily overlooked south Clifton, which contained very little open space compared to north Clifton. This oversight suggests the power of the new metropolitan vision of the city as a system of functionally and structurally differentiated groups and parts, a vision so powerful that it led even close and honest observers to concoct conceptions of reality compatible with the "need" to assign special roles to each of the parts of the city, and to ignore contradictory evidence, or to gloss over perceptions dissonant with those conceptions. For accounts of Clifton as parklike, see Daniel J. Kenny, *Illustrated Cincinnati* (Cincinnati: Robert Clarke, 1875), 33–36, 92; Max Burgheim, *Der Führer von Cincinnati* (Cincinnati: Burgheim, 1875), 160–62, 189; Max Burgheim, *Cincinnati im Wort und Bilt* (Cincinnati: Burgheim, 1891), 353–54, 408; Moses King, ed., *King's Pocket-Book of Cincinnati* (Cincinnati: Moses King, 1880), 18, 22; Henry A. Ford and Mrs. Kate B. Ford, *History of Cincinnati, Ohio, with Illustrations and Biographical Studies* (Cleveland: L. A. Williams, 1881), 9–11, ch. 48; W. W. Spooner, ed., *A Guide to Picturesque Cincinnati* (Cincinnati: O. Reich, P. T. Schulz, and F. L. Plympton, 1883), vii-viii, 19–21; John W. Leonard, *Centennial Review of Cincinnati: One Hundred Years of Progress in Commerce, Manufacturing, the Professions, and in Social and Municipal Life* (Cincinnati: H. M. Elstner, 1888), 151; *The City of Cincinnati and Its Resources* (Cincinnati: Cincinnati Times-Star, 1891), n.p.; Daniel J. Kenny, *Illustrated Guide to Cincinnati and the World's Columbian Exposition* (Cincinnati: Robert Clarke, 1893), 207, 215–17, 226; *History of Cincinnati and Hamilton County, Ohio* (Cincinnati: S. B. Nelson, 1894), 73–74, 420–21; *Kraemer's Picturesque Cincinnati* (Cincinnati: A. O. and G. A. Kraemer, 1898), 12–13; George W. Engelhardt, *Cincinnati: The Queen City* (Cincinnati: George W. Englehardt, 1901), 9; Charles Theodore Greve, *Centennial History of Cincinnati and Representative Citizens* (Chicago: Biographical, 1904),

1:17; Henry Howe, *Historical Collections of Ohio* (Cincinnati: State of Ohio, 1908), 1: 788, 864.

5. Attempts to separate groups geographically seemed sensible then because the identity and behavior of group members no longer appeared as malleable as at midcentury. Social theory in the late nineteenth and early twentieth centuries rested on biological determinism, the notion that groups inherited their physical constitutions, mental and moral capacities, and culture. This idea made the groups seem intractable and suggested that they should be segregated to stabilize property values, keep the peace, and discourage interbreeding of superior and inferior groups. See Zane L. Miller and Bruce Tucker, *Changing Plans for America's Inner Cities: Cincinnati's Over-the-Rhine and Twentieth-Century Urbanism* (Columbus: Ohio State University Press, 1998), 3–4, 172–73n. 3. The "racialism" of the late nineteenth and early twentieth centuries yielded significant consequence in all aspects of American life. For a stunning example from legal history, see Linda Przybyszewski, *The Republic According to John Marshall Harlan* (Chapel Hill: University of North Carolina Press, 1999), 10–11.

6. Urban historians have produced a large body of literature since 1950 dealing with suburbs and big city neighborhoods of various kinds. But most share a culturally individualistic concern with two closely related problems: the extent to which individuals succeeded in inventing their own identities as a basis for making choices about where and how to live, and the extent to which such liberated individuals succeeded in creating groups—class, race, ethnic, religious, gender, age, occupational, or sexual preference groups, for example—that more or less managed in their competition with other self-constructed groups to establish and maintain their self-constructed group identities and to carve out or redesign social and physical environments compatible with those group identities. This book attempts to avoid that approach for the periods before the 1950s, which ushered in the era of cultural individualism, a general social imperative that did not exist before that decade. For an elaboration on this point, see Zane L. Miller, "The Crisis of Civic and Political Virtue: Urban History, Urban Life, and the New Understanding of the City," *Reviews in American History* 24, no. 3 (September 1996): 361–70. See also Marcus, "Back to the Present," 7–26, esp. 7–10. Marcus names some of the chief practitioners of the conventional approach (he identifies two schools) and also the authors of some works that take an approach similar to that used in this book.

For other introductions to and assessments of the historical literature on suburbs and big city neighborhoods, see Carol A. O'Connor, "The Suburban Mosaic: Patterns of Land Use, Class, and Culture"; Michael Ebner, "Re-reading Suburban America: Urban Population Deconcentration, 1810–1980"; and Patricia Mooney Melvin, "The Neighborhood-City Relationships," all in *American Urbanism: A Historiographical Review*, ed. Gillette and Miller, 227–70. See also Robert Fisher and Peter Romanofscky, eds., *Community Organization for Urban Social Change: A Historical Perspective* (Westport, Conn.: Greenwood Press, 1981); and Patricia Mooney Melvin, ed., *American Community Organizations: A Historical Dictionary* (Westport, Conn.: Greenwood Press, 1986).

Besides Mayer and Wade, *Chicago,* and Jackson, *Crabgrass Frontier,* some of the more important recent books on suburbs and/or neighborhoods include Henry C. Binford, *The First Suburbs: Residential Communities on the Boston Periphery, 1815–1860* (Chicago:

University of Chicago Press, 1985); Robert Fishman, *Bourgeois Utopias: The Rise and Fall of Suburbia* (New York: Basic Books, 1987); Louise C. Wade, *Chicago's Pride: The Stockyards, Packingtown, and Environs in the Nineteenth Century* (Urbana: University of Illinois Press, 1987); Michael H. Ebner, *Creating Chicago's North Shore: A Suburban History* (Chicago: University of Chicago Press, 1988); John Stilgo, *Borderland: Origins of the American Suburb, 1820–1939* (New Haven: Yale University Press, 1988); Ann Durkin Keating, *Building Chicago: Suburban Developers and the Creation of a Divided Metropolis* (Columbus: Ohio State University Press, 1989); David R. Contestee, *Suburb in the City: Chestnut Hill, Philadelphia, 1850–1990* (Columbus: Ohio State University Press, 1992); Alexander von Hoffman, *Local Attachments: The Making of an American Urban Neighborhood, 1850–1920* (Baltimore: Johns Hopkins University Press, 1994); Evan McKenzie, *Privatopia: Homeowner Associations and the Rise of Residential Private Government* (New Haven: Yale University Press, 1994), esp. 175–98; Edward J. Blakely and Mary Gail Snyder, *Fortress America: Gated Communities in the United States* (Washington, D.C.: Brookings Institution Press, 1997), esp. 161–77; Jon C. Teaford, *Post-suburbia: Government and Politics in the Edge Cities* (Baltimore: Johns Hopkins University Press, 1997); and Ray Suarez, *The Old Neighborhood: What We Lost in the Great Suburban Migration, 1966–1999* (New York: Free Press, 1999). See also the short study by Kevin O'Connor and Edward J. Blakely, "Suburbia Makes the Central City: A New Interpretation of City-Suburb Relationships," working paper no. 485, Institute of Urban and Regional Development, University of California at Berkeley, August 1988.

7. For nationally prominent exceptions to the silence on race in regionalist discussions, see David Rusk, *Cities Without Suburbs* (Washington, D.C.: Woodrow Wilson Center Press, 1993); David Moberg, "How to Heal Our Cities: Myron Oldfield Has a Radical Solution to Suburban Sprawl—Social Justice," *Sierra*, May/June 2000, 74–77, 100.

8. John D. Fairfield, "Democracy in Cincinnati: Civic Virtue and Three Generations of Urban Historians," *Urban History*, 24, no. 2 (August 1997): 200–219; Zane L. Miller, *Suburb: Neighborhood and Community in Forest Park, Ohio, 1935–1976* (Knoxville: University of Tennessee Press, 1981), esp. xiv–xvii. For a sociological study of some other similar and similarly situated neighborhoods in other cities, see Richard P. Taub, *Paths of Neighborhood Change: Race and Crime in Urban America* (Chicago: University of Chicago Press, 1987).

Chapter One

1. Geoffrey J. Giglierano and Deborah A. Overmyer, with Frederic L. Propas, *The Bicentennial Guide to Greater Cincinnati: A Portrait of Two Hundred Years* (Cincinnati: Cincinnati Historical Society, 1988), contains historical sketches of Cincinnati suburbs and documents the variety of such places in the mid-nineteenth century as well as after. This same generalization holds for the suburbs of other cities as well. See, e.g., Carol A. O'Connor, "The Suburban Mosaic," in *American Urbanism: A Historiographical Review*, ed. Howard Gillette Jr. and Zane L. Miller (Westport, Conn.: Greenwood Press, 1987), 243–56, esp. 243–45.

2. Suburbs appeared around Cincinnati as early as the 1820s, but the directory/guidebooks (this genre did not become two separate categories until the 1870s) either ignored

them or said very little about them until the last third of the century. See Richard C. Wade, *The Urban Frontier: The Rise of Western Cities, 1790–1830* (1959; reprint, Urbana: University of Illinois Press, 1996), 305–7; B. Drake and E. D. Mansfield, *Cincinnati in 1826* (Cincinnati: Morgan, Lodge, and Fisher, 1827); Charles Cist, *Cincinnati in 1841: Its Early Annals and Future Prospects* (Cincinnati: privately published, 1841), 35–36; Cist, *Sketches and Statistics of Cincinnati in 1851* (Cincinnati: Wm. M. Moore, 1851), 15, 45, 268–70; and Cist, *Sketches and Statistics of Cincinnati in 1859* (Cincinnati: privately published, 1859), which refers to just two suburbs and then only for the purpose of discussing the colleges located in them (236–38). Cist's 1851 volume put suburbs in the book's last chapter, entitled "Miscellaneous" (268–70).

3. For a recent and most elegant description of the grand houses and estates of Clifton see John Clubbe, *Cincinnati Observed: Architecture and History* (Columbus: Ohio State University Press, 1992), 291–320.

4. Henry D. Shapiro and Zane L. Miller, *Clifton: Neighborhood and Community in an Urban Setting* (Cincinnati: Laboratory in American Civilization, Department of History, University of Cincinnati, 1976), 9–12, 22.

5. Ibid., 17–18; Andrea T. Kornbluh, "Parks and the People: The Place of the Kessler Park Plan [for Cincinnati] in the History of Parks and Public Recreation," *Queen City Heritage: The Journal of the Cincinnati Historical Society* 51, no. 1 (spring 1993): 53–55.

6. George E. Stevens, *The City of Cincinnati: A Summary of Its Attractions, Advantages, Institutions and Internal Improvements, with a Statement of Its Public Charities* (Cincinnati: Geo. S. Blanchard, 1869), 10, 27, 29.

7. Ibid., iii, 34, 201, 213.

8. Sidney Maxwell, *The Suburbs of Cincinnati: Sketches Historical and Descriptive* (Cincinnati: George E. Stevens, 1870), v-vi.

9. Ibid., 10.

10. Ibid., 27–52, 125, 170–72.

11. Ibid., 129–32, 165–66, 173–74.

12. Ibid., 30, 186.

13. On the disdain for the use of animal power for rapid transit, see Clay McShane, *Down the Asphalt Path: The Automobile and the American City* (New York: Columbia University Press, 1994), 41–56.

City dwellers generally, not just Cliftonites and Cincinnatians, saw the city in the late nineteenth century and for the first time as a congeries of different but interdependent neighborhoods, such as immigrant neighborhoods, and black, working-class, middle-class, and upper-class ones, each with its own character and "needs." City dwellers thought too that each of these neighborhoods should develop a civic sense, a sense of the neighborhood's community interest as it related to the welfare of the city as a whole, the larger community. This way of thinking made it seem appropriate that neighborhoods should develop vehicles for cultivating and expressing this sense, such vehicles as a settlement house, or an "institutional" church, or a public school social center. Of course, "outsiders" organized most of these institutions, and they did not seem appropriate for places like Clifton, the residents of which seemed quite capable of acquiring unassisted by outsiders appropriate institutions for community development and expression, in this case, a neighborhood improvement association.

The notion of neighborhood as a differentiated and interdependent unit of the city and possessing a sense of local community also carried ramifications for land use patterns. This way of thinking defined the neighborhood not merely as a place to reside but as a *community* in which to live. This definition gave the word *residence* new meaning and gave rise to the phrase *residential neighborhood,* to distinguish it from local places with different patterns of activities and land uses, such as industrial districts or commercial districts. It meant, that is, that each residential neighborhood should contain things that geographic parts of the city lacked in the mid-nineteenth century. It meant, for example, that each neighborhood should have rapid transit lines for ready and speedy access to that other new and centrally located "neighborhood" of concentrated work, leisure, and commercial facilities known as "downtown." It also meant that residential neighborhoods should be complete and convenient local arenas for residential life, places supplied with the amenities and services necessary for raising a family and conducting the daily routine of life. It meant, in short, that Clifton and other residential neighborhoods should contain a shopping district to supply everyday needs for groceries, medicines, refreshments, and delicacies such as candy, an array of churches, a neighborhood improvement association, and a modern public elementary school, all of which Clifton acquired in the late nineteenth and very early twentieth centuries.

14. Richard M. Wagner and Roy J. Wright, *Cincinnati Streetcars, No. 2. The Inclines* (Cincinnati: Wagner Car, 1968), 30, 47, and *Cincinnati Streetcars, No. 3. Cable Cars and Earliest Electrics* (Cincinnati: Wagner Car, 1969), 92; Greve, *Centennial History of Cincinnati,* 1:1007–8; "Slow but Sure," *Cincinnati Times-Star,* August 22, 1984, in *Street Railways,* Scrapbook, n.p., Cincinnati Historical Society.

15. The Public Library of Cincinnati and Hamilton County, Newspaper Clippings on Cincinnati, vol. 1, "Clifton: Most Lovely of All the Suburbs of Cincinnati," 205–6, 250–51. These scrapbooks contain two more newspaper articles from the early 1890s on rapid subdividing in Clifton, both of which emphasized the activity in "south" Clifton. See vol. 1, 208, and vol. 2, 205–6. Not all Cliftonites applauded this kind of development, even though the village council courted it. One resident in 1895 thought it might go too far if Cincinnati annexed Clifton, and in that event hoped that Clifton, Lafayette, and Central Avenues might remain "rural highways" and that other thoroughfares would be spared the "disfigurement of car tracks and a cat's cradle of wire overhead, which would sacrifice beautiful trees. After all," she wrote, "citizens of the city drive through our village on pleasant days and bring visitors to see Clifton, and if our streets are to be laid out on grade lines, paved and ruined by car tracks, the glory will have departed forever and Clifton will have ceased to share with Lenox the proud title of the two most beautiful villages in the United States." The Public Library of Cincinnati and Hamilton County, Newspaper Clippings on Cincinnati, vol. 2, 174, "Annexation Sentiment."

16. Clifton franchises (routes) to the Cincinnati Street Railway Company, under which name all the city's street railways were consolidated in 1896, are listed in Annexation Proceedings, p. 12, which may be found in the city of Cincinnati's Clerk of Council's Office, City Hall, Cincinnati.

17. Land use information is based on a compilation made by Tracy Thomas from *Williams' Cincinnati Directories.* Among the implications to be drawn from her study, Thomas notes that Clifton "was not an independent community." Its businesses could not provide all the essential services a community would need to exist independently. It contained no bakeries, barber shops, coal dealers, ice companies, dentists, restaurants,

hotels, or service-type businesses. See Tracy Thomas, "Clifton: Businesses and Institutions, 1896" (Laboratory in American Civilization, Department of History, University of Cincinnati, December 4, 1974). For an introduction to the history of churches in Clifton see Maxwell, *Suburbs of Cincinnati,* 50; and Greve, *Centennial History of Cincinnati,* 773–76.

18. Zane L. Miller, *Boss Cox's Cincinnati: Urban Politics in the Progressive Era* (New York: Oxford University Press, 1968), 240.

19. The size of the population for 1910 comes from an estimate by University of Cincinnati sociologists who used census tract boundaries for 1930 and projected population figures for those tracts back to 1900. Clifton still rang up low numbers in the density of people per inhabited acre (7, 6, and 4 for the three tracts that roughly corresponded with the old village boundaries, well below the figure for the tracts immediately to its south, which came in at 13, 36, and 52 persons per inhabited acre, and way below tracts near the center of the old city, six of which showed densities of over one hundred souls per inhabited acre, and the most dense of which came in with a score of 173). See James A. Quinn, Earle Eubank, and Lois E. Elliott, *Population Changes: Cincinnati, Ohio, and Adjacent Areas, 1900–1940* (Columbus: Bureau of Business Research, Ohio State University, 1947), research monograph no. 47, 12–13, 28–29. The Clifton tract boundaries ran south to north, so that the spacious north Clifton countered the more densely settled south Clifton area, the density of parts of which (in the apartment district) probably ran as high as 52 persons per inhabited acre. The population figures are for 1900 and 1910, from Miller, *Boss Cox's Cincinnati,* 27. For land uses see Tracy Thomas, "Clifton: Businesses and Institutions: 1896."

Most of the rest of the businesses lay along Vine, three clustered at the southern extreme near Ludlow, sixteen on either side of Woolper south of the German Evangelical Protestant cemetery, and five between Glenwood and Wuest on northern Vine Street in St. Bernard. Except for the florists on McAlpin and Biddle, a professional office on McAlpin, a business on Wood at the corner of Middleton and another on Lafayette Circle (B. Morrison & Co., table decorations).

20. Iola O. Silberstein, "Diversity on Converging Pathways: Mary H. Doherty and Helen G. Lotspeich," *Queen City Heritage: The Journal of the Cincinnati Historical Society* (hereinafter cited as *Queen City Heritage*), 41, no. 4 (winter 1983): 10, 13–20.

21. The parish lines ran west on the south side of Nixon Street from Vine to Burnet Woods and from Clifton Avenue to Marshall Street on the south side of Riddle Road; then north on Marshall Avenue to the canal and on the east side of the canal north to Mitchell Avenue; then east on Mitchell to Purdue Avenue and south on the west side of Purdue to the Zoo on Vine Street, then south again to Nixon. The parish income for its first year came to $14,289.83 and its debt stood at $3,500 at the end of the year. The parish paid $7,000 for 130 feet of the hospital tract on Resor and $33,000 for the rest of the plot. Father James Kelly, like many other priests in the Cincinnati archdiocese in this period, complained frequently that other priests "raided" his parish by performing sacraments for Catholics who resided in his territory (parish). This information, like that in the text about the parish, comes from James Kelly, "The Story of Annunciation Parish," October 14, 1919, pp. 1–2, and "Silver Jubilee, 1910–1935. Church of the Annunciation, B.V.M. Clifton," p. 5, both in Annunciation, Clifton: Parish History file, drawer 1, folder 12, Archives of the Catholic Archdiocese of Cincinnati; from the *Wil-*

liams Cincinnati Directory for 1909; from Geoffrey Giglierano, "Catholics and Clifton" (Laboratory in American Civilization, Department of History, University of Cincinnati, n.d.); from James H. Campbell, "New Parochialism: Change and Conflict in the Archdiocese of Cincinnati, 1878–1925," in *Ethnic Diversity and Civic Identity: Patterns of Conflict and Cohesion in Cincinnati Since 1820,* ed. Henry D. Shapiro and Jonathan D. Sarna (Urbana: University of Illinois Press, 1992), 106–16; and from Sister Benadicta Mahoney, *We Are Many: History of the Sisters of Charity of Cincinnati, 1898–1971* (Cincinnati: Sisters of Charity, 1982), 21.

22. Cincinnati *Catholic-Telegraph,* October 22, 1931, p. 6.

23. Clifton requested a new firehouse at the time of annexation but failed to secure it in the annexation agreement. See *Annexation Proceedings,* 4–6, 91. On the persistence of Clifton's "genteel" ambiance, see *The Cincinnati Address Book: Elite Family Directory, Club List, 1898* (Cincinnati and Buffalo: Dau, 1898), 115ff., which lists many Clifton streets and the names of many people on each one.

24. Cincinnati Board of Park Commissioners, report, 1911, 7. For a biography of Bowler, see Greve, *Centennial History of Cincinnati,* 978–79. On Strauch, see Blanche Linden-Ward, "The Greening of Cincinnati: Adolph Strauch's Legacy in Park Design," *Queen City Heritage* 51, no. 1 (spring 1993): 20.

25. Giglierano and Overmyer, *Bicentennial Guide,* 214; Linden-Ward, "The Greening of Cincinnati," 24. For the shift in the 1890s of the concept of city parks, see Kornbluh, "Parks and People," 55–58.

26. Cincinnati Board of Education, *67th Annual Report* (1896), viii, 23.

27. Cincinnati school officials laid cornerstones for Hughes and Walnut Hills comprehensive high schools in 1908, and hoped, as in the past, to permit parents from all over the city to select the high school in which to enroll their children. In 1911, however, when enrollment at Hughes exceeded its capacity of 1,500 by 300 students, the Board of Education decided to create high school attendance districts. The board also ran small high schools offering only "academic" courses. Cincinnati Board of Education, *79th Annual Report* (1908), 39; *81st Annual Report* (1910), 33–34; and *82d Annual Report* (1911), 27–29.

28. Cincinnati Board of Education, minutes, January 20, p. 381, February 17, p. 394, March 16, p. 408, March 30, p. 419, and September 28, 1896, p. 526.

29. The enumeration of youth for Clifton in 1894 found 513 of potential school age (between ages six and twenty-one), and the enumeration of youth in 1896 found 494, of whom 251 attended the public school, 51 attended a church school, 47 attended a private school, and 135 did not attend school at all. *Annexation Proceedings,* 90; Cincinnati Board of Education, *67th Annual Report* (1896), 111, 114, and *72d Annual Report* (1901), 90, 96.

30. On the school development program, see Janet A. Miller, "Urban Education and the New City: Cincinnati's Elementary Schools, 1870–1914" (D.Ed. diss., University of Cincinnati, 1974), 378–451, and esp. 427–51 for school building construction.

31. Cincinnati Board of Education, *78th Annual Report* (1907), 32.

32. The emergence of a "new" urban politics and a new urban political configuration is the subject of Miller, *Boss Cox's Cincinnati.* For Cincinnati politics in the 1910s and 1920s, see William A. Baughin, "Murray Seasongood, Twentieth-Century Urban Re-

former" (Ph.D. diss., University of Cincinnati, 1972), chs. 5–8, and Wilbert J. Cameron Jr., "Community Control of Education in Cincinnati, 1900–1921" (Ph.D. diss., University of Cincinnati, 1977), chs. 2–10.

33. Patricia Mooney Melvin, "Local Improvement Associations and the City-Building Process," 1–4, paper delivered at the Cincinnati Seminar on the City, Cincinnati Historical Society, November 9, 1994; William H. Wilson, *The City Beautiful Movement* (Baltimore: Johns Hopkins University Press, 1989), 35–50.

34. *Constitution of the Clifton and Burnet Woods Improvement Association, Adopted April 30, 1896* (Cincinnati, 1896), 1, 6.

35. *The North Cincinnati and Clifton Advocate: A Monthly Journal Devoted to the Interests of the Citizens of the 28th and 31st Wards* 1, no. 4 (October 1897): 1, 4.

36. Ibid., 4, 5.

37. Ibid., 5, 6.

38. Ibid., 2, 4, 5, 6.

39. Kornbluh, "Parks and the People," 55–56.

40. Ibid., 56.

41. Cincinnati Board of Park Commissioners, report, 1911, 10–13, 17, 32. Kessler did not mention automobiles, then growing rapidly in popularity among prosperous people, street railways or horse carriages but seems to have intended his parkways for use by all three modes of conveyance.

42. Ibid., 18, 30, 33, 35–36.

43. "Approved: General Park System," *Cincinnati Enquirer,* May 14, 1907, p. 12.

44. "Clifton," *Civic News* (organ of the Federated Improvement Associations of Hamilton County, Ohio) 1, no. 4 (January 1912): 6–7; "Clifton Welfare and Protective Association," *Civic News* 4, no. 7 (April 1915): 5. On the Ludlow Avenue improvements and viaduct see *Cincinnati Times-Star,* April 7, 1913, p. 5, col. 3, June 4, 1914, p. 9, col. 2, and *Cincinnati Commercial,* June 16, 1914, p. 10, col. 2.

45. "Conference of Representatives from Improvement Associations," *Cincinnati Enquirer,* May 10, 1907, p. 12.

46. "To Promote the Welfare of the City," *Cincinnati Enquirer,* May 28, 1907, p. 5.

47. Quoted in Zane L. Miller, *Boss Cox's Cincinnati,* 111.

48. "Clifton Welfare and Protective Association."

49. Shapiro and Miller, *Clifton,* 37–38.

50. See Zane L. Miller and Patricia Mooney Melvin, *The Urbanization of Modern America: A Brief History* (San Diego: Harcourt Brace Jovanovich, 1987), 136–43.

51. *Charter for the City of Cincinnati: Prepared and Proposed by the Charter Commission of the City of Cincinnati, Election Day, July 14, 1914* (copy in Main Branch, the Public Library of Cincinnati and Hamilton County), 4–8, 21–22, 25–27, 50–53.

52. The presence from 1897 to 1920 of Miss E. Antoinette Ely's Clifton School for Young Ladies, as well as the persistence of Sacred Heart Academy on Lafayette Avenue, fortified Clifton's identification with education in the early twentieth century. Miss Ely's school offered programs to prepare students "for admission into any of the colleges open to women." Giglierano and Overmyer, *Bicentennial Guide,* 228.

53. Ibid., 237, 241–42; *Cincinnati Times-Star,* April 25, 1940, 11, Sports sec.

54. Alvin F. Harlow, *The Serene Cincinnatians* (New York: E. P. Dutton, 1950), and

Zane L. Miller, introduction to Federal Writers' Project, Works Projects Administration, *Cincinnati: A Guide to the Queen City and Its Neighbors* (Cincinnati: Cincinnati Historical Society, 1987, orig. published, 1943), esp. xv-xviii.

Chapter Two

1. Municipal Art Society of Cincinnati, *City Plan for Cincinnati* (Cincinnati: Municipal Art Society, 1921), 2, 37–46. On the effort to establish metropolitan master planning in Cincinnati, see Andrea Tuttle Kornbluh, *Lighting the Way . . . : The Woman's City Club of Cincinnati, 1915–1965* (Cincinnati: Young and Klein, 1968), 15–19.

2. Municipal Art Society, *City Plan for Cincinnati*, 5–46.

3. Zane L. Miller, *Suburb*, xxiv, 3–6, 224, 240, 248–50; and Miller and Tucker, *Changing Plans for America's Inner Cities*, general introduction, prologue, and part 1.

4. Judith Spraul-Schmidt, "Local Government and Urban Community: Cincinnati and Hamilton County" (seminar paper, Zane L. Miller's files, University of Cincinnati, June 1977); Jon C. Teaford, *City and Suburb: The Political Fragmentation of Metropolitan America, 1850–1970* (Baltimore: Johns Hopkins University Press, 1979), chs. 4–9.

5. Cincinnati City Planning Commission, *Official Plan of the City of Cincinnati* (Cincinnati: Cincinnati City Planning Commission, 1925), 6 (Commission hereafter abbreviated as CCPC); Robert A. Burnham, "'Pulling Together' for Pluralism: Politics, Planning, and Government in Cincinnati, 1924–1959" (Ph.D. diss., University of Cincinnati, 1990), ch. 5.

6. Robert B. Fairbanks, *Making Better Citizens: Housing Reform and the Community Development Strategy in Cincinnati, 1890–1960* (Urbana: University of Illinois Press, 1988), esp. ch. 3.

7. Ibid., ch. 1; Patricia Mooney Melvin, *The Organic City: Urban Definition and Neighborhood Organization, 1880–1920* (Lexington: University Press of Kentucky, 1987), esp. ch. 1; Henry D. Shapiro, "Neighborhood and the Family: The Larger Setting. The Emergence of Ideas and Their Implications," in *Home and Family in the 1980s: Insights from Past, Present, and Future*, ed. Thomas H. Jenkins (Cincinnati: Better Housing League of Greater Cincinnati, 1981), esp. 45–46.

8. See L. B. Blackmore, clerk of council, and Carl G. Werner, codifier, *Charter (Adopted 1926) and Code of Ordinances (Revised June 28, 1928) of the City of Cincinnati* (Cincinnati: Council of the City of Cincinnati, Ohio, 1928), 9–34, and esp. 18–21 (on the planning commission). This form of government seems not to have stifled the neighborhood organization movement. The Federated Civic Association, for example, persisted into the 1950s, the decade of the repeal of proportional representation but not other important features of the charter of 1926. The association incorporated in 1927 and consisted in 1937 of fifty-five constituent organizations (forty-four of them from within the city of Cincinnati, claiming a combined membership of 45,000 to 50,000 people, including women by this time). That same year the association adopted a twenty-five project program. It also claimed to accept suggestions from its affiliate for projects but supported only those deemed for "the common good of the Community." Federated Civic Association, *Thirteenth Anniversary Souvenir and History of the Federated Civic Association and Its Fifty-five Affiliated Organizations of Hamilton County* (Cincinnati: Federated Civic Association, 1937 [copy in the Rare Book Department, the Pub-

lic Library of Cincinnati and Hamilton County]), 2–3, 10, 15–22, 45, 49, 53. This book contains no reference to the existence of a civic association representing Clifton.

9. CCPC, *Official Plan,* 17, 276.
10. Ibid., 250.
11. Ibid., 26.
12. Ibid., 26–28.
13. Ibid., 160–61, 166, 170–71, 176–78, 190, 197–98.
14. Fairbanks, *Making Better Citizens,* 46. The metropolitan planners of this era thought of the city in terms of dynamic equilibrium or homeostasis. They believed that particular localities within the metropolis inevitably changed functions with the growth of the city, but that a function or functions that left one locality appeared somewhere else. In case this process sometimes failed to occur naturally, homeostasis might be restored by the intervention of the planners, either to restore a lost function, remove an "intruding" function from an improper context, or to prepare a locality to receive an appropriate function. Planners, as noted in the discussion below of Clifton's future, applied this idea to residential land use types as well as to commercial, industrial, and residential land use districts generally.
15. CCPC, *Official Plan,* 210.
16. Ibid., 210–11. On Mariemont see also Bradley Cross, "New Jerusalems for a New World: The Garden City Idea in Modern Town Planning Thought and Practice in Britain, Canada, and the United States, 1900–1970" (Ph.D. diss., University of Cincinnati, 1997), part 3.
17. CCPC, *Official Plan,* 52–53. The plan contended that "well over three-quarters of the area of the city" remained undeveloped, leaving plenty of room for "the expansion of housing in general" (32). An observer of Cincinnati real estate prices in the 1920s noted that the large number of "suburban" subdivisions in the late nineteenth century held down the price of lots for so long that "only now . . . [are] prices for suburban lots . . . being obtained that should have prevailed for many years." He believed that prices for this kind of property had been even lower in Cincinnati than in much smaller cities. Hiram S. Mathews [untitled insert] in *Greater Cincinnati and Its People: A History,* ed. Lewis Alexander Leonard (New York: Lewis Historical, 1927), 2:703. Mathews probably used the word *suburban* to refer to subdivisions outside the basin but within the city of Cincinnati, as well as ones farther out.
18. The lobbying effort included sending to city council's city planning committee 150 letters protesting a proposed district for two-family houses. Robert A. Burnham, "Cincinnati's First Zoning Ordinance" (Cincinnati: Laboratory in American Civilization, Department of History, University of Cincinnati, May 31, 1983), 4–6.
19. Federated Civic Association, *Thirteenth Anniversary Souvenir.* This document notes that the association incorporated in 1927 and continued in 1937 as before to help affiliates secure "large projects" and to investigate and pursue questions affecting the welfare of the whole community. Nonetheless, the neighborhood improvement association movement within the city declined generally in vitality during the 1920s and 1930s, especially the extent to which associations initiated requests for particular physical improvements, a task they forfeited to the planners at city hall. See Lyle Koehler, "Westwood in [Cincinnati] Ohio: Community, Continuity, and Change" (Department of Archives and Rare Books, Blegen Library, University of Cincinnati, 1980), 98–105.

20. William Applebaum, *The Secondary Commercial Centers of Cincinnati* (Cincinnati: Institute for Industrial Research, for the Commercial Club of Cincinnati, June 10, 1932), 70–71. The population of the territory that once constituted the village of Clifton rose from 4,300 in 1920, to 6,343 in 1930, and to 6,528 in 1940. If you add to that territory the land south of Ludlow that came to be considered part of Clifton, the figures read 5,450 for 1920, 7,996 for 1930, and 8,340 for 1940. See Quinn, Eubank, and Elliott, *Population Changes*, 12–13.

21. Applebaum, *Secondary Commercial Centers*, 1.

22. Ibid., 48–51, 58–59, 71–72 and, for a map of the district, 84.

23. Writers' Program of the Work Projects Administration in the State of Ohio, *Cincinnati: A Guide to the Queen City and Its Neighbors* (Cincinnati: Wiesen-Hart Press, 1943). The spine of the book carried the title *The Cincinnati Guide*.

24. Ibid., viii, xix. For more information about Graff, see the reprint of this guide put out by the Cincinnati Historical Society in 1987.

25. Ibid., xx–xxiii.

26. Ibid., p. xxii.

27. Ibid., p. xx.

28. Ibid., p. 371.

29. Ibid.

30. Ibid., 374–81.

31. Ibid., 381–82.

32. Ibid., 383–91.

33. CCPC, *Residential Areas: An Analysis of Land Requirements for Residential Development, 1945–1970* (Cincinnati: CCPC, 1946), 127, 133.

34. CCPC, *The Cincinnati Metropolitan Master Plan and the Official City Plan* (Cincinnati: CCPC, 1948), 9; CCPC, *Residential Areas*, 48.

35. CCPC, *Residential Areas*, 17–18.

36. CCPC, *Communities: A Study of Community and Neighborhood Development* (Cincinnati: CCPC, December 1947), 52.

37. CCPC, *Cincinnati Metropolitan Master Plan*, 10.

38. CCPC, *The Economy of the Cincinnati Metropolitan Area* (Cincinnati: CCPC, 1946), 63–71.

39. CCPC, *Cincinnati Metropolitan Master Plan*, 11, 27–34, fig. 17. For a good black-and-white map of the communities and their constituent neighborhoods, see CCPC, *Residential Areas*, 16.

40. CCPC, *Communities*, 2–6.

41. Ibid., 6, 21–22.

42. Ibid., 21–22

43. Ibid., 9.

44. Ibid., 52–53.

45. CCPC, *Cincinnati Metropolitan Master Plan*, fig. 10.

46. CCPC, *Communities*, 53.

47. Ibid., p. 55. In 1952, the Hughes High School (a comprehensive, as opposed to a vocational, school district) drew not only from Clifton School but also from a territory served by the Central Fairmount, Chase, College Hill, Columbian, Fairview, Sayler Park, Schiel, South Avondale, Garfield, Hartwell, Kirby Road, North Avondale, Roosevelt,

Taft, Washington, Winton Place Elementary Schools and parts of the Bond Hill, Heberle, Roselawn, and Vine Street Elementary School districts. In addition, pupils from Central Fairmount, North Fairmount, and Sayler Park could choose between Western Hills or Hughes High Schools, and pupils living in the North and South Avondale elementary districts but east of Reading Road could choose between Withrow and Hughes High School. "Planning Your Future, Cincinnati High Schools," pamphlet, p. 22, in sec. D-4, Cincinnati Board of Education, Research Department Projects, 1951–52, vol. 2, secs. D-G, Offices of the Cincinnati Board of Education. In 1950–51, Hughes enrolled 1,540 students, 86 of them (5.58 percent) African American, and Clifton Elementary enrolled 533 pupils, none of them African American. See "Memberships, Percent, and Number of Negro Pupils, by School, Cincinnati Public Schools, 1950–51, 1960–61, 1963–64, and 1964–65," Office of Joseph Timmons, Head of the Administrative Research Section of the Evaluation Branch, Office of the Superintendent, Cincinnati Public Schools.

48. CCPC, *Communities*, 55–56.
49. See ibid., fig. 10B, for a map of the community civic center.
50. CCPC, *The Cincinnati Metropolitan Master Plan*, 82–84.
51. On the creation of Cincinnati's second ghetto, see Charles Casey-Leininger, "Making the Second Ghetto in Cincinnati, Avondale, 1925–1970" (master's thesis, University of Cincinnati, 1989), chs. 1–3.
52. Harlow, *Serene Cincinnatians*, esp. 413–19.
53. Public Library of Cincinnati and Hamilton County, newspaper clippings on Cincinnati, vol. 60, pp. 7–17, from *Cincinnati Enquirer Pictorial Magazine*, April 10, 1949; James Ratcliff, "Castles of Clifton's Barons Are Still Fit for Kings," *Cincinnati Enquirer*, April 10, 1949, sec. 3, p. 1.
54. Public Library of Cincinnati and Hamilton County, newspaper clippings on Cincinnati, vol. 60, pp. 11, 17, from the *Cincinnati Enquirer*, May 1, 1949.
55. Public Library of Cincinnati and Hamilton County, newspaper clippings on Cincinnati, vol. 71, pp. 25–26, from *Cincinnati Times-Star*, October 14, 1950.

Chapter Three

1. The federal Housing Act of 1954 placed more emphasis on the conservation and rehabilitation of old neighborhoods than on slum clearance and redevelopment, and stressed, albeit in vague language, the importance of securing the participation of citizens in the planning process. That same year, President Dwight D. Eisenhower led in the creation of the American Council to Improve Our Neighborhoods (ACTION) to promote the goals of the Housing Act of 1954, including conservation and citizen participation. See Mel Scott, *American City Planning since 1890* (Berkeley: University of California Press, 1971), 501–4. It should be remembered, however, that the Cincinnati metropolitan master plan of 1948 laid out a program for the conservation of some old neighborhoods, but only as a temporary step to forestall the inevitable decay of the neighborhood and its scheduling for clearance and redevelopment.

The new emphasis on citizen participation in neighborhood planning and implementation stemmed in the final analysis from growth after the mid-1930s which led in the 1950s to the abandonment of the racial and/or social determinism of culture on which both totalitarianism and metropolitan master planning rested. The revulsion also inaugurated an era of cultural individualism, the notion that individuals should be free to define their own lifestyles and to choose or design social and physical environments, including neighborhoods and nations, compatible with their lifestyles. See Miller and Tucker, *Changing Plans for America's Inner Cities,* esp. xvii–xviii, 43–46. For a corroborative but rather different take on the mid-twentieth-century thinking about democracy and the consequences of the new thinking, see Edward A. Purcell Jr., *The Crisis of Democratic Theory: Scientific Naturalism and the Problem of Value* (Lexington: University Press of Kentucky, 1973), parts 3 and 4.

2. Andrea Tuttle Kornbluh, "Clifton Meadows, Inc.," 1–3, 7, Clifton project files, n.d., Department of History, McMicken College of Arts and Sciences, University of Cincinnati (hereafter referred to as Clifton project files). Clifton Meadows apparently was a trendsetter. In the 1950s, the Yellow Pages of the phone book carried no entry for such community recreational clubs. It listed them for the first time in 1962 under the entry, "Swim Clubs, Private." There were nine such clubs in 1962, seventeen in 1963, twenty-five in 1964, thirty in 1965, and thirty-two in 1970. Ironically, the bulk of them were outside the city of Cincinnati.

3. CCPC, *Communities: A Study of Neighborhood and Community Development* (Cincinnati: CCPC, December 1947), 129.

4. Zane L. Miller and Geoffrey Giglierano, "Downtown Housing: Changing Plans and Perspectives," *Cincinnati Historical Society Bulletin* 40, no. 3 (fall 1982): 176.

5. At the same time, Warner was constructing on Mount Adams a luxury high-rise apartment embellished with a swimming pool and a view of downtown. Ibid., 176–177.

6. Ibid., 177–82.

7. Martha S. Reynolds, "The City, Suburbs, and the Establishment of Clifton Town Meeting, 1961–1964," *Cincinnati Historical Society Bulletin* 38, no. 1 (spring 1980): 9. On the creation of and other responses to the spread of the second ghetto in Cincinnati, see Miller, *Suburb,* 8–27; Robert B. Fairbanks and Zane L. Miller, "The Martial Metropolis: Housing, Planning, and Race in Cincinnati, 1940–1955," in *The Martial Metropolis: U.S. Cities in War and Peace,* ed. Roger W. Lotchin (New York: Praeger, 1984), 197–213; Charles Casey-Leininger, "Creating Democracy in Housing: Civil Rights and Housing Policy in Cincinnati, 1945–1980" (Ph.D. diss., University of Cincinnati, 1993). For a study of another city, see Arnold R. Hirsch, *Making the Second Ghetto: Race and Housing in Chicago, 1940–1960* (Cambridge: Cambridge University Press, 1983).

8. The Cincinnati Citizens Development Committee, which represented Cincinnati's largest business corporations, pushed for the renewal of Avondale and Corryville to "save" the University of Cincinnati and especially its medical center, despite acknowledged problems in finding relocation housing for persons displaced from this and other renewal and redevelopment projects. See George Stimson, "They Cared—The Citizens Development Committee, 1948–1968," 100–106, 116–122, Citizens Development Committee Collection, Cincinnati Historical Society.

9. Turn-of-the-century neighborhood organizations focused their educational efforts chiefly on a public *outside* the neighborhood, namely, the city government and voters in city elections. Between 1920 and 1950, the emphasis shifted inward to communities in the 20,000 to 40,000 population range, and after 1950 local civic education focused on individuals in the neighborhood area.

10. CCPC, *Avondale-Corryville General Neighborhood Renewal Plan* (Cincinnati: CCPC, 1960). See ch. 3, "Mutual Assistance Program," for the plan's neighborhood organization component, and p. 54 for the office district.

11. Reynolds, "The City, Suburbs," 8; Philip Walters, "My Years with Clifton Town Meeting," pp. 1–2, Clifton project files, ca. 1991. The ghettoization of south Avondale and the plan for Avondale-Corryville attracted a similar kind of attention in North Avondale. See Gary P. Kocolowski, "The History of North Avondale: A Study of the Effects of Urbanization upon an Urban Locality" (master's thesis, University of Cincinnati, 1971), ch. 3.

12. Reynolds, "The City, Suburbs," 11–12, 15–17.

13. Mrs. Van Meter Ames to Marshall Bragdon, director, Mayor's Friendly Relations Committee, May 22, 1962, CTM Papers (US-77-7), box 3, folder 30; Walters, "My Years with CTM," 6–7. On this point it is useful to remember that during the early 1960s the Greater Cincinnati Committee for Equal Opportunity in Housing lobbied the state legislature for the passage of a fair housing bill. The CTM Papers contain an undated copy of the committee's newsletter explaining the provisions of the bill and listing endorsements of the measure, including those of the Cincinnati city manager and city council. See CTM Papers (US-77-7), box 3, folder 30.

14. C. A. Harrell, city manager, to city council highway committee, Jan. 22, 1962, CTM Papers (US-77-7), box 8, folder 72. CTM leaders continued to monitor developments in Avondale-Corryville. See "Notes on Lecture, 'Control Measures in Planning,'" by Herbert Stevens, director of planning for Cincinnati, May 23, 1961, and Cincinnati Department of Urban Development, *Urban Renewal Plan: Avondale I-Corryville, Ohio R-6* (Cincinnati: Department of Urban Development, April 1961), CTM Papers (US-77-7), box 7, folder 68.

15. Memo, "As a result of discussion at meeting [of] July 25, 1961, at 5 P.M., home of Mrs. Sidney Miller," CTM Papers (US-77-7), box 8, folder 73.

16. Community meeting minutes, September 21, 1961, CTM Papers (US-77-7), box 3, folder 22.

17. C. A. Harrell to highway committee, January 22, 1962, CTM Papers (US-77-7), box 8, folder 72.

18. CTM constitution and bylaws, 1962, CTM Papers (US-77-7), box 1, folder 1.

19. Reynolds, "The City, Suburbs," 14.

20. CTM Papers (US-77-7), box 1, folders 5, 19, 20; Philip Walters to Zane L. Miller, interview, spring 1980. Juergens Avenue posed a particularly nettlesome and intractable problem. CTM representatives first met with residents of the street on May 28, 1962, and the organization kept a file of reports on the street's problems. These ranged from the absence of sidewalks and curbs to the presence of unsupervised teenage girls and their boyfriends. A special report in July 1964 noted that some residents of Juergens wanted to move out. They complained of too many children on the street, litter and loafing, fast automobiles, and the "proximity of Negro areas," which "keep property owners uneasy and [make] renters of the more permanent type . . . hard to find." See "Juergens Ave., . . . Report of July 3, 1964," CTM Papers (US-77-7), box 3, folder 35, and the other material in this folder.

21. "Negroes Next Door No Cause for Panic," Cincinnati *Catholic Telegraph-Reporter,* October 13, 1961, CTM Papers (US-77-7), box 8, folder 79; George Martin to

Mrs. Joseph Sagmaster, December 31, 1961 [a letter inviting CTM representatives to attend a North Avondale Neighborhood Association (NANA) meeting and enclosing a copy of *NANA News*, the organization's newsletter]; "A Report of Meeting of Kennedy Heights Neighborhood Assn.," May 18 [1962]; "Notes on East Walnut Hills Groups (no name yet)," November 1962; "What Is NANA?" ca. 1962. All of these found in CTM Papers (US-77-7), box 8, folder 79.

22. Draft of report made by E. K. McGee, hand notes, ca. 1962, CTM Papers (US-77-7), box 7, folder 68. McGee began his report by citing an attack on city planners by Robert L. Zion in the *New York Times Sunday Magazine*, June 1, 1962.

23. A board member of Clifton Enterprises resigned from the board of CTM to keep CTM "independent" of the real estate venture. Unsigned letter to "Dear Betty [Ames], September 16, 1962, CTM Papers (US-77-7), box 6, folder 62. See also "Progress Report . . . from the Board of Directors," Clifton Enterprises, Inc., ca. 1962, CTM Papers box 3, folder 34; Walters, "My Years with CTM," 6–7.

24. "Race and Reconciliation," sermon by Thomas W. Clayton, assistant minister, Immanuel Presbyterian Church, Cincinnati, August 5, 1962, CTM Papers (US-77-7), box 3, folder 30. Clayton wrote a note in the margin of this copy of his manuscript which said, "Thanks so much for the loan of . . . Town Meeting material."

25. John C. Vaughan, executive director, Better Housing League, "Housing for Negroes in Cincinnati, 1962," May 1962, CTM Papers (US-77-7), box 8, folder 74; Advance Mortgage Corporation, *Midwestern Minority Housing Markets: A Special Report*, December 1, 1962, CTM Papers (US-77-7), box 6, folder 57.

26. "Statement made by Mrs. Sagmaster at the hearing before Council on . . . the 'Shaker Heights' ordinance," May 1962, CTM Papers (US-77-7), box 3, folder 30. A representative of NANA said at the hearing that such tactics had been used in Cincinnati since 1954. *Cincinnati Post and Times-Star*, May 22, 1962, clipping, CTM Papers, box 3, folder 30. A month later, however, CTM refused to testify at an Ohio Civil Rights Commission hearing on housing discrimination in Cincinnati on the grounds that questions of "social planning" lay beyond the organization's competence. Mrs. Joseph Sagmaster to Albert J. Dellihay, June 21, 1962, CTM Papers (US-77-7), box 6, folder 62.

27. Mrs. Van Meter Ames to Marshall Bragdon, May 22, 1962, CTM Papers (US-77-7), box 3, folder 30.

28. Betty B. Ames, "Zoning," April 18, 1962, CTM Papers (US-77-7), box 6, folder 62.

29. Betty B. Ames to Erwin E. Hoffman (CCPC staff member), November 23, 1962, CTM Papers (US-77-7), box 6, folder 62.

30. Memo, "Dear Skippy," n.d., and *Cincinnati Enquirer*, January 9, 1962, clipping, CTM Papers (US-77-7), box 7, folder 70.

31. CTM board minutes, October 1963, CTM Papers (US-77-7), box 1, folder 5.

32. Philip G. Walters to Mrs. Donald Ross, October 17, 1963, and Francis L. Dale to Leo J. Brumleve, November 6, 1963, CTM Papers (US-77-7), box 7, folder 65.

33. General meeting minutes, May 7, 1963, CTM Papers (US-77-7), box 2, folder 1; zoning committee report, 1964, 1–2, CTM Papers (US-77-7), box 2, folder 1.

34. Walters, "My Years with CTM," 9–10.

35. Mrs. H. Rodenberg to I. A. Holdern, n.d., CTM Papers (US-77-7), box 2, folder 3; Mrs. Joseph Sagmaster, as quoted in *North Cincinnati Community News*, April 13, 1962, clipping, CTM Papers (US-77-7), box 1, folder 3.

36. CTM Papers (US-77-7), box 1, folder 3, box 5, folders 49 and 52; CTM board minutes, special meeting, April 28, 1965, CTM Papers (US-77-7), box 1, folder 1; Reynolds, "The City, Suburbs," 19–22; Tweddell and Wheeler, architects, AIA, "Study of the Problems Dealing with Residential Street Lighting," September 29, 1965, esp. p. 10, CTM Papers (US-77-7), box 5, folder 51.

37. CTM *Bulletin,* January 1964, p. 3; CTM Papers (US-77-7), box 4, folder 41; Mrs. Joseph Sagmaster to the National Trust for Historic Preservation, April 23, 1962, CTM Papers (US-77-7), box 3, folder 21.

38. CTM *Bulletin,* March-August 1963, CTM Papers (US-77-7), box 4, folder 41.

39. CTM *Bulletin,* November 1963, p. 2, CTM Papers (US-77-7), box 4, folder 41.

40. Mrs. Donald Ross to Mrs. Cramer, March 20, 1964; CTM to Al Schottelkotte, news director, WCPO-TV, n.d.; CTM, "Clifton Home Beautiful Tour," n.d., CTM Papers (US-83-3), box 6, folder 1. This folder also contains letters about the tour to Concordia Lutheran, Annunciation, Immanuel Presbyterian, Clifton Methodist, Calvary Episcopal, and the Clifton Church of Christ. Concerns about the spread of blight on Cincinnati's east side prompted the City Planning Commission to publish in 1964 a study of the structural integrity and conversion to other uses of old single-family detached houses, especially their conversion to multifamily use, considered a dangerous sign of neighborhood decay. Clifton fared well on both scores, and investigators even found examples of reconversion to single-family use of houses once changed to multifamily status. See Cincinnati City Planning Commission, *A Study of the Large Old Single-Family Houses in Cincinnati* (Cincinnati: CCPC, August 1964), 4, 12.

41. W. G. Roeseler, AIP, consultant, city planner, Ladislas Segoe and Associates, to CTM steering committee, September 21, 1961, CTM Papers (US-77-7), box 1, folder 2.

42. Kenneth E. Corey, *The Clifton Community Plan: Existing Conditions and Analysis of the Clifton Community* (Cincinnati: Division of Community Assistance, CCPC, ca. 1976), I-4, I-5, I-6.

43. Ibid., I-3; Mrs. Joseph Sagmaster to Robert Curry, February 5, 1963, and "Report of Meeting Between Representatives of the City Planning Department and the CTM, April 16, 1964, at City Hall," CTM Papers (US-77-7), box 1, folder 4; Reynolds, "The City, Suburbs," 23–29.

44. B. L. Abernathy to City Planning Commission, April 24, 1964, CTM Papers (US-77-7), box 1, folder 6.

45. Mrs. Joseph Sagmaster to City Planning Commission, April 27, 1964 and minutes, CTM planning committee, May 19, 1964, July 6, 1964, CTM Papers (US-77-7), box 1, folder 6.

46. Corey, *Clifton Community Plan,* I-7, I-8.

47. Mrs. Joseph Sagmaster to Willis D. Gradison, October 11, 1963, CTM Papers (US-77-7), box 3, folder 21.

48. Zoning committee report, 1964, p. 3, CTM Papers (US-77-7), box 2, folder 51.

Chapter Four

1. "Annual Survey: Housing," p. 1, Jewish Community Relations Committee (JCRC) Papers, American Jewish Archives, Collection #202, box 19, file 5; Jerry Belenker to Arnold Aronson, January 28, 1959, 1–3, JCRC Papers, Collection #202, box 20, file 1;

JCRC to Ohio Advisory Commission of the U.S. Commission on Civil Rights, March 20, 1959, 1–3, JCRC Papers, Collection #202, box 20, file 3; Regine Ransohoff to Zane L. Miller, December 1998, Clifton project files; Richard D. Spoor to Zane L. Miller, conversation, December 1998. CTM zoning committee, report, 1964, 2–3, CTM Papers (US-77-7), box 2, folder 51. My sense of religious tensions and residential patterns in Clifton derives from the experience of Henry D. Shapiro and myself as residents of the neighborhood during these years. American universities did not hire significant numbers of Jews as faculty members until the second half of the twentieth century. For an explanation of this phenomenon that also explores some of its consequences (but not its effects on urban residential patterns), see David A. Hollinger, *Science, Jews, and Secular Culture: Studies in Mid-Twentieth-Century American Intellectual History* (Princeton: Princeton University Press, 1996).

2. Tommy West, "Stress: Clifton," *Cincinnati Enquirer Magazine*, February 7, 1971, p. 6. West concluded that Clifton had changed. "It still has many of its beautiful old homes, but many of them are now apartment buildings. It still has its solid, conservative citizenry, but it also has its 'counter-culturists.' And every night, the old gas lights wink on to illuminate the changing face of one of Cincinnati's oldest and most historic communities."

3. CTM *Bulletin*, June-July 1966, p. 1; February 1966, p. 1; December 1966, p. 1; January 1968, pp. 1–2; June 1970, p. 2; report of the president, annual meeting, May 19, 1971, p. 1, all in CTM Papers (US-77-7), box 3, folder 22.

4. Walters, "My Years with Clifton Town Meeting," 14–15; S. Arthur Spiegel, "Hey Boys, Meet Your Dad!" 1993, pp. 289–90, in possession of S. Arthur Spiegel; David Lee Smith to Zane L. Miller, telephone interview, August 4, 1993, notes in Clifton project files. Spiegel compared the Ludlow Garage to Filmore East in New Jersey and Filmore West in San Francisco, and occasionally attended concerts at the Garage with his sons. He identified the financial backer of the project as Robert Stern of the U.S. Shoe Corporation. David Lee Smith, a faculty member at the University of Cincinnati, served as architect for Tarbell.

5. CTM *Bulletin*, February 1966, p. 1; June-July 1966, p. 1; January 1969, pp. 1–2; Theodore Hattemer to Mrs. Walter Langsam, March 7, 1966, CTM Papers (US-77-7), box 2, folder 15; John K. Rose to city council, March 11, 1966, CTM Papers (US-77-7), box 2, folder 19; CCPC, *A Report on the Traffic Survey of Clifton Ave., McAlpin Ave., and Woolper Ave.* (CCPC, April 1964), esp. 22–25. The city's traffic planners did not abandon plans to straighten the McAlpin-Clifton-Woolper intersection until 1979. After consultation with CTM, the city put on the market a house on the corner of Woolper and Clifton it acquired in 1953 in preparation for the improvement. See CTM board minutes, May 7, 1979, p. 2, CTM Papers (US-83-3), box 1, folder 46; CTM executive committee minutes, July 2, 1979, p. 2, CTM Papers (US-83-3), box 2, folder 11; CTM board minutes, March 2, 1981, p. 2, CTM Papers (US-88-18), box 1, folder 13.

6. CTM *Bulletin*, October 1968, p. 2.
7. CTM *Bulletin*, March 1967, p. 1; November 1967, p. 1; March 1968, p. 1.
8. Special events committee report, n.d., CTM Papers (US-77-7), box 6, folder 36.
9. CTM *Bulletin*, May 1965, CTM Papers (US-77-7), box 6, folder 36.
10. CTM *Bulletin*, clipping, n.d., CTM Papers (US-77-7), box 6, folder 36.
11. Walters, "My Years with CTM," 14.

12. Kathryn M. Borman and Joel H. Spring, *Schools in Central Cities: Structures and Process* (New York: Longman, 1984), 56–61; W. A. Montgomery, "Racial History of the Cincinnati and Suburban Public Schools, as It Has Been Influenced by Instances of Discriminatory Intent and Purpose," November 13, 1978, pp. 153, 156, 159, 169–70, 177, Urban Studies Collection, Department of Archives and Rare Books, University of Cincinnati Libraries.

13. *Cincinnati Post,* March 4, 1969, p. 22; *Cincinnati Enquirer,* March 5, 1969, p. 17.

14. Spiegel, "Hey Boys, Meet Your Dad!" 244–46, 288–89. Spiegel brought the action under the Civil Rights Act of 1866.

15. *Cincinnati Enquirer,* February 25, 1970, p. 13.

16. CTM *Bulletin,* June-July 1966, p. 2; January 1967, p. 2.

17. CTM *Bulletin,* February 1967, p. 1; March 1967, p. 2; January 1968. A Cliftonite served as the first president of the district foundation, known as the Cincinnati School Foundation. See CTM *Bulletin,* February 1968, p. 1.

18. CTM *Bulletin,* May 1967, p. 2.

19. CTM *Bulletin,* September 1968, p. 1.

20. CTM *Bulletin,* October 1968, pp. 1–2.

21. CTM *Bulletin,* February 1969, pp. 1, 2.

22. CTM *Bulletin,* March 1969, pp. 1–2.

23. CTM *Bulletin,* May 1969, p. 1; June 1969, p. 2. CTM dropped its affiliation with the Citizens School Committee in 1973. CTM board minutes, August 27, 1973, 2–3, CTM Papers (US-77-7), box 2, folder 18.

24. Education committee minutes, November 21, 1973, p. 2, CTM Papers (US-83-3), box 2, folder 8; *Cincinnati Post,* May 10, 1973, clipping, CTM Papers (US-83-3), box 5, folder 7. In 1979, the CTM education committee judged both elementary schools as "excellent academically." Education committee minutes, August 9, 1979, CTM Papers (US-88-18), box 1, folder 35.

25. CTM *Bulletin,* June 1970, pp. 1–2.

26. CTM *Bulletin,* June 1969, p. 2; October 1969, p. 2; December 1969, p. 1; April 1970, p. 2.

27. CTM *Bulletin,* February 1970, p. 2; March 1970, p. 2; November 1970, p. 2; February 1971, p. 1; March 1971, p. 2; CTM board minutes, June 5, 1972, p. 2, CTM Papers (US-83-3), box 1, folder 20; open meeting minutes, November 28, 1972, CTM Papers (US-83-3), box 1, folder 3. The board voted against locating a mental rehabilitation outpatient center in Clifton. CTM board minutes, November 6, 1972, p. 2, CTM Papers (US-83-3), box 1, folder 22.

28. CTM *Bulletin,* November 1969, p. 2; December 1969, pp. 1, 3.

29. CTM *Bulletin,* March 1970, pp. 1, 2–3; May 1970, pp. 2–3; June 1970, p. 2.

30. CTM *Bulletin,* June 1970, p. 3; October 1970, p. 2; November 1970, p. 2.

31. CTM board minutes, May 3, 1971, p. 2, and June 7, 1971, both in CTM Papers (US-83-3), box 1, folder 16.

32. CTM board minutes, May-June 1972, box 1, folder 20; board minutes, July 10, 1972, p. 1, box 1, folder 21; board minutes, November 6, 1972, pp. 2–3, box 1, folder 22, all in CTM Papers (US-83-3); CTM board minutes, January 17, 1973, p. 2, February 5, 1973, p. 2, March 5, 1973, p. 2, and December 3, 1973, p. 2, all in CTM Papers, box 2, folder 18; CTM *Bulletin,* January 1973, p. 2.

33. CTM *Bulletin,* January-February 1974, p. 1; March 1974, p. 1.

34. CTM board minutes, September 13, 1971, CTM Papers (US-83-3), box 1, folder 17.

35. Max C. Fleischmann, of the famous yeast family, sold his ten-acre estate, Edgewood, which adjoined Sacred Heart, to the Academy in 1920. The convent and the Academy moved to Clifton in 1876. See Cincinnati Hillside Landmark Grant Request, documentation, 1974, report on the Fleischmann Estate, CTM Papers (US-83-3), box 5, folder 7. On the Institute and the Sacred Heart part of the proposal, see E. Pope Coleman to Max C. Fleischmann Foundation, CTM Papers (US-83-3), box 5, folder 1.

36. CTM board minutes, May 7, 1973, p. 1, CTM Papers (US-77-7), box 2, folder 18; CTM *Bulletin,* March 1973, p. 3.

37. CTM board minutes, November 5, 1973, CTM Papers (US-77-7), box 2, folder 18.

38. Glaser and Meyers and Associates, Inc., *A Community Recreation Facilities Master Plan Study,* Study Area II, Clifton, Clifton Heights–Fairview, Corryville, University Heights (prepared for the Cincinnati Recreation Commission, September 1974), esp. pp. 16, 28.

39. J. Kenneth Dysart to Dear Councilmember, February 21, 1974, and Betty Ames to Dear Charley [Taft], March 11, 1974, both in CTM Papers (US-77-7), box 2, folder 20; CTM *Bulletin,* April 1974, p. 2; CTM board minutes, October 7, 1974, CTM Papers (US-77-7), box 2, folder 18.

40. CTM *Bulletin,* February 1972, p. 1, and summer 1972, p. 1; CTM board minutes, March 1972, p. 1, and CTM special meeting minutes, March 24, 1972, p. 1, both in CTM Papers (US-88-18), box 1, folder 7.

41. CTM board minutes, July 10, 1972, p. 1, CTM Papers (US-88-18), box 1, folder 7.

42. Real Estate Research Corporation, "City-Wide Economic Trends: Cincinnati Housing Strategy, Position Paper #7," April 13, 1973, pp. 1–3. The report noted that manufacturing was leaving the city, that the commercial, governmental, and service sectors were growing, and that as the tax base and population declined after 1960, government expenditures grew. Another report by the same firm contended that Cincinnati could not compete with its suburbs' new single-family homes because of high land costs and because its schools had too many blacks and low-income students and an excess of older buildings. It would therefore have to rely on the construction of multifamily dwellings to increase its housing stock. It also noted that Cincinnati had lower real estate taxes than almost all major cities in the United States and that its school taxes ranked below those of all major northern cities. See Real Estate Research Corp., "Cincinnati Residential Competitive Position: Cincinnati Housing Research Strategy, Position Paper #8," pp. 1–4, April 13, 1973, CTM Papers (US-77-7), box 5, folder 56.

43. In 1970, city council passed a resolution recognizing the decline of neighborhood business districts in the face of suburban shopping center competition and declaring it city policy to plan and carry out a program to improve the city's neighborhood business districts. See CCPC, *Neighborhood Business District Study: Inventory of Existing Conditions* (Cincinnati: CCPC, December 1970), p. 1. For an account of the progress in this area of activity to 1978, see CCPC, *Neighborhood Business Districts: Background, Current Status, and Recommendations* (Cincinnati: CCPC, October 1978).

44. One 1966 survey listed sixteen typed, double-spaced pages of neighborhood organizations in Cincinnati and Hamilton County. Better Housing League of Cincinnati

and Hamilton County, "Greater Cincinnati Neighborhood Organization Survey," December 1966, CTM Papers (US-77-7), box 7, folder 74.

45. Cincinnati Department of Urban Development, Development Services Division, *From Housing Rehabilitation to Neighborhood Development* (Cincinnati: Department of Urban Development, September 1972), 1, 21, 2.

46. Ibid., 96–104, esp. 100–104.

47. Pat Crum, public information subcommittee, working review committee on housing, "A Comprehensive Strategy for the City of Cincinnati," August 1973, pp. 1–3, CTM Papers (US-77-7), box 5, folder 56; CTM *Bulletin,* December, 1971, p. 4.

48. Real Estate Research Corporation, "Concept of Community Balance: Cincinnati Housing Strategy, Position Paper #10," June 29, 1972, pp. 1–2, CTM Papers (US-77-7), box 6, folder 56.

49. See the Real Estate Research Corporation position papers in the CTM Papers (US-77-7), box 5, folder 56 and box 6, folder 56. See also Anthony Downs, *Neighborhoods and Urban Development* (Washington, D.C.: Brookings Institution, 1981), esp. 86–102. It should be noted that Downs's conceptual apparatus did not permit him to discuss stable, racially integrated neighborhoods, only "transitional" ones, those in passage from white to black, from middle to low income, from health to deterioration.

50. CTM board minutes, October 1, 1973, p. 1, and November 5, 1973, p. 2, CTM Papers (US-77-7) box 2, folder 18; working review committee on housing, "On the Horizon: A Housing Strategy for Cincinnati," December 8, 1973, CTM Papers, box 1, folder 8; CTM *Bulletin,* November 1973, p. 2, and January 1975, p. 2.

51. Real Estate Research Corporation, "Concept of Community Balance," 21–24; Real Estate Research Corporation, "Description and Partial Analysis of Cincinnati's 44 Statistical Areas: Cincinnati Housing Strategy, Position Paper #9," May 18, 1973, CTM Papers (US-77-7), box 5, folder 56; Real Estate Research Corporation, "Inventory of Means of Action: Cincinnati Housing Strategy, Position Papers #11," October 19, 1973, pp. 5–6, CTM Papers (US-77-7), box 6, folder 56. The working review committee submitted to the city manager a draft resolution for city council to endorse the committee's report on October 29, 1974. Arnold J. Rosenmeyer to E. Robert Turner, October 29, 1974 (copy), CTM Papers (US-77-7), box 5, folder 56.

52. CTM board minutes, November 11, 1972, p. 1, CTM Papers (US-88-18), box 1, folder 7.

53. CTM board minutes, October 1, 1973, 4, 8, CTM Papers (US-77-7), box 2, folder 18; CTM *Bulletin,* June 1973, p. 1, and September 1973, p. 3; Charlotte T. Birdsall, "Project COPE: A Cincinnati Experiment in Citizens Participation" (master's thesis, University of Cincinnati, 1975).

54. CTM board minutes, June 4, 1973, p. 1, CTM Papers (US-77-7), box 2, folder 10.

55. CTM *Bulletin,* April 1973, p. 2.

56. CTM *Bulletin,* June 1973, p. 2.

57. CTM board minutes, October 7, 1974, 1–2, CTM Papers (US-77-7), box 2, folder 18.

58. CTM *Bulletin,* September 1973, p. 1; CTM board minutes, June 25, 1973, p. 3, and August 27, 1973, p. 2, CTM Papers (US-77-7), box 2, folder 18.

59. CTM board minutes, June 4, 1973, p. 2, CTM Papers (US-77-7), box 2, folder 18.

60. CTM *Bulletin,* summer 1974, p. 3.

Chapter Five

1. CTM board minutes, September 9, 1974, p. 4, CTM Papers (US-77-7), box 2, folder 18; CCPC, *The Coordinated City Plan,* vol. 1: *Strategies for Current Physical Development* (Cincinnati: CCPC, 1979), esp. 1–2, and vol. 2: *Strategies for Comprehensive Land Use* (Cincinnati: CCPC, December 1980).

2. For the emergence of this form of city planning and its consequences for another neighborhood, see Miller and Tucker, *Changing Plans for America's Inner Cities,* pt. 2.

3. CTM board minutes, February 3, 1975, p. 1 (US-77-7), box 2, folder 18.

4. CTM planning committee report, October 25, 1974, p. 1 (US-77-7), CTM Papers, box 2, folder 18; "Tentative Objectives for the Clifton Community—Critique," 1974, CTM Papers, box 1, folder 7.

5. CTM *Bulletin,* December 1974, p. 4; CTM planning committee report, January 6, 1975, pp. 1–2, and CTM historic preservation committee report, February 24, 1975, pp. 1–2, both in CTM Papers (US-77-7), box 2, folder 18; CTM *Bulletin,* February 1975, p. 2. For the historic preservation committee, see CTM *Bulletin,* March 1975, p. 2, which also reported that Clifton had seven homes on the National Register and that the preservation committee was considering both Sacred Heart Academy and the Abbe Observatory for such listing. The CTM board endorsed the designation of the Lafayette Avenue Circle area as a historic district in the spring of 1975. See CTM *Bulletin,* April 1975, p. 2.

6. "Neighborhood Profile: Clifton" and working review committee on housing, "Cincinnati Statistical Neighborhoods," map, January 1973, both in CTM Papers, box 1, folder 8.

7. Clifton Town Meeting and Cincinnati City Planning Commission, *The Clifton Community Plan: The First Report of a Planning Series. Goals and Objectives.* (Cincinnati: CCPC, May 1975), 2–3, 4–7, 8–9, 27–32 (hereafter pages cited in text).

8. CTM *Bulletin,* June 1975, p. 1, and September 1975, p. 1; CTM board minutes, September 8, 1975, p. 1, CTM Papers (US-77-7), box 2, folder 18; Pat O'Connor [the Kroger Company] to Barry Wakeman [CTM president], September 15, 1975, CTM Papers (US-77-7), box 2, folder 20.

9. CTM housing and planning committee report, April 1975, CTM Papers (US-77-7), box 2, folder 18.

10. CTM *Bulletin,* October 1975, p. 1, November 1975, p. 2, December 1975, p. 1, January 1976, p. 1; CTM board minutes, October 6, 1975, pp. 1–2, November 3, 1975, p. 1, December 1, 1975, p. 2, CTM Papers (US-77-7), box 2, folder 18; Barry Wakeman to William R. Donaldson [city manager], November 3, 1975, CTM Papers (US-77-7), box 2, folder 20.

11. CTM *Bulletin,* January 1976, p. 1, July 1976, p. 1, August 1976, p. 1, January-February 1977, p. 1; CTM board minutes, August 2, 1976, pp. 10–12, CTM Papers (US-83-3), box 1, folder 27; CTM land use committee minutes, December 15, 1976, CTM Papers (US-83-3), box 2, folder 16; Cincinnati Department of Urban Development, *Clifton Neighborhood Business District Urban Design Plan* (Cincinnati: Department of Urban Development, Approved by Clifton Town Meeting, May 2, 1977), 1 fold-out page, map and text.

12. *Cincinnati Post,* editorial, March 1, 1977, newsclip, CTM Papers (US-83-3), box 5, folder 42. This folder contains two other *Post* articles on the business district plan fight from February 23 and March 10, 1977.

13. Cincinnati Department of Urban Development, *Clifton Neighborhood Business District Urban Design Plan;* CTM *Bulletin,* January-February 1977, p. 1; CTM economic review committee, progress report, February 1977, pp. 1–6, CTM Papers (US-83-3], box 2, folder 22. On the Telford Avenue apartment fight, see Barbara Davis-Venn to Martin P. Walsh Jr., Department of Buildings and Inspections, February 19, 1976, CTM Papers, box 2, folder 15.

14. CTM *Bulletin,* May 1977, p. 1; Barbara Davis-Venn to Clifton residents, April 11, 1977, CTM Papers, box 1, folder 9.

15. CTM *Bulletin,* May 1977, editorial, p. 2, and president's report, p. 3.

16. CTM board minutes, May 2, 1977, pp. 2–3, CTM Papers (US-83-3), box 1, folder 34.

17. H. W. Stevens to City Planning Commission, "Broader Boundaries for the Clifton EQ-UD #2, August 21, 1978," CTM Papers (US-83-3), box 5, folder 11. The Stevens memo contains a map of the compromise boundaries.

18. CCPC, *Coordinated City Plan and Process: Policy Paper* (Cincinnati: CCPC, December 1976, updated, February 1977), esp. i, 1–7, 39.

19. QUEST Research, "The Community Assistance Program: A Report on Its Design and Operations," prepared for the City Planning Commission and the Division of Community Assistance, Office of the City Manager, January 1, 1977, pp. 1–5, CTM Papers (US-88-18), box 3, folder 43. Making the writing of history optional and placing it at the end of the process seems curious, for surely such a task would be useful if not essential in establishing the concept of what a community wanted to become. It should be noted, too, that the CAT neighborhood planning program formed an integral part of the city's new budget process, which established priorities without reference to available revenues and then funded them to the maximum extent possible with available funds. A corollary of the planning part of the process held that the solicitation of community desires and needs had to be comprehensive, that those plans could be amended "at will" or annually, and that the process would "lead to equity among communities." The QUEST analysis concluded that the budget process had not been working well, except for its utility in selecting projects for funding with federal community development money.

20. Kenneth E. Corey, *The Clifton Community Plan: Existing Conditions and Analysis of the Clifton Community* (Cincinnati: CCPC, 1977), 1–8. For the quotes, see p. 1. See also CTM board minutes, October 3, 1977, p. 1, CTM Papers (US-83-3), box 1, folder 35. At this same time the organizers of the annual Clifton house tour arranged for the preparation of a history of Clifton in an undergraduate research seminar conducted by Henry D. Shapiro and Zane L. Miller in the McMicken College of Arts and Sciences at the University of Cincinnati. It appeared as a booklet in 1976 and 1981: Shapiro and Miller, *Clifton: Neighborhood and Community in an Urban Setting.* The production of this booklet convinced us of the feasibility of doing a longer study of Clifton's past.

21. Corey, *Clifton Community Plan,* 8-1 to 8-6.

22. City Planning Commission, *Coordinated City Plan,* 39; Corey, *Clifton Community Plan,* 8–1.

23. Corey, *Clifton Community Plan,* appendix E. This appendix suggested a similarity between the implicit principles guiding Clifton's "early planners" and the principles and concepts of Clarence Perry's neighborhood unit theory, elaborated in the 1920s, and of Ebeneezer Howard's garden city idea, set down at the turn of the century.

Although the appendix did not say so, both Perry and Howard planned for the welfare of the entire urbanized unit, the metropolis, Howard for the purpose of controlling the size of such units and Perry for the purpose of encouraging their expansion in an orderly manner to preserve a sense of community within them. The appendix did contend, however, that the "concepts of Howard and Perry as applied to Clifton need to be re-examined in light of today's context." On Howard and Perry, see Robert F. Fairbanks, *Making Better Citizens,* 50, 192n. 43; and Cross, "New Jerusalems for a New World," esp. ch. 1.

24. David Lee Smith to Charles Collins (HUD), July 29, 1977, CTM Papers, box 3, folder 15; CTM board minutes, December 5, 1977, pp. 2–3, box 1, folder 36; CTM housing and zoning committee minutes, January 12, 1978, p. 2, box 2, folder 15; CTM board minutes, August 17, 1978, p. 1, box 1, folder 39; CTM board minutes, September 10, 1979, p. 2, box 1, folder 47, all in CTM Papers (US-83-3).

25. CTM board minutes, August 2, 1976, p. 4, box 1, folder 27; CTM board minutes, September 22, 1977, p. 1, box 2, folder 18; and CTM Sacred Heart committee minutes, January 23, 1978, p. 1, all in CTM Papers (US-83-3).

26. Betty Ames to Warren Bennis, January 21, 1977, CTM Papers (US-77-7), box 2, folder 20.

27. CTM board minutes, March 3, 1978, p. 1, CTM Papers (US-83-3], box 1, folder 38; CTM board minutes, May 1, 1978, p. 1, 2, box 1, folder 39; CTM board minutes, December 12, 1978, p. 1, box 1, folder 42; CTM board minutes, January 8, 1979, p. 3, box 1, folder 43; "Sacred Heart Development: Planning and Time Phases, January 1, 1979 thru September 30, 1979," n.d., CTM Papers (US-83-3), box 1, folder 41. Also, CTM board minutes, September 10, 1979, p. 2, CTM Papers (US-83-3), box 1, folder 47; CTM board minutes, October 8, 1979, p. 2, CTM Papers (US-83-3), box 1, folder 48; CTM board minutes, November 3, 1980, p. 1, CTM Papers (US-88-18), box 1, folder 12; CTM board minutes, March 2, 1981, p. 2, CTM Papers (US-88-18), box 1, folder 13.

28. CTM executive committee minutes, January 6, 1977, p. 1, February 3, 1977, p. 1, April 1, 1977, p. 1, and September 27, 1977, p. 1, all in CTM Papers (US-88-18), box 1, folder 37; CTM recreation committee report, February 7, 1977, 1–2, CTM Papers (US-83-3), box 2, folder 38; CTM board minutes, September 15, 1977, p. 2–3, CTM Papers (US-83-3), box 1, folder 35. The race issue is not reported in any of the documents in the CTM papers, but both Henry D. Shapiro and I heard it expressed by several residents of Clifton during the contest.

29. CTM board minutes, September 15, 1977, p. 3, CTM Papers (US-83-3), box 1, folder 35; CTM executive committee minutes, September 29, 1977, p. 1, CTM Papers (US-83-3), box 2, folder 1; CTM *Bulletin,* September 1977, p. 6.

30. CTM board minutes, October 3, 1977, pp. 1–2, and October 3, 1977, pp. 1–2, both in CTM Papers (US-88-18), box 1, folder 9; "Resolution, 10/3/77," CTM board minutes, October 3, 1977, p. 3, CTM Papers (US-88-18), box 1, folder 35; CTM *Bulletin,* October 1977, p. 2.

31. CTM *Bulletin,* October 1977, p. 4.

32. CTM board minutes, June 2, 1977, p. 1, CTM Papers (US-83-3), box 1, folder 34; CTM board minutes, December 4, 1978, CTM Papers (US-83-3), box 1, folder 42.

33. CTM board minutes, August 17, 1978, p. 1, box 1, folder 39; May 7, 1979, p. 2,

box 1, folder 46; November 5, 1978, box 1, folder 48; June 9, 1980, box 1, folder 49; and August 4, 1980, box 1, folder 50, all in CTM Papers (US-83-3).

34. CTM board minutes, December 1, 1980, p. 2, box 1, folder 12; October 8, 1979, p. 2, box 1, folder 11; and November 3, 1979, 1–2 (US-88-18), box 1, folder 11, all in CTM Papers (US-88-18).

35. CTM board minutes, January 8, 1979, p. 2, CTM Papers (US-83-3), box 1, folder 43.

36. CTM board minutes, June 4, 1979, p. 2, box 1, folder 11; and August 4, 1980, p. 2, box 1, folder 12, both in CTM Papers (US-88-18).

37. CTM board minutes, September 9, 1980, p. 1, box 1, folder 50; November 3, 1980, p. 2, box 1, folder 51; April 6, 1981, p. 2, box 1, folder 53; April 5, 1982, p. 1, box 1, folder 55, all in CTM Papers (US-83-3).

38. CTM board minutes, September 10, 1979, CTM Papers (US-83-3), box 1, folder 47; Nell D. Surber, director, Department of Development, to urban development, planning, zoning and housing committee [of city council], "Neighborhood Business Districts and Town Centers—First Up-dated Quarterly Report," June 26, 1979, p. 6, CTM Papers (US-83-3), box 4, folder 37.

39. The city's CAT teams, which now operated out of the city's new Department of Neighborhood Housing and Conservation, assisted in finishing the work, but additional aid came through the city by way of a Mott Foundation grant to provide community councils funds with which to hire part-time community coordinators. CTM hired its first such coordinator ($5,000) in 1978, but she spent only 50 percent of her time planning, 30 percent in helping to secure greater community involvement with CTM, and the rest in assisting various CTM committees and in representing CTM at meetings outside of Clifton. CTM minutes, October 8, 1979, p. 1, CTM Papers (US-83-3), box 1, folder 47; CTM executive committee, Recommendation for 1979 SNAP Proposal, ca. February 1979, p. 2, CTM Papers (US-83-3), box 1, folder 44.

40. Gerard A. Hyland to Zane L. Miller, memo, September 30, 1993, pp. 1–2.

41. Brent E. Owens, assistant director of parks, to Barbara Lichtenstein, community assistant Team-Quadrant 4, Clifton Community Plan, April 20, 1981, folder "Clifton Plan—Comments of Departments," Gerard A. Hyland Papers, possession of Zane L. Miller.

42. G. Franklin Miller to Barbara Lichtenstein, October 28, 1980 and July 6, 1981, Hyland Papers, possession of Zane L. Miller.

43. Steven Bloomfield, director, Department of Neighborhood Housing and Conservation, to Herb Stevens, director of city planning, December 9, 1981, Hyland Papers, possession of Zane L. Miller; Proceedings of the City Planning Commission, January 8, 1982, 1–2, copy in Hyland Papers, possession of Zane L. Miller; Clifton Town Meeting and Cincinnati Department of Neighborhood Housing and Conservation, *Clifton Community Plan* (Cincinnati: Clifton Town Meeting and Department of Neighborhood Housing, December 1982), 34.

44. Clifton Town Meeting and Cincinnati Department of Neighborhood Housing and Conservation, *Clifton Community Plan* (Cincinnati: Clifton Town Meeting and Department of Neighborhood Housing, December 1982), 11–14.

45. Ibid., n.p.

46. B. H. Wiers, "Hamilton County Housing Trends: Are We Getting What We

Want?" 1–9, and exhibits, presented to the Community Housing Resources Board annual meeting, September 6, 1984 (copy in Zane L. Miller's possession); "HOME Charter," Housing Opportunities Made Equal (HOME), report to the executive committee, August 13, 1984, HOME Papers [unprocessed], Urban Studies Collection, Department of Archives and Rare Books, University of Cincinnati Libraries. The *Clifton Community Plan* did, of course, endorse the scattering of federally subsidized housing units for low income and elderly people (p. 28).

Chapter Six

1. Erwin E. Hoffman, administrator, land use and zoning, to Cincinnati City Planning Commission, "A Report on the Application of an EQ-HS District," March 21, 1980, 1–2, 4, CTM Papers (US-83-3), box 2, folder 29.

2. CTM board minutes, March 1, 1982, p. 2, March 5, 1982, p. 1, CTM Papers (US-83-3), box 1, folder 55; CTM board minutes, August 2, 1982, p. 2, CTM Papers (US-83-3), box 1, folder 57.

3. CTM board minutes, January 4, 1982, p. 2, CTM Papers (US-83-3), box 1, folder 54; CTM board minutes, March 5, 1982, box 1, folder 55; Geraldine E. Turbeville, "Neighborhood Support Program: Self-Help Project" (master's thesis, University of Cincinnati, 1983), 10–16.

4. CTM board minutes, August 2, 1982, p. 2, September 13, 1982, CTM Papers (US-83-3), box 1, folder 57.

5. Nancy Shapiro, report of boundary review committee, ca. October 1984, CTM Papers (US-83-3), box 1, folder 58; Clifton Town Meeting and Cincinnati Department of Neighborhood Housing and Conservation, *Clifton Community Plan* (Cincinnati: Clifton Town Meeting and Cincinnati Department of Neighborhood Housing and Conservation, December 1981), 8, appendix.

6. CTM board minutes, October 4, 1982, p. 1, CTM Papers (US-83-3), box 1, folder 8; Gerard Hyland, Department of Neighborhood Housing and Conservation, telephone interview (untaped) with Zane L. Miller, September 6, 1984.

7. The Uptown plan, moreover, which emerged in 1989, said little about Clifton, and the absence of city funds to implement proposed projects elsewhere that might have ramifications for Clifton rendered it a document that posed no threat to the interests of Clifton as the CTM board understood them. Robert Duffy, senior planner, guest lecture, Department of History, University of Cincinnati, September 22, 1986, tape recording, esp. side A, Clifton project files; Cincinnati Department of City Planning and Department of Neighborhood Housing and Conservation, *Uptown: Planning Program and Priorities* (Cincinnati: Department of City Planning, 1986), 8–9; CTM board minutes, October 7, 1985, p. 2, September 8, 1986, p. 1, October 6, 1986, p. 2, May 1, 1989, p. 2, CTM Papers (US-93-10), box 1 (no folders); *Clifton Living*, November 1986, 10; *Cincinnati Enquirer*, April 20, 1989, B4, Metro edition. Charlotte T. Birdsall, a Planning Department staff member, described Clifton as "never seriously involved" with Uptown planning and said the implementation of the plan "fizzled out" because of the lack of city dollars. Birdsall to Zane L. Miller, telephone interview, September 13, 1993.

8. CTM *Bulletin*, May 1980, p. 3.

9. CTM board minutes, June 6, 1983, p. 1, CTM Papers (US-86-5), box 1, folder "Extra Copies"; CTM board, resolution to CCURC, n.d., CTM Papers (US-86-5), box 1, folder CCURC; CTM board minutes, June 11, 1984, p. 2, CTM Papers (US-86-5), box 1, folder "Blue Loose Leaf Binder"; CTM board minutes, September 10, 1984, p. 2, November 4, 1985, p. 1, CTM Papers (US-93-10), box 1 (no folders).

10. CTM board minutes, November 7, 1983, p. 1, CTM Papers (US-86-5), box 1, folder "Blue Loose Leaf Binder."

11. CTM board minutes, April 2, 1984, 1–2, CTM Papers (US-86-5), box 1, folder "Minutes and Scraps."

12. CTM board minutes, May 6, 1984, p. 1, CTM Papers (US-86-5), box 1, folder "Blue Loose Leaf Binder"; *Cincinnati Enquirer,* May 8, 1984, C1.

13. *Cincinnati Enquirer,* May 22, 1984, B1, B2; Sidney Weil, oral history interview with Nancy K. Shapiro, June 9, 1985, side A, Clifton project files.

14. CTM board minutes, June 4, 1984, p. 2, CTM Papers (US-86-5), box 1, folder "Blue Loose Leaf Binder."

15. Weil, oral history interview; "Appeal by Clifton Town Meeting to the Council of the City of Cincinnati," May 25, 1984, 1–5, CTM Papers (US-86-5), box 1, folder 4.

16. CTM board minutes, June 4, 1984, p. 2, CTM Papers (US-86-5), box 1, folder "Blue Loose Leaf Binder"; CTM board minutes, September 10, 1984, p. 2, October 1, 1984, p. 1, July 1, 1985, p. 1, September 9, 1985, p. 2, CTM Papers (US-93-10), box 1 (no folders); CTM *Bulletin,* June 1984, p. 1, October 1984, p. 1, December 1984, p. 1.

17. CTM *Bulletin,* December 1984, p. 1; CTM board minutes, May 6, 1985, p. 2, CTM Papers (US-86-5), box 1, folder "Blue Loose Leaf Binder"; CTM board minutes, December 2, 1985, p. 1, January 6, 1986, p. 4, February 3, 1986, p. 1, CTM Papers (US-93-10), box 1 (no folders); Franchise Developers, Inc. v. Cincinnati, 30 Ohio St. 3d, 31–33.

18. CTM board minutes, special meeting, February 10, 1986, p. 1, CTM Papers (US-93-10), box 1 (no folders); *Cincinnati Post,* February 6, 1986, B1, B2; *Cincinnati Enquirer,* February 12, 1986, E3, February 15, 1986, C6, February 16, 1986, G4, March 11, 1986, E9; *Clifton Living,* March 1986, 3, 4–5; April 1986, 4; May 1986, 4. The press coverage of the issue noted that two city council members opposed making the appeal and that many Cliftonites did not object to a Wendy's on Ludlow Avenue. At least one lawyer used the appeals court decision to argue that Cincinnati's historic district overlay zoning ordinance was unconstitutional. See Charles Wm. Anness, counsel to McAlpin's [department store] to Councilman James C. Cissell, re: Cincinnati Historic Conservation Ordinance and Guidelines, March 31, 1986, esp. p. 8, copy in Clifton project files. The lawyer did not take the city to court on this issue, however.

19. *Brief of Appellants,* no. 86–513 In the Supreme Court of Ohio, Franchise Developers . . . v. The City of Cincinnati and . . . Clifton Town Meeting, Defendants-Appellants, esp. p. 19, City Solicitor's Office, Files of Ely Ryder, City Hall, Cincinnati, Ohio.

20. *Cincinnati Post,* May 29, 1986, B1; 30 Ohio St. 3d, 32–34.

21. CTM board minutes, November 3, 1986, p. 2, December 1, 1986, pp. 1–2, January 5, 1987, p. 2, and April 6, 1987, p. 1, all in CTM Papers (US-93-10), box 1 (no folders); *Clifton Living,* November 1986, 10; December 1986, 8; January 1987, 10; February 1987, 14; CTM *Bulletin,* May 1987, p. 6, June 1987, p. 6; *Cincinnati Enquirer,* November 20, 1986, A1, A15; *Cincinnati Enquirer,* December 11, 1986, Metro sec., p. 3; *Cincinnati Post,*

November 26, 1986, B1, April 13, 1990, C1. The state supreme court decided the case without hearing both sides on the grounds that the "matter appealed is one of great public or general interest." 30 Ohio St. 3d, p. 29. For other versions of the Wendy's conflict, see Karen Gregg, "Wendy's vs. the Movies: A Community Takes on Business," *Urban Resources* 5, no. 1 (fall 1988): C1-C8; Pamela Whissel, "Coming Up Roses," *Clifton Magazine* [University of Cincinnati student magazine], spring 1990, 32–35.

22. Leon Meyer, administrator, land use/environment, to Cincinnati City Planning Commission, a report and recommendation on proposed amendments, November 21, 1986, pp. 2–5, copy in Clifton project files. Meyer also traced the history of the passage of environmental quality legislation and found no intent to include in it authority to regulate land uses. See p. 1. See also CCPC, minutes, vol. 51, November 21, 1986, 217–21, Department of City Planning, City Hall, Cincinnati, Ohio. For the legislative alterations, see City of Cincinnati, ordinance no. 439 and 440-1986, Clerk of Council's Office, City Hall, Cincinnati, Ohio.

23. CCPC, "Environmental Quality District Development Guidelines Report, . . . EQ-HS #2, . . . Clifton Hillsides in the vicinity of Lafayette Avenue, Clifton Avenue, Ludlow Avenue and Vine Street," n.d., p. 102, copy in Clifton project files; CCPC, minutes, vol. 42, June 3, 1977, p. 68; Clifton Town Meeting and Department of Neighborhood Housing and Conservation, *Clifton Community Plan* (Cincinnati, 1982, approved by CTM in October 1979), 7, 9–11.

24. CTM *Bulletin*, December 1979, p. 2, November 1980, p. 1; Department of City Planning, Historic Conservation Office, *Cincinnati's Historic Properties*, vol. 1, *National Register Listings* (Cincinnati: Department of City Planning, Historic Conservation Office, May 1982), 2–3.

25. CTM board minutes, November 2, 1981, p. 2, and January 4, 1982, p. 3, both in CTM (US-86-5), box 1, folder CTM-8182; CTM *Bulletin*, March 1982, p. 1, January-February 1983, p. 1; CTM board minutes, September 12, 1983, p. 2, CTM Papers (US-86-5), box 1, folder CTM September 83; CTM board minutes, October 3, 1983, p. 3, December 7, 1983, p. 1, February 4, 1984, p. 1, and June 4, 1984, p. 1, all in CTM Papers (US-86-5), box 1, folder "Blue Loose Leaf Binder"; CTM *Bulletin*, January-February 1984, p. 1, March 1984, p. 3; CTM board minutes, February 6, 1984, p. 1, CTM Papers (US-86-5), box 1, folder 1.

26. Steven Bloomfield, director, Department of Neighborhood Housing and Conservation, to Sylvester Murray, city manager, Transmittal of Ordinance Pertaining to Sale of Sacred Heart Academy, March 13, 1985, copy in Clifton project files.

27. John M. Kurak Jr. to Genevieve Ray, urban conservator, November 12, 1986, pp. 1–2, copy in Clifton project files. The PUD regulations may be found in *Zoning Code of Cincinnati* (Cincinnati: Office of the Clerk of Council, January 1983, ch. 9, esp. pp. 172–73, 447. The zoning code described the intention of PUD regulations as fostering the use of property "in a manner not permitted by the existing district regulations, without detriment to neighboring properties," and their purpose as providing "for orderly development of a specific property while protecting the natural open space, ecological, topographical, geological, and historic features of the property from damage which might occur from development permitted by conventional zoning and subdivision regulations." See *Zoning Code*, p. 169.

28. CTM board minutes, December 15, 1986, pp. 1–2, CTM Papers (US-93-10), box 1 (no folders).

29. CTM board minutes, January 1987, p. 1, and April 6, 1987, 2–3, both in CTM Papers (US-93-10), box 1 (no folders); David B. Beran, president, CTM, to James Selonick, chair, Historic Conservation Board, April 1987, pp. 1–2, copy in Clifton project files.

30. Citizens Association for the Preservation of Sacred Heart to Honorable Historic Conservation Board, Regards to: Application for Sacred Heart Redevelopment Permission . . . , April 12, 1987, n.p., copy in Clifton project files.

31. Christopher A. Cain, acting urban conservator, to Honorable Historic Conservation Board, Subject: Planned Unit Development in the Sacred Heart/Mount Storm Park Historic District and the Environmental Quality Hillside District no. 2, April 13, 1987, esp. p. 7, copy in Clifton project files; *Cincinnati Enquirer*, April 19, 1987, B3, June 3, 1987, F5; *Clifton Living*, June 1987, 12; CTM *Bulletin*, January 1989, p. 1.

32. Department of City Planning, Historic Conservation Office, *Cincinnati's Historic Resources*, vol. 1, *National Register Listings* (Cincinnati: Department of City Planning/Historic Conservation Office, May 1982), 5, 11, 13; CTM *Bulletin*, June 1981, p. 1.

33. CTM board minutes, January 10, 1983, p. 2, CTM Papers (US-86-5), box 1, folder "Extra Stuff"; CTM board minutes, January 7, 1985, p. 1, February 4, 1985, p. 2, May 6, 1985, p. 1, all in CTM Papers (US-86-5), box 1, folder "Blue Loose Leaf Binder"; CTM board minutes, October 7, 1985, p. 2, CTM Papers (US-93-10), box 1 (no folders).

34. CTM board minutes, January 6, 1986, p. 1, CTM Papers (US-93-10), box 1 (no folders); *Clifton Living*, March 1986, 9; *Cincinnati Enquirer*, June 27, 1989, A12; CTM *Bulletin*, September 1989, p. 1; *Clifton Living*, September 1989, 5.

35. CTM board minutes, December 4, 1989, p. 2, CTM Papers (US-93-10), box 1 (no folders); *Clifton Living*, January 1990, 4; CTM *Bulletin*, January 1990, p. 1, March 1990, p. 2.

36. CTM *Bulletin*, February 1990, p. 1; CTM board minutes, March 5, 1990, p. 2, and April 2, 1990, p. 2, both in CTM Papers (US-93-10), box 1 (no folders); *Cincinnati Enquirer*, April 29, 1990, B8; CTM board minutes, May 7, 1990, pp. 1–2, CTM Papers (US-93-10), box 1 (no folders).

37. *Cincinnati Post*, May 21, 1990, 6A, May 22, 1990, 4A.

38. CTM board minutes, June 4, 1990, p. 1, CTM Papers (US-93-10), box 1 (no folders); CTM *Bulletin*, June 1990, pp. 1, 3; *Cincinnati Post*, June 6, 1990, 8A; *Cincinnati Enquirer*, June 8, 1990, D2; *Cincinnati Post*, June 18, 1990, 4A. One member of the library board, however, wondered why his colleagues assumed that CTM accurately represented the residents of Clifton on this issue. *Cincinnati Enquirer*, June 19, 1990, A9.

39. CTM board minutes, January 7, 1991, p. 3, February 4, 1991, p. 2, March 4, 1991, p. 3, November 4, 1991, p. 4, CTM Papers (US-93-10), box 1 (no folders); CTM *Bulletin*, January 1991, p. 2, February 1991, p. 2, January/February 1992, pp. 1, 5, September 1992, p. 9, March 1993, pp. 1, 5; *Cincinnati Enquirer*, Extra/Central, June 7, 1991, p. 3, August 2, 1991, p. 1, February 28, 1993, p. 1.

40. CTM board minutes, January 7, 1991, p. 1, CTM Papers (US-93-10), box 1 (no folders); CTM *Bulletin*, January 1991, p. 2; *Cincinnati Enquirer*, January 18, 1991, p. 9, Extra/Central.

41. CTM board minutes, February 4, 1991, p. 2, CTM Papers (US-93-10), box 1 (no folders); CTM *Bulletin,* February 1991, p. 2.
42. Mr. and Mrs. Jack Brand to Mr. Christopher Cain, February 22, 1991, Historic Conservation Office, City Hall, Cincinnati, copy in Clifton project files.
43. CTM board minutes, September 9, 1991, p. 4, October 7, 1991, p. 4, CTM Papers (US-93-10), box 1 (no folders); *Cincinnati Post,* Central Neighbors sec., September 24, 1991, 5A, September 26, 1991, p. 1, October 3, 1991, p. 1.
44. City Planning Department, Historic Conservation Office, *Clifton Historic District: Designation Report,* September 1991, esp. pp. 1–9, copy in Clifton project files; Cincinnati City Planning Department, Historic Conservation Office, *Clifton Historic District: Conservation Guidelines,* August 1991, esp. pp. 1, 9–11, copy in Clifton project files.
45. CTM board minutes, November 4, 1991, CTM Papers (US-93-10), box 1 (no folders).
46. *Cincinnati Enquirer,* November 13, 1991, B2; *Cincinnati Post,* November 14, 1991, 13A, November 27, 1991, 5A, December 3, 1991, p. 7, Central Neighbors sec.; CTM board minutes, December 2, 1991, p. 4, CTM Papers (US-93-10), box 1 (no folders).
47. *Cincinnati Post,* January 7, 1992, p. 5, Central Neighbors sec.
48. CTM *Bulletin,* January 1992, p. 3.
49. *Cincinnati Enquirer,* January 16, 1992, A11.
50. *Cincinnati Post,* Central Neighbors sec., January 30, 1992, p. 1, January 13, 1992, p. 1, March 12, 1992, p. 1, August 27, 1992, p. 1, November 10, 1992, p. 1; CTM *Bulletin,* June 1992, p. 7.
51. Jerry H. Lawson, Center for Resolution of Disputes, "The Working Group on Clifton Historic Designation," n.d., copy in Clifton project files.
52. *Cincinnati Enquirer,* October 25, 1988, pp. 1–2, Extra sec.; *Cincinnati Post,* November 8, 1988, p. 11, Central Neighbors sec.
53. *Cincinnati Enquirer,* October 25, 1988, p. 1, Extra sec.; *Cincinnati Post,* January 17, 1989, p. 10, Central Neighbors sec.; CTM *Bulletin,* June 1989, p. 1.
54. CTM board minutes, March 6, 1989, p. 1, May 1, 1989, p. 1, September 5, 1989, p. 9, CTM Papers (US-93-10), box 1 (no folders); *Cincinnati Enquirer,* November 21, 1989, p. 7, Extra sec.
55. CTM board minutes, April 2, 1990, p. 2, September 4, 1990, 2, 5, November 5, 1990, 3–4, CTM Papers (US-93-10), box 1 (no folders); *Cincinnati Enquirer,* December 25, 1990, pp. 1–2, Extra sec.
56. CTM board minutes, January 7, 1991, p. 2, March 4, 1991, p. 1, April 1, 1991, p. 1, May 6, 1991, p. 1, November 4, 1991, p. 2, February 3, 1992, p. 3, March 2, 1992, p. 5, May 4, 1992, p. 6, CTM Papers (US-93-10), box 1 (no folders); *Cincinnati Post,* May 30, 1992, 8D, CTM *Bulletin,* June 1992, p. 4.
57. CTM *Bulletin,* June 1992 (no pagination, see article entitled "Reaching Closure on the Closure: Report of the Hosea Closure Improvements Committee").
58. *Cincinnati Post,* August 27, 1992, p. 3, Central Neighbors sec. Only one of the three plaintiffs lived on Loraine.
59. *Cincinnati Post,* September 8, 1992, p. 1, Central Neighbors sec.
60. CTM *Bulletin,* September 1992, p. 4. The constitutional review committee came up with amendments, adopted in May of 1994, making it easier for members to vote on

major issues of broad concern. See Article IV, as amended, of the revised CTM constitution, copy in CTM Office, 325 Ludlow Avenue.

61. CTM *Bulletin,* September 1992, pp. 1–2.

62. CTM *Bulletin,* November 1992, p. 5. The disclaimer appeared on p. 4 of this issue of the *Bulletin.*

63. CTM *Bulletin,* May 1993, pp. 1, 5. A Hamilton County Common Pleas Court judge subsequently ruled in favor of the city in the Hosea case, and the district appellate court upheld that decision. Plaintiffs attempted to carry the case to the Ohio Supreme Court, but it refused to consider the issue. City of Cincinnati, ex. rel. Jack Brand, Taylor Fitchett and Gordon C. Cain, Realtors-Appellants v. The City of Cincinnati and Gerald Newfarmer, City Manager, Respondents-Appellees, and the Clifton Town Meeting, Respondent. Nos. C-930546, A-9207567. Court of Appeals of Ohio, Hamilton County, January 25, 1995 (Cincinnati: West, 1997), 1–7; Ely M. T. Ryder, assistant city solicitor, to Zane L. Miller, telephone interview, July 30, 1997.

64. An "outsider" and author of a walking tour of Clifton said in 1992 that it gave him "a sense of community both self-aware and self-confident, even a trifle smug in its sense of the rightness of its priorities." Clubbe, *Cincinnati Observed,* 292.

65. CTM constitution and bylaws, January 8, 1979, CTM Papers (US-83-3), box 1, folder 1. CTM filed for incorporation and amended its constitution to indicate its new status before receiving official notice of the fact from the Ohio Secretary of State.

66. CTM board minutes, March 1992, p. 2, May 4, 1992, p. 5, CTM Papers (US-93-10), box 1 (no folders).

67. Michael E. Maloney and Janet R. Buelow, *The Social Areas of Cincinnati: An Analysis of Social Needs, Patterns for Three Decades, 1970–1990* (Cincinnati: School of Planning, University of Cincinnati, 1997), esp. 2–4, 86–100; Douglas S. Massey, "The Age of Extremes: Concentrated Affluence and Poverty in the Twenty-first Century [United States]," *Demography* 33, no. 4 (November 1996): 395–412.

68. James M. Murray to Zane L. Miller, September 25, 1997, conversation. Murray has been a Clifton resident since 1985.

Epilogue

1. For an examination of the question of race and a suburban gilded ghetto in the Cincinnati metropolitan area, see Zane L. Miller, *Suburb,* 234–41. For a national study that reaches conclusions compatible with those expressed in this epilogue, see Rusk, *Cities Without Suburbs,* esp. 129–30, on the role of neighborhood associations.

2. Orlando Patterson, "What to Do When Busing Becomes Irrelevant," *New York Times,* July 18, 1999, p. 17.

3. CTM appears a likely candidate for this role not only because of Clifton's situation vis-à-vis the city's black ghetto but also because of some other facts of its condition. It escaped the post-1950 white flight that drained many city neighborhoods of valuable fiscal and civic resources (between 1940 and 1990, Clifton's population rose from 8,340 to 9,029), and in that perspective it seems "stable." But it is also diverse, more so than many people think and more than CTM acknowledged in the 1990s. Its population in 1990 included 1,163 blacks, 388 Asians, and 245 Hispanics, not all of them

affluent. The neighborhood's white households boasted a mean income of $41,845, while blacks came in at $25,181, Asians at $24,545, and Hispanics at $29,009. In addition, 12.7 percent of whites, 17.8 percent of blacks, 38.9 percent of Asians, and 28.6 percent of Hispanics lived below the poverty level. Data compiled from federal census numbers by the Institute for Policy Research, University of Cincinnati, for the Cincinnati City Planning Department.

Appendix

1. Some of these maxims are laid out more elaborately in Henry D. Shapiro, *Appalachia on Our Mind: The Southern Mountains and Mountaineers in the American Consciousness* (Chapel Hill: University of North Carolina Press, 1978), ix–xix; Miller, *Suburb*, introduction; and Miller and Tucker, *Changing Plans for America's Inner Cities*, 3–5, 9–12, 43–46.

Bibliography

Applebaum, William. *The Secondary Commercial Centers of Cincinnati.* Cincinnati: Institute for Industrial Research, for the Commercial Club of Cincinnati, June 10, 1932.
Baughin, William A. "Murray Seasongood, Twentieth-Century Urban Reformer." Ph.D. diss., University of Cincinnati, 1972.
Binford, Henry C. *The First Suburbs: Residential Communities on the Boston Periphery, 1815–1860.* Chicago: University of Chicago Press, 1985.
Blackmore, L. B., Clerk of Council, and Carl G. Werner, Codifier. *Charter (Adopted 1926) and Code of Ordinances (Revised June 28, 1928) of the City of Cincinnati.* Cincinnati: City Council, 1928.
Blakely, Edward J., and Mary Gail Snyder. *Fortress America: Gated Communities in the United States.* Washington, D.C.: Brookings Institution Press, 1997.
Borman, Kathryn M., and Joel H. Spring. *Schools in Central Cities: Structures and Process.* New York: Longman, 1984.
Burgheim, Max. *Der Führer von Cincinnati.* Cincinnati: Burgheim, 1875.
———. *Cincinnati im Wort und Bilt.* Cincinnati: Burgheim, 1891.
Burnham, Robert A. "'Pulling Together' for Pluralism: Politics, Planning, and Government in Cincinnati, 1924–1959." Ph.D. diss., University of Cincinnati, 1990.
———. "Cincinnati's First Zoning Ordinance." Cincinnati: Laboratory in American Civilization, Department of History, University of Cincinnati, May 31, 1983.
Cameron, Wilbert J., Jr. "Community Control of Education in Cincinnati, 1900–1921." Ph.D. diss., University of Cincinnati, 1977.
Campbell, James H. "New Parochialism: Change and Conflict in the Archdiocese of Cincinnati, 1878–1925." In *Ethnic Diversity and Civic Identity: Patterns of Conflict and Cohesion in Cincinnati Since 1820,* ed. Henry D. Shapiro and Jonathan D. Sarna (Urbana: University of Illinois Press, 1992), 106–16.
Casey-Leininger, Charles. "Making the Second Ghetto in Cincinnati, Avondale, 1925–1970." M.A. thesis, University of Cincinnati, 1989.
———. "Creating Democracy in Housing: Civil Rights and Housing Policy in Cincinnati, 1945–1980." Ph.D. diss., University of Cincinnati, 1993.
Chapin, Rev. E. H. *Humanity in the City.* 1854; reprint, New York: Arno Press, 1974.
Cincinnati City Planning Commission. *Official Plan of the City of Cincinnati.* Cincinnati: City Planning Commission, 1925.
———. *The Economy of the Cincinnati Metropolitan Area.* Cincinnati: City Planning Commission, 1946.

———. *Residential Areas: An Analysis of Land Requirements for Residential Development, 1945 to 1970*. Cincinnati: City Planning Commission, December 1946.
———. *Communities: A Study of Community and Neighborhood Development*. Cincinnati: City Planning Commission, December 1947.
———. *The Cincinnati Metropolitan Master Plan and the Official City Plan*. Cincinnati: City Planning Commission, 1948.
———. *Avondale-Corryville General Neighborhood Renewal Plan*. Cincinnati: City Planning Commission, 1960.
———. *A Report on the Traffic Survey of Clifton Ave., McAlpin Ave., and Woolper Ave*. Cincinnati: City Planning Commission, April 1964.
———. *Neighborhood Business District Study: Inventory of Existing Conditions*. Cincinnati: City Planning Commission, December 1970.
———. *Coordinated City Plan and Process: Policy Paper*. Cincinnati: City Planning Commission, December 1976, updated, February 1977.
———. *Neighborhood Business Districts: Background, Current Status and Recommendations*. Cincinnati: City Planning Commission, October 1978.
———. *The Coordinated City Plan*, vol. 1: *Strategies for Current Physical Development*. Cincinnati: City Planning Commission, 1979.
———. *The Coordinated City Plan*, vol. 2: *Strategies for Comprehensive Land Use*. Cincinnati: City Planning Commission, December 1980.
Cist, Charles. *Cincinnati in 1841: Its Early Annals and Future Prospects*. Cincinnati: privately printed, 1841.
———. *Sketches and Statistics of Cincinnati in 1851*. Cincinnati: Wm. M. Moore, 1851.
———. *Sketches and Statistics of Cincinnati in 1859*. Cincinnati: privately printed, 1859.
The City of Cincinnati and Its Resources. Cincinnati: Cincinnati Times-Star, 1891.
Clifton Town Meeting and Cincinnati City Planning Commission. *The Clifton Community Plan: The First Report of a Planning Series. Goals and Objectives*. Cincinnati: City Planning Commission, May 1975.
Clubbe, John. *Cincinnati Observed: Architecture and History*. Columbus: Ohio State University Press, 1992.
Contosta, David R. *Suburb in the City: Chestnut Hill, Philadelphia, 1850–1990*. Columbus: Ohio State University Press, 1992.
Corey, Kenneth E. *The Clifton Community Plan: Existing Conditions and Analysis of the Clifton Community*. Cincinnati: City Planning Commission, 1977.
Cross, Bradley D. "New Jerusalems for a New World: The Garden City Idea and Modern Town Planning Thought and Practice in Britain, Canada, and the United States, 1900–1970." Cincinnati: Ph.D. diss., University of Cincinnati, 1997.
Downs, Anthony. *Neighborhoods and Urban Development*. Washington, D.C.: Brookings Institution, 1981.

Drake, B., and E. D. Mansfield. *Cincinnati in 1826*. Cincinnati: Morgan, Lodge, and Fisher, 1827.
Ebner, Michael H. "Re-reading Suburban America: Urban Population Deconcentration, 1810–1980." In *American Urbanism: A Historiographical Review*, ed. Howard Gillette Jr. and Zane L. Miller. Westport, Conn.: Greenwood Press, 1987.
———. *Creating Chicago's North Shore: A Suburban History*. Chicago: University of Chicago Press, 1988.
Engelhardt, George W. *Cincinnati: The Queen City*. Cincinnati: Geo. W. Englehardt, 1901.
Fairbanks, Robert B. *Making Better Citizens: Housing Reform and the Community Development Strategy in Cincinnati, 1890–1960*. Urbana: University of Illinois Press, 1988.
Fairbanks, Robert B., and Zane L. Miller. "The Martial Metropolis: Housing, Planning and Race in Cincinnati, 1940–1955." In *The Martial Metropolis: U.S. Cities in War and Peace*, ed. Roger W. Lotchin, 197–213. New York: Praeger, 1984.
Fairfield, John D. "Democracy in Cincinnati: Civic Virtue and Three Generations of Urban Historians." *Urban History* 24, no. 2 (August 1997): 200–219.
Federated Civic Association. *Thirteenth Anniversary Souvenir and History of the Federated Civic Association and Its Fifty-five Affiliated Organizations of Hamilton County*. Cincinnati: Federated Civic Association, 1937.
Fisher, Robert, and Peter Romanofscky, eds. *Community Organization for Urban Social Change: A Historical Perspective*. Westport, Conn.: Greenwood Press, 1981.
Fishman, Robert. *Bourgeois Utopias: The Rise and Fall of Suburbia*. New York: Basic Books, 1987.
Ford, Henry A., and Mrs. Kate B. Ford. *History of Cincinnati, Ohio, with Illustrations and Biographical Studies*. Cleveland: L. A. Williams, 1881.
Foster, George C. *New York by Gas-Light and Other Sketches*. Edited by Stuart M. Blumin. Berkeley: University of California Press, 1990.
Giglierano, Geoffrey J., and Deborah A. Overmyer. *The Bicentennial Guide to Greater Cincinnati*. Cincinnati: Cincinnati Historical Society, 1988.
Gillette, Howard, Jr., and Zane L. Miller, eds. *American Urbanism: A Historiographical Review*. New York: Greenwood Press, 1987.
Gregg, Karen. "Wendy's vs. the Movies: A Community Takes on Business." *Urban Resources* 5, no. 1 (fall 1988): C1-C8.
Greve, Charles Theodore. *Centennial History of Cincinnati and Representative Citizens*. Chicago: Biographical, 1904.
Harlow, Alvin F. *The Serene Cincinnatians*. New York: E. P. Dutton, 1950.
Hirsch, Arnold R. *Making the Second Ghetto: Race and Housing in Chicago, 1940–1960*. Cambridge: Cambridge University Press, 1983.
History of Cincinnati and Hamilton County, Ohio. Cincinnati: S. B. Nelson, 1894.

Hollinger, David A. *Science, Jews, and Secular Culture: Studies in Mid-Twentieth-Century American Intellectual History.* Princeton: Princeton University Press, 1996.

Howe, Henry. *Historical Collections of Ohio.* Cincinnati: State of Ohio, C. J. Krehbield & Co., Printers and Binders, 1908.

Jackson, Kenneth T. *Crabgrass Frontier: The Suburbanization of the United States.* New York: Oxford University Press, 1985.

Keating, Ann Durkin. *Building Chicago: Suburban Developers and the Creation of a Divided Metropolis.* Columbus: Ohio State University Press, 1989.

Kenny, Daniel J. *Illustrated Cincinnati.* Cincinnati: Robert Clarke, 1875.

———. *Illustrated Guide to Cincinnati and the World's Columbian Exposition.* Cincinnati: Robert Clarke, 1893.

King, Moses, ed. *King's Pocket-Book of Cincinnati.* Cincinnati: Moses King, 1880.

Kocolowski, Gary P. "The History of North Avondale: A Study of the Effects of Urbanization upon an Urban Locality." Master's thesis, University of Cincinnati, 1971.

Koehler, Lyle. "Westwood in [Cincinnati] Ohio: Community, Continuity, and Change." Department of Archives and Rare Books, Blegen Library, University of Cincinnati Libraries, 1980.

Kornbluh, Andrea Tuttle. *Lighting the Way . . . : The Woman's City Club of Cincinnati, 1915–1965.* Cincinnati: Young and Klein, 1968.

———. "Parks and the People: The Place of the Kessler Park Plan [for Cincinnati] in the History of Parks and Public Recreation." *Queen City Heritage: The Journal of the Cincinnati Historical Society* 51, no. 1 (spring 1993): 53–55.

Kraemer's Picturesque Cincinnati. Cincinnati: A. O. and G. A. Kraemer, 1898.

Leonard, John W. *Centennial Review of Cincinnati: One Hundred Years of Progress in Commerce, Manufacturing, the Professions, and in Social and Municipal Life.* Cincinnati: H. M. Elstner, 1888.

Leonard, Lewis Alexander, ed. *Greater Cincinnati and Its People: A History,* vol. 2. New York: Lewis Historical, 1927.

Linden-Ward, Blanche. "The Greening of Cincinnati: Adolph Strauch's Legacy in Park Design." *Queen City Heritage* 51, no. 1 (spring 1993): 20.

Mahoney, Sister Benadicta. *We Are Many: History of the Sisters of Charity of Cincinnati, 1898–1971.* Cincinnati: Sisters of Charity, 1982.

Maloney, Michael E., and Janet R. Buelow. *The Social Areas of Cincinnati: An Analysis of Social Needs, Patterns for Three Decades, 1970–1990.* Cincinnati: School of Planning, University of Cincinnati, 1997.

Marcus, Alan I. *Plague of Strangers: Social Groups and the Origins of City Services in Cincinnati, 1819–1870.* Columbus: Ohio State University Press, 1991.

———. "Back to the Present: Historians' Treatment of the City as a Social System During the Reign of the Idea of Community." In *American Urbanism: A Historiographical Review,* ed. Howard Gillette Jr. and Zane L. Miller. New York: Greenwood Press, 1987.

Massey, Douglas S. "The Age of Extremes: Concentrated Affluence and Poverty in the Twenty-first Century [United States]." *Demography* 33, no. 4 (November 1996): 395–412.
Maxwell, Sidney. *The Suburbs of Cincinnati: Sketches Historical and Descriptive.* Cincinnati: Geo. E. Stevens, 1870.
Mayer, Harold M., and Richard C. Wade. *Chicago: The Growth of a Metropolis.* Chicago: University of Chicago Press, 1969.
McKenzie, Evan. *Privatopia: Homeowner Associations and the Rise of Residential Private Government.* New Haven: Yale University Press, 1994.
McShane, Clay. *Down the Asphalt Path: The Automobile and the American City.* New York: Columbia University Press, 1994.
Melvin, Patricia Mooney. *The Organic City: Urban Definition and Neighborhood Organization, 1880–1920.* Lexington: University Press of Kentucky, 1987.
———. "The Neighborhood-City Relationships." In *American Urbanism: A Historiographical Review,* ed. Howard Gillette Jr. and Zane L. Miller. Westport, Conn.: Greenwood Press, 1987.
———. "Local Improvement Associations and the City-Building Process." Paper delivered at the Cincinnati Seminar on the City, Cincinnati Historical Society, Cincinnati, Ohio, November 9, 1994.
———, ed. *American Community Organizations: A Historical Dictionary.* Westport, Conn.: Greenwood Press, 1986.
Miller, Janet A. "Urban Education and the New City: Cincinnati's Elementary Schools, 1870–1914." D.Ed. diss., University of Cincinnati, 1974.
Miller, Zane L. *Boss Cox's Cincinnati: Urban Politics in the Progressive Era.* New York: Oxford University Press, 1968.
———. Introduction to *Cincinnati: A Guide to the Queen City and Its Neighbors* (1943), by Writers' Program of the Work Projects Administration in the State of Ohio. Cincinnati: Cincinnati Historical Society, 1987.
———. *Suburb: Neighborhood and Community in Forest Park, Ohio, 1935–1976.* Knoxville: University of Tennessee Press, 1981.
———. "The Crisis of Civic and Political Virtue: Urban History, Urban Life, and the New Understanding of the City." *Reviews in American History* 24, no. 3 (September 1996): 361–70.
Miller, Zane L., and Geoffrey Giglierano. "Downtown Housing: Changing Plans and Perspectives." *Cincinnati Historical Society Bulletin* 40, no. 3 (fall 1982): 176.
Miller, Zane L., and Patricia Mooney Melvin. *The Urbanization of Modern America: A Brief History.* San Diego: Harcourt Brace Jovanovich, 1987.
Miller, Zane L., and Henry D. Shapiro. "Learning History by Doing: The Laboratory in American Civilization." *History Teacher* 11, no. 4 (spring 1978): 483–95.
Miller, Zane L., and Bruce Tucker. *Changing Plans for America's Inner Cities: Cincinnati's Over-the-Rhine and Twentieth-Century Urbanism.* Columbus: Ohio State University Press, 1998.
Moberg, David. "How to Heal Our Cities: Myron Oldfield Has a Radical Solution

to Suburban Sprawl—Social Justice." *Sierra: The Magazine of the Sierra Club,* May/June 2000, 74–77, 100.

O'Connor, Carol A. "The Suburban Mosaic: Patterns of Land Use, Class, and Culture." In *American Urbanism: A Historiographical Review,* ed. Howard Gillette Jr. and Zane L. Miller, 243–56. Westport, Conn.: Greenwood Press, 1987.

O'Connor, Kevin, and Edward J. Blakely. "Suburbia Makes the Central City: A New Interpretation of City-Suburb Relationships." Working paper no. 485, Institute of Urban and Regional Development, University of California at Berkeley, August 1988.

Writers' Program of the Work Projects Administration in the State of Ohio. *Cincinnati: A Guide to the Queen City and Its Neighbors.* Cincinnati: Wiesen-Hart Press, 1943.

Przybyszewski, Linda. *The Republic According to John Marshall Harlan.* Chapel Hill: University of North Carolina Press, 1999.

Purcell, Edward A., Jr. *The Crisis of Democratic Theory: Scientific Naturalism and the Problem of Value.* Lexington: University Press of Kentucky, 1973.

Quinn, James A., Earle Eubank, and Lois E. Elliott. *Population Changes: Cincinnati, Ohio, and Adjacent Areas, 1900–1940.* Research monograph no. 47. Columbus: Bureau of Business Research, Ohio State University, 1947.

Reynolds, Martha S. "The City, Suburbs, and the Establishment of Clifton Town Meeting, 1961–1964." *Cincinnati Historical Society Bulletin* 38, no. 1 (spring 1980): 9.

Rusk, David. *Cities Without Suburbs.* Washington, D.C.: Woodrow Wilson Center Press, 1993.

Scott, Mel. *American City Planning Since 1890.* Berkeley: University of California Press, 1971.

Shapiro, Henry D. *Appalachia on Our Mind: The Southern Mountains and Mountaineers in the American Consciousness.* Chapel Hill: University of North Carolina Press, 1978.

———. "Neighborhood and the Family: The Larger Setting. The Emergence of Ideas and Their Implications." In *Home and Family in the 1980s: Insights from Past, Present, and Future,* ed. Thomas H. Jenkins. Cincinnati: Better Housing League of Greater Cincinnati, 1981.

———. "The Place of Culture and the Problem of Identity." In *Appalachia and America: Autonomy and Regional Dependence,* ed. Allen Batteau. Lexington: University Press of Kentucky, 1983.

Shapiro, Henry D., and Zane L. Miller. *Clifton: Neighborhood and Community in an Urban Setting. A Brief History.* Cincinnati: Laboratory in American Civilization, Department of History, University of Cincinnati, 1976.

Shapiro, Henry D., and Jonathan D. Sarna, eds. *Ethnic Diversity and Civic Identity: Patterns of Conflict and Cohesion in Cincinnati Since 1820.* Urbana: University of Illinois Press, 1992.

Silberstein, Iola O. "Diversity on Converging Pathways: Mary H. Doherty and Helen G. Lotspeich." *Queen City Heritage: The Journal of the Cincinnati Historical Society* 41, no. 4 (winter 1983): 10, 13–20.
Spooner, W. W., ed. *A Guide to Picturesque Cincinnati*. Cincinnati: O. Reich, P. T. Schulz, and F. L. Plympton, 1883.
Stevens, George E. *The City of Cincinnati: A Summary of Its Attractions, Advantages, Institutions and Internal Improvements, with a Statement of Its Public Charities*. Cincinnati: Geo. S. Blanchard, 1869.
Stilgo, John. *Borderland: Origins of the American Suburb, 1820–1939*. New Haven: Yale University Press, 1988.
Suarez, Ray. *The Old Neighborhood: What We Lost in the Great Suburban Migration, 1966–1999*. New York: Free Press, 1999.
Teaford, Jon C. *City and Suburb: The Political Fragmentation of Metropolitan America, 1850–1970*. Baltimore: Johns Hopkins University Press, 1979.
———. *Post-suburbia: Government and Politics in the Edge Cities*. Baltimore: Johns Hopkins University Press, 1997.
von Hoffman, Alexander. *Local Attachments: The Making of an American Urban Neighborhood, 1850 to 1920*. Baltimore: Johns Hopkins University Press, 1994.
Wade, Louise C. *Chicago's Pride: The Stockyards, Packingtown, and Environs in the Nineteenth Century*. Urbana: University of Illinois Press, 1987.
Wade, Richard C. *The Urban Frontier: The Rise of Western Cities, 1790–1830*. 1959; reprint, Urbana: University of Illinois Press, 1996.
Wagner, Richard M., and Roy J. Wright. *Cincinnati Streetcars, No. 2. The Inclines*. Cincinnati: Wagner Car, 1968.
———. *Cincinnati Streetcars, No. 3. Cable Cars and Earliest Electrics*. Cincinnati: Wagner Car, 1969.
Whissel, Pamela. "Coming Up Roses." *Clifton Magazine*, spring 1990, 32–35.
Wilson, William H. *The City Beautiful Movement*. Baltimore: Johns Hopkins University Press, 1989.

INDEX

A
Abbe, Cleveland, 53
Abbe Meteorological Observatory, 53
African Americans: 4, 75; exclusion of, 82–83; inner-city neighborhoods, 5; population in Cincinnati, 162 map 15; metropolitan area, 163; Wendy's franchise 136–40
Aiken High School, 83, 100
Amazon Park (subdivision), 18, 21
American Civic Association, 26
American Guide Series, 48
American League for Civic Improvement, 26
American Park and Outdoor Association, 26
"American stock" people, 2, 4
Ames, Betty, 83, 109; vision of Clifton, 111–12
annexation, 9, 10, 14, 49, 158, 174n. 15
Annunciation (Roman Catholic) Parish, 3, 22–23, 175n. 21; church, 52, 99; school, 23, 147
Anti-Catholic sentiment, 19. *See also* Cincinnati Woman's Club
Anti-Semitism, 6, 93–94, 186n. 1
apartment construction (1940–45), 53
auto repair shop, Ludlow controversy, 95–96
Avondale, 7, 14, 47, 74, 183n. 14; south Avondale, 76
Avondale-Corryville urban renewal plan/project, 74–76, 77, 107, 134, 182n. 8

B
Ball, Mayor Flamen, vision of Clifton, 9
Bartholomew-Clifton School, 22
"Basin," the, 44
Berger, Bill, 163
Bethesda Home for the Aged, 53
Better Housing League, 82

Bettman, Alfred, 37
Bishop Street, 133, 152–53
blight, 54, 68, 74–75, 158, 185n. 40
block-busting, 81
Bond Hill, 93
boss rule, 25
Bowler, Robert Bonner, 23, 53
Brand, Mr. and Mrs. Jack, 148
Brookline Avenue, 20, 21
Brush, Tom, 110
Bryant Avenue, 21
Burnet, Robert, 24
Burnet Woods, library proposal, 147
Burnet Woods Park, 24, 29, 66
Burnham Plan (Chicago), 34
Burton Elementary School, 100

C
Calhoun Street, 96, 102; businesses, 137, 151
Camp Washington, 59, 60
Central Avenue, 174n. 15. *See also* McAlpin Avenue
central business district, 39, 47; core, 120
Central Parkway, 29, 37
Charleton Street, 27
Chicago, 27
Children's Hospital, 66
Cincinnati
  Board of Park Commissioners, 24, 113
  characterized, 49–53
  central business district, 68, 69
  Citizens Development Committee, 182n. 8
  city charter: of 1914, rejected, 35, 37; revised, 1918, 37; amended, 1924, 38–39; of 1926, 40
  City Charter Committee, 39
  compared with Paris, 85
  conditions (1973), 188n. 42
  coordinated city plan, 114, 121, 123–24
  defined, 4

Cincinnati (*continued*)
  Department of Neighborhood Housing and Conservation, 130, 134, 193n. 39
  Department of Public Works, 105
  Department of Urban Development, 119; on neighborhood development, 107
  Department of Urban Renewal, 74
  Division of Buildings and Inspection, 138
  Division of Community Assistance, 122
  economy, 56–57
  Fire Department, 23
  growth projected, 32
  Health and Welfare Council, 102
  Historic Conservation Board, 144; designation process, 151
  Historic Conservation Office, 145
  Historic District, boundaries, 146, 147, 148
  Human Relations Committee, 95
  Metropolitan Housing Authority, 124
  metropolitan region, 56
  Ohio River, and formation of city's character, 49
  park plan, 147
  personality of, 49
  Planning Commission 34, 40, 83, 96, 119, 121, 137–38, 145, 185n. 40
  Planning Department, 88, 134
  Planning Division, 115
  population, 106, 161
  population density: (1900), 16; (1940), 17 map 3a
  Recreation Commission, 102, 103, 143
  as residence site, 70–71 (*see also* downtown)
  as serene, 65
  Urban Development Department, 119
Cincinnati Catholic-Telegraph, 23
Cincinnati City Council, 53, 82, 149–50, 152; new zoning code (1963), 86; and parks (1903) 29–30
Cincinnati Crematory, 26, 52
Cincinnati Enquirer, 70, 86, 100, 153, 165
Cincinnati, Hamilton, and Dayton Railroad, 7, 30
Cincinnati Post, 190n. 12
Cincinnati Public Schools, Board of Education, 24–25, 98; high school districts, 176n. 27; racial integration, 98
Cincinnati Roman Catholic Archdiocese, 22

Cincinnati School Foundation, 189n. 17
"Cincinnati School" of urban history, 6, 172n. 8
Cincinnati Statistical Neighborhood #7, 116
Cincinnati Street Railway Company, 18
Cincinnati Times-Star, 66
Cincinnati tour, WPA guides, 50–53
Cincinnati Woman's Club, 83–84, 87
Cincinnati Woodlands Fund, 104
Cincinnati Zoological Gardens, 26
Circuit Court, Sixth, U.S., 99
citizen participation, 181–82n. 1. *See also* neighborhood planning; neighborhoods
Citizens Association for the Preservation of Sacred Heart (CAPSH), 103, 144–45
Citizens School Committee, 100–101, 187n. 23
Citizens United for Good Schools, 98
city, the: conception of (1948), 56; defined, 2–4; and homeostasis, 179n. 14; as placeless, 169n. 2; as social system, 15; as system of groups and parts, 170n. 4, 173–74n. 13
city guidebooks, 170n. 4, 172–73n. 2. *See also* Cincinnati tour, WPA guides
city manager government, 25, 40
city planning, municipal, 35
civic boosterism, 27
Civic identity, role of, 15
Civil Rights Act (1866), 187n. 14
civil rights movement, 98
Civil War, 6
class, socioeconomic, 200n. 3
Clayton, Rev. Thomas, 184n. 24
Cleveland, President Grover, 23
Clifton
  as academic neighborhood, 50
  age of, 46 map 8
  beginnings, 1–2
  as biracial community, 131
  boundaries of, 30, 36, 49, 50, 51 map 9, 60–61, 66, 67, 69, 86, 96, 101, 115, 129, 133
  business district plan, 119–120; approved, 121; hearings, 120–21; implementation, 129
  "center" of, 48
  characterized, 186n. 2
  as city neighborhood, 3, 25
  compared with Cincinnati, 116
  core and periphery, 120

as cosmopolitan, 36
as "Dutch," 66
firehouse, 176n. 23
fire station, 23
grand houses, 173n. 3
historic district, 147–52, 155; enlarged boundaries, 147–48
historic resources (National Register), 145
history of, 5, 149
as "home" neighborhood, 42
incorporation of, 2
as in-town suburb, 74, 68, 69, 81, 90
library, new, 146–47
location of, 1
Maxwell's vision of, 14
as middle-aged, 54
as national example, 92
neighborhood business district urban design plan, 119; environmental quality district, 119, 138; public facilities, 125
"new," 67
north, 2, 3, 14, 30, 36, 170n. 4
"old," 66
parking problem, 66
as parklike, 2, 9, 10, 25, 170–71n. 4 (see also suburbs)
planning goals (1964), 106
as political reform neighborhood, 25–26
as political ward, 21
population, 116; density, 1830 and 1840, 17; 1850–1880, 2; 1860 and 1870, 8; 1895, 21; 1910, 21; 1940, 53, 174n. 19, 180n. 20, 197–200n. 3
prospects (in 1925), 42, 45
public library: new, 127–28, 134; 128 figure 6; search for site, 136
razing and redevelopment, 53
as serene, 65
as "solid" neighborhood, 108
south, 2, 3, 14, 30, 36, 170n. 4
smoke problem, 66
as stable, 115
subdivisions, 174n. 15
visions of, 111–12, 116, 120, 133
youths, enumeration of, 176n. 29
Clifton and Burnet Woods Improvement Association, 26
Clifton Auto Repair, 152, 155
Clifton Avenue, 20, 21, 22, 29, 30, 174n. 15;
new lights, 129; widening of, 60, 77–78, 85, 96, 105
Clifton Business Association, 88
Clifton Business and Professional Association, 147
Clifton Citizens for Open Housing, 102
Clifton Coalition on Aging, 147
Clifton Community Association, 77
Clifton Community kiosk, 129
Clifton Community plan: approved by CTM board, 129–30, 157; contents, 130–31; draft (1975), 116–18; description, 116; goals and objectives, 117–18; guidelines, 132, ii frontispiece; to city hall, 130; status, 137
Clifton Community Urban Redevelopment Corporation, 142
Clifton Enterprises, Inc., 82
Clifton Golf Club, 36
Clifton Heights, 18
Clifton Hills, 53, 59; civic center, 62; Community Center, 63
Clifton Improvement and Welfare Association, 30, 33, 45
Clifton Is a Neighborhood for Children (CLINCH), 104
Clifton Library Committee, 147
Clifton Meadows Swim Club, 69–70; and racial integration, 98–99; too expensive, 102–3, 104; as trendsetter, 182n. 2
Clifton Open Air School, 21–22
Clifton Professional Men's Association, 88
Clifton Public School, 52, 61, 187n. 24; as integration model, 101; racial integration, 99–100; recreation 105; vacant land controversy, 126–27
Clifton Recreation Commission, 104
Clifton ridge, 133–34
Clifton School, 22, 24; new building (1907), 24–25
Clifton School Annex, 102
Clifton School for Young Ladies, 179n. 52
Clifton School Foundation, 101
Clifton Summer Activities Organization, 102
Clifton Theater Corporation, 138, 140
Clifton Town Meeting (CTM), 68; as analogue to City Planning Commission, 123; and annexation, 133; annual house tour, 86–91, 191n. 20; artists' exhibit, 96; assessed, 157–59; and branch post office,

Clifton Town Meeting (CTM) (*continued*) 85; clean-up campaign, 96; and Clifton Avenue, 76, 77–78; and Clifton's reputation, 80; city budget priorities, 110–11; city-wide issues as problem, 102, 110; community control, 95; community council, ix; and comprehensive neighborhood planning, 109–12; constitution, 155–56, 198–99n. 60; Constitutional Review Committee, 198–99n. 60; as corporation, 95; crime and drugs, 94; crimes of late 1960s, 97–99; depressed housing prices, 94; fair housing bill, 183n. 13; founding of, 74–77; gas lights, 85; ghettoization, 81–84; historic preservation, 84–85, 150–51, 190n. 5; historic preservation committee, 115, 146; Hosea Ave, 152, 155; Memorial Day Parade, 96–97; neighborhood plan, 86–87; objectives (1962), 79; open housing, 101; parking, 78–79; passive, 127–29; planning goals, 116–17; — (1964), 89–91; as political party, 95; property maintenance, 80; public school politics, 100–101; race, 77–79; razing and redevelopment, 53; recreation, 79; rejects new library site, 147; riverfront and convention bonds, 91; senior citizens association, 96; street lighting, 78–79; welcome signs, 79–80; territory, 80; turning inward, 158–59; zoning, 83, 87

Clifton Town Meeting *Bulletin*, 95–96, 99, 102, 121, 156, 157

Clifton Urban Redevelopment Corporation, 126

Clifton Village, 3; early problems, 8–9

Committee for the Children of Clifton, 126

Committee to Keep Clifton Green and Preserve Trees, 126

Community Assistance Teams, 121–22, 124, 191n. 19, 193n. 39

Community Chest Social Planning Council, 102

Community Council endowment, 132

Community Development Act, 115

Community Development grant, 119

Community Mental Health Program, 102

Community Organization and Planning (COPE) task force, 109

comprehensive metropolitan planning, 38

comprehensive planning, 5

Concerned Clifton Citizens Committee, 118

Concordia Lutheran Church, 132–33

Congress of Neighborhood Groups, 127

Congress of Racial Equality, 98

conservation and rehabilitation, 181–92n. 1

Constitution, U.S., 155

Coordinated City Plan, on Clifton, 130

Corey, Kenneth, 111

Corinthian Restaurant, 129–32

Cornell Place, 30, 33

Corryville, 11, 18, 26, 47, 61, 74, 104, 183n. 4

Cox, George B., 21, 52

culture: biological determinism, 171n. 5; as individualism, 164; as individual training and experience, 169n. 2; as lifestyle, 90, 182n. 1; mid-nineteenth-century view, 1, 3; racial determinism, 181–82n. 1; social determinism, 181–82n. 1; as way of life, 15

cultural individualism, 182n. 1; era of, 171n. 6

Cummings, Marcus, 98

commercial centers, secondary, 47

D

Dale, Frances L., 70

Deaconess Hospital, 36, 52

Democratic-Charterite coalition, 106

Department of Housing and Urban Development, 115, 125

District Court, First, Ohio, 138

District Court, U.S., 98, 99

diversity, as problem, 15

Dixmyth Avenue, 22, 29, 60

Doherty, Mary H., 175n. 20

Downs, Anthony, 108, 189n. 49

downtown, 174n. 13; fringe, 73; housing, 71–73; new conception, plan (1957), 71–72, (1964), 73–74

drugs, drop-in treatment center, 102; users, 94, 95

dwelling unit densities, 46

E

Economic Recovery Act, 142

Edgewood Estate, 187n. 35

Ely, Miss E. Antoinette, 177n. 52

empathy, and public interest, 164

environment, conservation of, 6; quality control, hillside, 133; quality district legislation, 109
environmental quality districts (EQD), 109
Esquire Theater, 141 figure 8; closes, 136; donated to city, 140; deeded to Clifton Theater Corporation, 140; reopens, 140
existing conditions study, 118, 121–24; plan of action proposal, 123; concept of Clifton, 124

F
Federal Housing Act: of 1949, 71; of 1954, 181n. 1
Federal Interregional Highway Plan (1944), 64
Federated Civic Association, 178n. 8, 179n. 19
Federated Improvement Association of Hamilton County, 33–34, 69. *See also* Federated Civic Association
First National Bank, 199
Fleischmann, Max, 23, 104, 188n. 35
Fountain Square, 18
Franz, W. G., 33
Frey, J. D., 33
Friends of the Library and Burnet Woods, 147

G
garden city idea, 191–92n. 23
Garfield Park, 72, 73
German Home for the Elderly, 26
German Methodist Episcopal Deaconess Home, 60–61
German Protestant Orphan Asylum, 26
ghettos, 64, 65, 74, 75, 77, 81, 93, 126, 131; African American, consequences, 158; significance, 161–64; size in 1990, 161; boundaries in 1960s, 93; — in 1977, 131; white backlash, 65
Gilded Age, 6
Glaser and Myers, consultants on recreation complex, 117
Glendale, 7, 13
Good Samaritan Hospital, 22, 36, 52
Goss, Charles Frederic, 33
Graff, Harry, 49
Greater Cincinnati Committee for Equal Opportunity in Housing, 182n. 13

Greater Park League (Cincinnati), 29
Greek Orthodox Church, 83
Greenhills, 39, 71
Groesbeck, William S., 23–24
guidebooks: late nineteenth century, 13; mid-nineteenth century, 7; Maxwell's, 10, 11, 14; Stevens's, 9–10

H
Hamilton County Court of Common Pleas, 138
Hanks, Louise, 22
Harrell, C. A., 78
Hebrew Union College, 36, 52, 102
hippies, 94, 96
historic districts: legislation, 109; libertarian reservations about, 148
historic preservation, Clifton, 6; mediator hired to resolve disputes over, 151–52; tax benefits of, 142
Historic Preservation Act, 145
history: Clifton booklet, 191n. 20; and Clifton planning, 123; and cultural individualism, 171n. 6; and planning, 57–58; legal, 171n. 5; lessons from, 168; "liberation," 6, 167–68; as marketing device, 158; of neighborhoods, 116, 122; role in planning, 191n. 19
home rule charter proposal, 34
horses, as urban problem, 15
Hosea Avenue, 18, 21; cul-de-sac controversy, 152–57; lawsuit, 155–57, 199n. 63
housing: for elderly, subsidized, 124–25; integration, class, 131; "open," 131; in-fill, 133; rehabilitation, 6, 107; religious discrimination, 93; strategy (comprehensive), 108–9; working review committee on, 189n. 51
Howard, Ebeneezer, 191–92n. 23
Hughes High School, 24, 36, 52, 61, 176n. 27; district, 180–81n. 47; predominantly black, 83, 100

I
Ibold, Michael, 22
IGA supermarket, 119; new parking for, 121
Immanuel Presbyterian Church, 82
immigrants, 2, 4, 49

individualism, cultural, 164
inner-city neighborhoods, 5, 69, 158. *See also* neighborhoods
integration: racial, 98; racial residential, 81, 161–65. *See also* ghettos
interdependence: mechanical, 28; ecological, 38, 39
interim development control zoning, 118
in-town suburbs, 69. *See also* suburbs
I-75 (Mill Creek Expressway), 60, 64, 72
isolationism, 158

J
Jewish cemetery, 20, 21, 148
Jewish Community Relations Committee, 93
Jewish Home and Hospital, 26
Jews, 14; housing, 93–94
Juergens Avenue, problem, 80, 111, 182n. 20

K
Kelly, Father James, 22, 23, 175n. 21
Kessler, George K.: and enthusiasm for local improvement, 30; park system plan, 29, 31 map 6, 37–38, 177n. 41

L
Lafayette Avenue, 174n. 15; barons, 8, 20; characterized, 53; tour (1949), 65
Lafayette Avenue Circle historic district, 115, 190n. 5
Lafayette Investments, Ltd. (LIL), 143–45
Lafayette View Park, 29
land use patterns: Clifton in 1890s, 20; Clifton in 1910, 21–23; segregation of, 62
Laurel-Richmond (urban redevelopment), 64
League of Women Voters (Cincinnati), Metropolitan Project, 109; Clifton branch, 76
"liberation" history, 167–68
Lillard Law, 21
Loraine Avenue, 152–53
Lotspeich, Helen G., 21–22, 175n. 20
Ludlow Avenue, 20, 21; apartments, 53; business district, 3, 14, 29; curves, 30; interim development control, 119; residential construction, 33; traffic problem, 66; viaduct, 30

Ludlow Garage, 97 figure 5, 186n. 4; as shopping mall, pizzeria, 128; teen center, 95–96
Lytle Park, 71, 72, 73

M
Mariemont, 44
maximum feasible participation, 69, 107
Maxwell, Sidney, 10–12
Mayor's Friendly Relations Committee, 82
McAlpin Avenue, 14. *See also* Central Avenue
McAlpin-Clifton-Woolper intersection, 186n. 5
McMillan Street, 52; commerce, 61
Merry Junior High School, 100
metropolis, conception of, 3–4, 8–9, 15; new view (1950s–1960s), 69; twentieth century, 62
Metropolitan Master Plan (1925), 39 54, 56, 62; analyzed, 40–45; on Clifton, 42–44, 45, 54, 56, 62
Metropolitan Master Plan (1948), analyzed, 53–64; 73–74, 76; on Clifton, 54–55, 59–64
metropolitan planning, 39; master planning, 38, 178n. 1
Meyer, Leon, 196n. 22
Miami and Erie Canal, 9, 20, 29
Miami Purchase Association, 115
Middleton Avenue, 20, 21, 26–27
migrants, white rural, 4
Mill Creek Expressway (I-75), 60, 64, 72
Mill Creek Valley, 29, 64
Miller, G. Franklin, 130
Miller, Zane L., 191n. 20
Model Cities programs, 5–6, 106
Mott Foundation, 193n. 39
Mount Adams, 102, 182n. 5; revival, 70–73
Mount Auburn, 7, 9–10, 26, 60
Mount Storm Park, 24, 53, 97, 103
Mount Storm (villa), 23; Venus's Temple of Love (replica), 23
Municipal Art Society of Cincinnati, 37–38

N
National Association for Advancement of Colored People, 98, 100
National Conference on City Planning, 37

National League of Improvement Associations, 26
National Register of Historic Places, 115, 142, 145, 190n. 5
neighborhood "balance" (integration), 108
Neighborhood Assistance Program (Cincinnati), 114
neighborhood business district, 20, 47, 61, 88–89; buffer, 152; survey, 47; urban design plan guidelines, 132
neighborhood improvement association movement, 26–36 106, 109, 178n. 19; civic participation in, 173n. 13; education focus, 182n. 8
neighborhood planning: comprehensive, 111 (*see also* Clifton Town Meeting); critique of, 163; new breed of planners, 38; process of, 191n. 19; as psychological welfare, 118
Neighborhood Planning Service, 88, 89
neighborhoods: autonomy, 69, 106, 109, 157; as basic unit, 68–69, 114; as communities, 174n. 13; community relations, 90 (*see also* Metropolitan Master Plan, 1925 and 1945); as community units, 39, 44, 47; competition, 28, 69, 70–71, 110–12, 188n. 42; conservation and rehabilitation, 5, 55; decay, 37; defined, 3–5; development, new campaign for, 106–8; empowerment, 6; idea of, 59; life cycle, 54; organization revolution, 5, 65, 66; organizations, number of (1966), 188n. 44; racially integrated, 6; self-determination, 111; sweepstakes, 69; transitional, 189n. 49; treatments (1948), 53–54; unit theory, 191–92n. 23
Neighborhood Support Program (Cincinnati), 156
new breed planners, 38
North Avondale, 74, 81, 107, 110
North Avondale Neighborhood Association, 184n. 6
North Cincinnati and Clifton Advocate, 26

O
Office of Community Affairs, 110
Ohio Civil Rights Commission, 184n. 26
Ohio-Kentucky-Indiana Regional Council of Governments, 105
Ohio Supreme Court, 196n. 21, 199n. 62
Ohio Writers' Program, 49
"old city," 4, 13, 14, 18, 26, 28, 29
"Old Clifton," 66, 67
Operation Head Start, 99
outer-city neighborhoods, 5–6, 69. *See also* neighborhoods
Over-the-Rhine, 9, 71, 73

P
parking corridor, 119
park movement, 28–33
participatory democracy, 110; planning, 113. *See also* citizen participation
Patterson, Orlando, 163–64
Pedretti, Francis, 53
Perry, Clarence, 191–92n. 23
Pinword Development Corporation, 142, 143
place: and cultural individualism, 171n. 6; and mid-nineteenth-century cities and suburbs, 7; Clifton as, 154; new role of, 3; role of in social theory, 6, 169n. 1, 171n. 5, 171n. 6; suburbs and cities, 1
plan, Clifton's first, 86–89
Planned Unit Development (PUD) districts, 196n. 27; zoning, 143, 144
planning, city, 34; comprehensive community, 106 (*see also* Metropolitan Master Plan of 1926 and 1948); conservationist, 113–14; coordinated, 114; and idea of dynamic equilibrium, 56
politics: machine, 25; "new" urban, 176–77n. 52; welfare-of-the-whole, 21
policy problem, central, 6; solutions, 163–65, 199–200n. 3
populism, new, 112
Probasco Fountain, 60, 61
Progressive Era, 6
proportional representation, 40
public housing, 39
public interest, 158, 159, 163, 164. *See also* welfare of the whole
Public Library of Cincinnati and Hamilton County, 146
public schools, taxes, 188n. 42
public transportation: urban transportation revolution (1870s), 18; street car routes (1910), 21; street car system and

public transportation (*continued*)
  inclines (1880s) 19 map 4; street railways, franchises, 15; transportation network, 20; trolley and bus map (1924), 43 map 7
  public works, rationale for, 34

Q
Queensgate I (urban redevelopment), 64, 65, 72, 73
quota system, residential, 131

R
race: as issue, 5, 77–78, 81–84, 97–99, 192n. 28; race relations, 1990s, 163; racism, 6
"racialism," 171n. 5
real estate prices, 179n. 17; taxes, 188n. 42
Real Estate Research Corporation, 108
recreation survey and master plan, 104–5
redevelopment, 53
regional race strategy, 165–66
regionalism, 5, 172n. 7
rehabilitation, as ongoing treatment, 74, 76. *See also* Metropolitan Master Plan, 1948; neighborhood planning
Republican Party, 20–21, 106
residential apartheid, 6, 161; quota system, 81, 108
residential neighborhood idea, invention of, 39, 174n. 13
residential racial quotas, 131
residential segregation: class, 111, 131; Jewish-Gentile, 93–94
Resor Academy and Literary Institute, 1, 24
riverfront plan (1961), 72
Roanoke apartments, endangered, 118–19
Rochelle Avenue, 27
Roeseler, W. G., Clifton plan, 86–87
Roselawn, 93, 108

S
Sabin, Albert B., 66
Sacred Heart Academy, 23; endangered, 115; preservation efforts (1970s), 103–5; proposals (late 1970s), 125; saved, 142–45; move to Clifton, 188n. 35
Sacred Heart/Mount Storm Historic District, 142
Saengferfest Hall, 27
Sagmaster, Mrs. Joseph, 66
Schoenberger, George K. 23
school taxes, increase, 24
Senior Citizens Center, 125
Shaker Heights ordinance, 184n. 26
Shapiro, Henry D., 167, 186n. 1, 191n. 20, 192n. 28
Sheblessey, John, 115
Skyline Chili, 152
slums, 36, 39; clearance of, 181–82n. 1; clearance and redevelopment, 5
Smith, David Lee, 186n. 4
social problems (mid-nineteenth century), 169–70n. 2
social theory, 6, 171n. 5
South Clifton Grammar School, 42
Spiegel, S. Arthur: Ludlow Garage, 96; Clifton Meadows Swim Club fight, 98–99, 186n. 4, 187n. 14
Spring Grove Avenue, widening of, 105
Spring Grove Cemetery, 24
Stern, Robert, 184n. 4
Stevens, George E., 9
Stevens, Herbert, 88
St. John's Unitarian Church, 86
St. Monica's Cathedral, 52
Strauch, Adolph, 23, 24, 26
streetlights, 30
subdivision boom, 18
suburban boom: mid-nineteenth century, 1, 7; drift, 70; flight, 6; gilded ghetto, 199n. 1; types, 10–11; defined, 179n. 17; neighborhoods, 4, 5. *See also* neighborhoods
suburbanization, late nineteenth century, 11, 14–15, 49
suburbs: Cincinnati (1875), 12–13 map 2; defined, 2–5; mid-nineteenth century, 7; and neighborhoods, literature on, 171–72n. 6; as parklike, 4; respectable, 1; as slums, 169n. 1; suburb-city relationship (mid-nineteenth century), 170n. 3
Supreme Court of Ohio, on Wendy's and zoning, 138–39
Supreme Court, U.S., 98

T
Tarbell, Jim, 95
taxonomies: residential, 4; of social reality, 6, 167

territoriality, 169n. 1
Thomas, Tracey, 174n. 17
totalitarianism, 181n. 1

U
U. S. Shoe Corporation, 186n. 4
University of Cincinnati: College of Design, Art, Architecture, and Planning, 125–26; Division of Metropolitan Services, 134; McMicken College of Arts & Science, 191n. 20; planning, 74–76; growth, 93; stabilizes, 158–59
Uptown (community): boundaries, 134; map 135
Uptown Plan, 194n. 7
Uptown Task Force, 134
Urban Conservator (Cincinnati), 146, 150
Urban Development Corporation (Clifton), 120
urbanization, 11, 14–15, 18
urban planning. *See* planning, city

V
violence, racial, 5, 82
vision of the city, 35; Clifton founder's, 7–8; metropolitan, 3, 39; 1870s–1910s, 170n. 4, 173–74n. 13; 1910s–1950s, 37; 1950s–present, 171n. 6

W
Wade, Richard C., quoted, 170n. 3
Walnut Hills, 7, 9, 45, 65

Walnut Hills Junior High School, 100
Walnut Hills Senior High School, 100, 176n. 127
war on poverty, 5, 106
Warner, Marvin, 71, 182n. 5
WCPO-TV, 86
Weil, Sidney, 138
"Welcome to Clifton Village" (sign), 158
welfare of the whole, 4–5, 38. *See also* public interest
Wendy's Old-Fashioned Hamburger Restaurant, 136–140, 195n. 18
West End, 9, 14; demolition proposal, 62, 64, 72
West, Tommy, 186n. 2
"Windings," the (estate), 23
Woolper Street, 60, 72, 80, 82. *See also* McAlpin-Clifton-Woolper intersection
Work Projects Administration, 48
World War II, 5, 64

Z
Zion, Robert L., 184n. 22
zoning code, 196n. 27
zoning, 5, 41–42, 44, 45, 87, 95, 103; environmental, 109, 196n. 22 ; historical, 109, 195n. 18; interim development, 118; and Wendy's, 137; overlap districts, 139–140; lobbying, 179n. 18. *See also* Clifton Town Meeting; Planned Unit Development districts

Urban Life and Urban Landscape Series
Zane L. Miller, General Editor

The series examines the history of urban life and the development of the urban landscape through works that place social, economic, and political issues in the intellectual and cultural context of their times.

Cincinnati, Queen City of the West, 1819–1838
Daniel Aaron

Domesticating the Streets: The Reform of Public Space in Hartford, 1850–1930
Peter C. Baldwin

Proportional Representation and Election Reform in Ohio
Kathleen L. Barber

Fragments of Cities: The New American Downtowns and Neighborhoods
Larry Bennett

The Lost Dream: Businessmen and City Planning on the Pacific Coast, 1890–1920
Mansel G. Blackford

Planning for the Private Interest: Land Use Controls and Residential Patterns in Columbus, Ohio, 1900–1970
Patricia Burgess

Cincinnati Observed: Architecture and History
John Clubbe

Lancaster, Ohio, 1800–2000: Frontier Town to Edge City
David R. Contosta

Suburb in the City: Chestnut Hill, Philadelphia, 1850–1990
David R. Contosta

Main Street Blues: The Decline of Small-Town America
Richard O. Davies

The Mysteries of the Great City: The Politics of Urban Design, 1877–1937
John D. Fairfield

Cincinnati in 1840: The Social and Functional Organization of an Urban Community during the Pre–Civil War Period
Walter Stix Glazer

The Poetics of Cities: Designing Neighborhoods That Work
Mike Greenberg

History in Urban Places: The Historic Districts of the United States
David Hamer

Getting around *Brown:* Desegregation, Development, and the Columbus Public Schools
Gregory S. Jacobs

Building Chicago: Suburban Developers and the Creation of a Divided Metropolis
Ann Durkin Keating

Silent City on a Hill: Landscapes of Memory and Boston's Mount Auburn Cemetery
Blanche Linden-Ward

Plague of Strangers: Social Groups and the Origins of City Services in Cincinnati, 1819–1870
Alan I Marcus

Changing Plans for America's Inner Cities: Cincinnati's Over-The-Rhine and Twentieth-Century Urbanism
Zane L. Miller and Bruce Tucker

Polish Immigrants and Industrial Chicago: Workers on the South Side, 1880–1922
Dominic A. Pacyga

The Rise of the City, 1878–1898
Arthur Meier Schlesinger

The New York Approach: Robert Moses, Urban Liberals, and Redevelopment of the Inner City
Joel Schwartz

Designing Modern America: The Regional Planning Association and Its Members
Edward K. Spann

Hopedale: From Commune to Company Town, 1840–1920
Edward K. Spann

Visions of Eden: Environmentalism, Urban Planning, and City Building in St. Petersburg, Florida, 1900–1995
R. Bruce Stephenson

Welcome to Heights High: The Crippling Politics of Restructuring America's Public Schools
Diana Tittle

Washing "The Great Unwashed": Public Baths in Urban America, 1840–1920
Marilyn Thornton Williams

www.ingramcontent.com/pod-product-compliance
Lightning Source LLC
Chambersburg PA
CBHW020946230426
43666CB00005B/194